GEORGIAN LONDON

JOHN SUMMERSON

GEORGIAN LONDON

BARRIE & JENKINS
LONDON

To my wife
ELIZABETH

Contents

Preface

THIS book originated in a series of lectures prepared for the Courtauld Institute in 1939, but not delivered owing to the turn of events. In 1940 it was suggested to me that the material might usefully be expanded into a book and I set about the work, completing some of the earlier chapters by the end of the year. More urgent things then intervened and the manuscript, less than half finished, was put away and only taken up again in the summer of 1944. The whole period has, of course, been somewhat unpropitious for a book of this sort. The subject-matter has been bombed from time to time and many papers, plans, and drawings of whose existence I was aware have been totally inaccessible. The book cannot therefore claim to be much more than an outline. As an outline I hope it will be useful. I hope most especially that it will show what an immense amount of research remains to be done on the building-history of London since the seventeenth century. This research needs doing now, before the age of reconstruction blots out all that vast quantity of minor evidence which, battered and often derelict, cannot be expected to survive long.

Some of the chapters are based on papers and articles prepared for certain occasions and periodicals. Chapters 2, 7, and 12 contain material assembled for a paper on 'The Great Land-owners' Contribution to the Architecture of London', read to the R.I.B.A. in 1939. Chapter 3 embodies parts of an article which appeared in the *Architect and Building News* in 1938. Chapter 13 is the substance of a lecture given at the Courtauld Institute in 1941, while Chapter 16 was read as a paper to the Ecclesiological Society in 1943.

The line-drawings in the text are, with certain exceptions, the work of Alison Shepherd, A.R.I.B.A., and my warmest thanks are due to her for the care and critical thought she has given to their execution. The only line-drawings not by Mrs Shepherd are as follows: Figs. 9 and 10, which are reproduced from the *Survey of London*, vol. x, by courtesy of the London County

Council; Fig. 25, which is from my own book, *John Nash*, by courtesy of Messrs George Allen & Unwin; and Fig. 36, which is a National Buildings Record drawing by Miss B. G. Bryan-Brown. I am indebted to Mr W. R. Headley for the loan of the drawing from which Figs. 7 and 27 were made. The half-tone plates are derived from a variety of sources, named in the list of illustrations, and I should like to acknowledge the kind permission of the Earl of Pembroke, the Editor of the *Builder*, the librarian of the R.I.B.A., and the Secretary of the School of Oriental Studies, to reproduce illustrations in their possession. My final obligation is to Miss Dorothy Stroud for reading the proofs.

J. S.

London, August 1945

Preface to the Revised Edition

IN revising this book more than twenty years after its inception I have made no attempt to change it from what it set out to be – an outline sketch of the subject from a particular and personal angle. The stuff within the outline, however, has been subjected to rigorous scrutiny in the light of present knowledge and with access to sources not available to me at the start. This has involved some re-writing and the elimination not only of crass error and ill-founded speculations but of what now seem to me immature or pedantic judgements.

While the final disintegration of Georgian London proceeds apace the definitive study of its fabric moves all too slowly. Nevertheless I must pay respectful and grateful tribute to the magnificent post-war volumes of the L.C.C.'s *Survey of London* – the finest things of their kind. I am also much indebted to Mr B. H. Johnson and Mr Donald J. Olsen for kindly allowing me to benefit from their unpublished studies of the Hanover Square area and the Bloomsbury estates respectively. Mr Howard Colvin's *Biographical Dictionary of English Architects, 1640–1840*, has, I need hardly say, been my constant companion and I have continually compared notes with Professor Pevsner through his two London volumes in the 'Buildings of England' series.

J. S.

London, May 1962

List of Plates

Where not otherwise stated, the prints reproduced are in the author's possession.

1 (a) Covent Garden. Painting at Wilton, reproduced by permission of the Earl of Pembroke
(b) Lindsey House, Lincoln's Inn Fields. Photograph: National Monuments Record

2 (a) Mansion House. Engraving from the *London Magazine*, October 1752
(b) Fenchurch Street. Detail from engraving published by Bowles

3 Neville's Court. Photograph: Society for Photographing Old London

4 (a) Plate from *The Builder's Jewel* by B. and T. Langley, 1740
(b) Doorway, 42 Great Ormond St. Photograph: H. Felton

5 No. 44 Berkeley Square. Photograph: London County Council

6 St Mary-le-Strand. Photograph: National Monuments Record (E. J. Mason)

7 (a) St Martin-in-the-Fields: model. Photograph: Warburg Institute (H. Gernsheim)
(b) St Martin-in-the-Fields. Aquatint by T. Malton, 1795

8 Christchurch, Spitalfields. Photograph: National Monuments Record (S. W. Newbery)

9 (a) St Paul's, Deptford. Engraving by W. H. Toms, after Thos. Allin
(b) St John's, Smith Square. Engraving published by R. Sayer (Gough Collection, Bodleian)

10 St George's, Hanover Square. Aquatint by T. Malton, 1800

11 Cavendish Square. Aquatint by T. Malton, 1800

12 (a) Horse Guards. Aquatint by T. Malton, 1794
(b) Spencer House. Engraving by T. Miller, 1763

13 Burlington House. Engraving from the *Builder,* 28 October 1854

14 Westminster Bridge. Engraving from *Illustrations of the Public Buildings of London* by Britton and Pugin, 1827

15 (a) Middlesex Hospital. Engraving by E. Rooker, after J. Paine
(b) Foundling Hospital. Engraving by B. Cole for Maitland's *History of London*, 1756

16 No. 37 Portland Place. Photograph: National Monuments Record (S. W. Newbery)

13

(b) St Pancras Church. Engraving by J. Tingle, after T. H. Shepherd, 1827, in *Metropolitan Improvements*
(c) Hanover Chapel. Engraving by J. Tingle, after T. H. Shepherd, 1827, in *Metropolitan Improvements*
39 St Peter's, Regent Square. Photograph: National Buildings Record (S. W. Newbery)
40 (a) All Saints, Camden Town. Engraving by T. Dale, after T. H. Shepherd, 1828, in *Metropolitan Improvements*
(b) Holy Trinity, Marylebone Road. Engraving by H. W. Bond, after T. H. Shepherd, 1828, in *Metropolitan Improvements*
(c) St Mary's, Wyndham Place. Engraving by Archer, after T. H. Shepherd, 1827, in *Metropolitan Improvements*
(d) St John's, Waterloo Road. Engraving by J. Cleghorn, after T. H. Shepherd, 1828, in *Metropolitan Improvements*
41 (a) Catholic Chapel, Moorfields. Engraving by H. Melville, after T. H. Shepherd, in *London Interiors*
(b) Lambeth Chapel. Aquatint by Ch. Rosenberg, after T. D. W. Dearn
42 Plate from *Contrasts in Architecture*, by A. W. Pugin, 1836
43 (a) Lancaster House. Photograph: H. Felton
(b) Lancaster House. Watercolour by Joseph Nash in the London Museum
44 (a) Waterloo Bridge. Engraving published by Richard H. Laurie, 1823
(b) Southwark Bridge. Engraving published by Richard H. Laurie, 1822
45 (a) United Service Club. Engraving by W. Wallis, after T. H. Shepherd, 1827, in *Metropolitan Improvements*
(b) Travellers' Club. Engraving from *The Travellers' Club House* by W. H. Leeds, 1839
46 (a) Drury Lane Theatre. Engraving by B. Pastorini in *The Works in Architecture of Robert and James Adam*
(b) Drury Lane Theatre. Engraving published by Richard Phillips, 1804
47 (a) Covent Garden Theatre. Engraving by G. Hawkins, 1809
(b) Drury Lane Theatre. Engraving by J. Le Keux, after T. Wyatt, in *Illustrations of the Public Buildings of London* by Britton and Pugin
48 (a) Covent Garden Market. Engraving by F. J. Havell after W. and F. J. Havell
(b) London Docks. Photograph: Newton & Co.

CHAPTER I

Air-View

It was not of profound consequence to architecture that George I ascended the throne in 1714 or that George IV died in 1830, but for the purpose of this book the dates are singularly convenient. They allow us to attach the word 'Georgian' to a period for which other, more significant merestones would do as well, while suggesting no equally simple and memorable inscription. Thus, the Georgian period begins with the building boom which followed the Treaty of Utrecht and continues to the end of the boom signalled by Waterloo. Or again, it begins with the rise of the Palladian movement and ends with the whole classical tradition tottering. The venerable Wren saw its beginning; young Pugin cursed its end. But while the little piece of history contained in this book is easily detachable from its context, there are certain long threads at either end which cannot be cut. We must glance backwards and forwards, therefore – backwards to the heroic, creative seventeenth century and forwards to the years when the steam age fogs the picture and the girthless London of our own time begins – the London whose boundaries are unknowable except as administrative hypotheses and whose sky-line is the bed of an ocean where the nineteenth century has foundered.

The story is made up of topography, biography, and architecture, and I shall try to weave these three together, illustrating the general in the particular and switching from one kind of detail to another as the situation suggests. But first, I propose to take a quick view of the landscape in which all the detail is to be found, and I ask you to imagine yourself suspended a mile above London; and to imagine yourself staying up there for a period of time proportional to two centuries, with the years speeding past at one a second. The spectacle below you proceeds like those nature films which accelerate into immodest realism the slow drama of plant life. The life of a city, condensed so, would be as dramatic. It would give the same startling impression of automatic movement, of mindless growth. For a town, like a plant or an ant-hill, is a product of a collective, unconscious will, and only to a very small extent of formulated intention.

Suppose we start our time-accelerator a century back from the year when our story begins – say 1615. Below us is the inconstant ribbon of the Thames, curving backwards and forwards among marshes and meadows. London is on one of the shallower curves, a tessellation of red roofs pricked with plots of green and the murlon-shadowed patches which are the lead roofs of churches. Within the blurred margin, the line of the ancient wall takes the eye, zigzagging away from the river northwards, eastwards, and down to the river again where a white concentric of fortifications focuses the Tower.

Away to the west, clearly separate, is Westminster. The abbey church and the cloister are distinct, and so is the tent-like roof of the hall. Round them is a red-roofed colony, less compact, less imposing, and much smaller than London.

Between London and Westminster a line of building fringes the river – the palaces along the Strand, with their halls, courts, and gardens, like Oxford colleges; and behind them the close gables of the road which joins the two cities – the merchant metropolis on the east, the court metropolis on the west – and serves the back entrances of the palaces, whose great highway and approach is the river itself.

During the first few 'years' of our watch, little changes. King James, a spendthrift in his own palaces, would, like Elizabeth, halt London if he could – rebuild but not expand. So we see change in density, not in size. We see that in the City green plots and great buildings become fewer and brick gables multiply; we see the belt around the walls swell with smoke and poverty and communicate its teeming pressure to the lanes off the Strand and to Holborn and the streets around the Inns of Court. Along the river, too, there is movement – eastwards where the mariners' and chandlers' houses cluster down by the water, and along the south bank behind the wharves and warehouses. At Whitehall the new Banqueting House lifts its white balustrade out of the Tudor chaos.

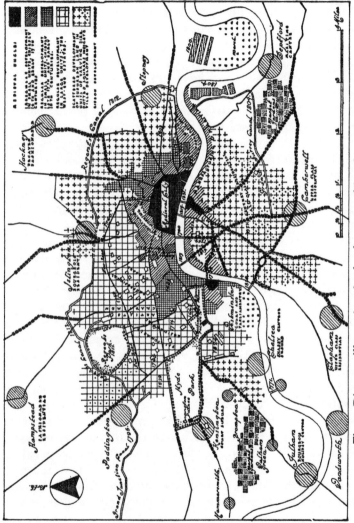

Fig. 1. Diagram illustrating the development of London up to 1830.

19

Sixteen-thirty, thirty-one, thirty-two ... A more energetic movement begins. The bonds of Royal Proclamation, which have constricted growth for two reigns, are being loosed. Within a few years, two great rectangles crystallize north of the Strand, in the 'Convent Garden' and the fields by Lincoln's Inn; and the houses which border them are conspicuous by trim discipline – uniform, ungabled fronts. Scaffolding comes and goes at St Paul's and leaves the Gothic hulk frilled with Italian lace. Again there is an idle pause, this time because of civil war. Cromwell's earthen forts heave up a sinister pattern in the northern and southern fields.

At 1660, the outlines quicken. A third square forms, as scraps of old suburbia are swept away in Bloomsbury, and a fourth as houses range themselves decorously in St James's Fields. Piccadilly becomes alive; classical palaces spring up on its north side. Measured tree-planting and path-making introduce the brisk order of an age of intelligence and expense.

Suddenly, as our clock ticks on to 1666, smoke and flame issue and vanish in the east, and the Great Fire of London has set all the contours of the city vibrating. Long before the charred patch glows again with fresh brickwork there is commotion in the west. The streets around Lincoln's Inn, Covent Garden, and St James's fill up with houses. Squares spring into being in Gray's Inn Fields and Soho, and packed streets close in upon them; new streets shoot northwards, eastwards, and westwards. The star of Seven Dials makes a pin-point nucleus for yet more building, which links St Giles's to St Martin's. Along the Strand, palaces disappear as russet furrows of houses drive across their sites. The Inns of Court make nests of rectangles. Meanwhile, the effects of the monstrous disaster are repaired. The new city, with red, regular streets and white churches, makes a brave show and, as the rotund bulk of new St Paul's looms into the clouds, we reach the end of the century. London is now no longer two linked cities, but one huge dragon of a town spread along the arc of the Thames.

And so we enter the great period. Queen Anne's reign is quiet, adding to the sum of London only a load of fine red brickwork and a seasoning of avenues and parterres; but at the

end of it, when a victorious peace heralds a dramatic change
of dynasty and government, come great adventures. A square,
named after the new Royal House, makes its florid appearance
on the north-west edge of the town; instantly two more squares
emerge from the fields north and south of Oxford Street, taking
their cue from the first and forming, with the surrounding
streets, an emphatic, martial, uniform criss-cross. This is the
texture of the new London. It finds an echo to the north, near
the Charterhouse, and again to the east in the squares of tiny
houses off the Ratcliffe Highway. In a hundred years it will
have wrapped all London in a net of pavements and covered
hundreds of acres of meadow and marsh.

Seventeen-twenty, year of crisis, sees a slackening, and our
attention is held only by the stately white churches emerging
from scaffolding in the new suburbs; they are the last we shall
see for nearly a century.

Now, for a while, we must observe more closely, for although
there is constant change, great building salients in the outskirts
cease. But we notice the shabby gabled streets in the inner west
end very slowly yielding to neatly parapeted rows. And we
notice that now the new brickwork tends to be grey and brown
rather than red. Whitehall becomes truer to the colour of its
name, the slow operations for a new bridge are seen at Westminster; in the outer parts, hospitals and asylums rise in the
fields; and the New Road creeps across the north from Paddington to Islington.

And so we pass from the period of Walpole and Burlington
and Chesterfield, past the '45 and into the Seven Years War. By
1760 the London of George III is eager to expand, to transform
itself into the great Imperial Capital which it is qualifying to
become. Within a few years a third bridge is thrown across the
Thames at Blackfriars, new roads strike down into Southwark
and Lambeth, and the skeleton of a great suburbia is etched on
the flats beyond the river. To the north-west there are stirrings
which break into activity just as war comes again; but the need
to expand is irresistible; the barrage of brown streets and squares
drives steadily north from Oxford Street and west from
Bloomsbury; and the New Road, which just now was a rural

track from Paddington to Islington, becomes the northern boundary of the town. The city, too, drives northward and plants a huge square on the fields of Finsbury. Now watch the river. In two places a new kind of scenery is rising. Two panoramas – the Adelphi in brick, Somerset House in stone – take their places on the sites of the last remaining palaces. Their arcaded terraces breast the Thames and make the first gesture towards embankment, instead of the broken shambling lines of wharves, piers, and watergates.

As we reach the London of the nineteenth century, England is once more at war. The short reprieve of 1801–3 coincides with the making of the first docks, and we notice how their shining oblongs break up the marshy isthmus beyond the city. To the dock area come line upon line of brown cottage streets, each carrying the east-end invasion further towards the Essex fields.

Now, for six or eight years, the picture scarcely moves. Prices are high; invasion threatens. Bankrupt builders desert the brick carcasses too hopefully begun. Depression reigns; but the cycle must turn and, with victory still barely in sight, the ascent begins. The Regency, in 1811, marks the turn. Brown, blue-slated terraces go up along main roads; the Thames is spanned by a fourth bridge, then a fifth and a sixth, and we see begun that great highway which is to be the stucco sceptre of the metropolis of George IV.

We watch the fields north of the New Road, and see digging and planting, farmsteads under the pick. We identify Regent's Park, and can hardly miss the fresh stucco of the crescent springing up just south of the Park. It is this pale stucco, a new-comer to the brick city, which helps us to follow the course of the new works. Where a ploughed line of demolition makes its way southwards to St James's Park, stucco façades line up. Later, they parade round the circumference of the Park, while stucco villas in clumps of young trees start up in this flat landscape. At the same time, the brickwork of Buckingham House disappears into scaffolding and emerges, much magnified, in yellow dress. Finally, the yellow pieces are joined into one streak and the Royal mile of John Nash, from Park to Palace, is complete.

That has brought us past the years of victory won and secured, and right to the end of the story. Having nailed our attention to this single operation we have, perhaps, failed to see how the perimeter of London has been moving at a ramping, devouring pace. Every outward road, now, is lined with terraces and villas. In the wedges of country between, streets and squares are filling in, London's satellite villages are villages no longer : Hackney, Islington, Paddington, Fulham, and Chelsea are suburbs. In Surrey a charming villadom – fresh-textured with greenery, garden walls, and slate-roofed stucco houses – spreads civilized grace over Clapham and Camberwell; and in the midst of this advance come churches again – some stone, some brick – some Greek, Roman, Gothic; all adding their quota of curious variety to a city in which standards of taste are adrift.

The crescendo is furious. It becomes impossible to distinguish particular movements. Vast estates in Pimlico and Bayswater borrow Nash's stucco uniform and advance into the Victorian west. Only St John's Wood bravely resists and makes, with its gardened villas, London's most humane suburb.

London assumes a new, balanced completeness. Linked by metalled roads to the regional turnpikes, it is the appropriate capital of its age; as appropriate and finished as the walled city in the circumscribed days of the Plantagenets. As we leave it, the future asks the terrible question : can London still grow – and yet be a *city*, a rounded place of human habitation? The Victorian age provides the answer. Iron fingers point to the stucco terraces in Euston Square, to the fields by Paddington, to Bishopsgate and Southwark. Steam brings new trade, new population, new ways of living; the man who walked for half an hour to his work two miles away will soon be riding for half an hour in a train covering seven times the distance. In a couple of decades more, the London of the Georgians begins to be locked in by vast dormitories which blot out the life of the village satellites and create anonymous wildernesses, neighbour-hoods without neighbours, whence the rich flee, and where poverty presses always on the heels of hard gentility. That is the end.

The end, I mean, of Georgian London. Victorian and modern

London make another story, a story of industrial conquest, of technical ingenuities, of the great battle for public hygiene, safety, and health, of the awakening of public responsibility for the condition of the poor, and, latterly, of the dawning of the conception that a city is a living creature which must be controlled and which, to be controlled, must be understood.

And now looking back, in a more critical and prosaic way, on the London drama which we have watched from our observation post in the clouds, what has it shown us? One thing, for sure; that London's growth has not been a matter of gradual and even incrementation, but of distinct waves of activity at intervals roughly of about fifty years. It is not a coincidence that this interval corresponds with the cycle which economic historians have detected in eighteenth-century trade. More closely studied, it bears an obvious relation to the alternation of periods of peace and war, and a less obvious relation to the increase of London's population. Each burst of house-building had a character of its own – a different social character, representing a different stratum of the national wealth and bringing into prominence a different kind of taste. Thus, Restoration building actively represented the consolidation of aristocrats in the west end, and, particularly after the Fire, the westward trek of luxury trades; taste was uncertain and retained a vernacular roughness. The next wave had its origin towards the end of Marlborough's wars and broke after the Treaty of Utrecht. This time, the central figure was the country lord setting up a town house and calling about him a genteel population of professional men. Taste was strictly Palladian. The third great wave of building began, likewise, in the middle of a war – this time the Seven Years War. It was slow in breaking, and the peak came ten to fifteen years later. The demand in this instance came from two quarters – from the country gentleman getting a foothold in town and from the citizen migrating to the west end. Taste was less assertive, less a matter of class *décor*, and advanced greatly in refinement and maturity. Finally, there came the first Napoleonic building boom, the contributory factors to which may be expressed as the sum of those which

24

affected the two previous periods with the addition of an enormous impetus from the rapidly increasing shopkeeper, artisan, and labouring classes. Taste began to be eclectic on the one hand, and strictly standardized on the other.

It is only in the last phase that the population figures have an emphatic relation to building output; for during the eighteenth century the increase in London's population was small. In 1700 it is calculated to have been about 674,500. In 1750 it was probably 676,750 – an increase of only 2,250. In 1801, however, the year of the first official census, it had risen to 900,000; and in 1831 it was 1,654,994. Thus, the earlier building booms appear to represent chiefly the expansion of particular classes of Londoners – expansion in the sense of families moving from small to larger houses – rather than a net increase in population. On the other hand, it should be remembered that increase in the upper classes of Londoners was off-set by an enormous death-rate in the lower classes, especially during the first part of the eighteenth century; and this, too, may be held to account for the considerable increase in the west at a time when the northern and eastern contours of London hardly changed.

Another conclusion to be drawn from our bird's-eye view is the rather obvious one that London has never been planned. Beside other eighteenth-century capitals, London is remarkable for the freedom with which it developed. It is the city raised by private, not by public, wealth; the least authoritarian city in Europe. Whenever attempts have been made to overrule the individual in the public interest, they have failed. Elizabeth and her Stuart successors tried bluntly to stop any expansion whatever. They failed. Charles II and his pet intellectuals tried to impose a plan after the Great Fire. They failed. Nearly every monarch in turn projected a great Royal Palace to dominate at least part of his capital. All failed until George IV conspired with Nash to cheat Parliament into rebuilding Buckingham House, scoring no triumph in the process. The reasons for all this are embedded deep in England's social and political history. London is one of the few capitals where church property and church interests have not been an overriding factor; where Royal prestige and prerogative in building matters have been set at naught; where defence has never, since the Middle Ages, dictated a permanent circumvallation to control the limits of development. London is above all a metropolis of merchandise. The basis of its building history is the trade cycle rather than the changing ambitions and policies of rulers and administrators. The land speculator and the adventuring builder have contributed more to the character of the Georgian city than the minister with a flair for artistic propaganda, or the monarch with a mission for dynastic assertion.

Yet taste has played as great a part as money, for taste has always formed, and still forms, a vital factor in the economics of building. It gives the psychological *élan* to the building market corresponding to the speculator's urge to enrich himself. Taste and wealth – these two are the basic things in Georgian London, so fundamental to our story that they must have a chapter apiece.

CHAPTER 2

Foundation Stones: Taste

TASTE in architecture reached London about 1615: taste, that is, in the exclusive, snobbish sense of the recognition of certain fixed values by certain people. Taste was a luxury import from abroad, received and cherished by a small group of noblemen and artists whose setting was the not very polished Court of James I. Architecture was a late comer to this little circle of intelligence in a still half-medieval England. But its arrival had been expected. Taste in other things – poetry, manners, the stage – was already tolerably well started. There were people about the Court who had not only been to Italy, but were un-affectedly familiar with the kind of culture to be found at the Courts of Florence, Milan, and Venice. People interested in such things talked about the possibilities of real Italian buildings – buildings with the antique stamp – being built in England. Sooner or later it was bound to happen. All that was needed was the right man and the right opportunities, and both came in 1615, the year that Inigo Jones, just back from his second visit to Italy, was appointed Surveyor to the King.

Inigo was forty-four. Though he had already held the office of Surveyor to Prince Henry for a few years preceding the Prince's death, his opportunities for building had been small. His fame rested on his incomparable ability to design the *décor* for Masques, which he did in a style perfectly Italian. He knew, probably, more about Italian design than any Englishman living. He had the whole thing at his finger-tips. He could sketch like an Italian; he had the deft Italian way of scribbling a head or a torso, a portico or a cartouche; every touch of his pen had the correct Italian swagger. Even in Italy, he was well thought of and would have cut a respectable figure among *seicento* architects had he chosen to practise there. He knew his own measure. He was confident of his own taste and knew what not to copy from Michelangelo.

He was therefore a unique asset at the English Court, and, like other men of singular talents and no estate – Donne, for instance, or Wotton – felt justified in expecting that a place could be found for him in the Royal service. The Surveyorship was his reward. It was an administrative post, chiefly concerned with the management of public works and the passing of accounts. There were collateral opportunities for architectural design, however, and before he had been in office a month he had made the first sketches for the Queen's House at Greenwich and for a new Star Chamber.

The freshness, the stark novelty, of Jones's work in Jacobean London cannot be overstressed. Here was a city built by generations of closely organized carpenters and masons, a city of gables, mullioned windows, carved barge-boards, corner-posts and brackets, a city in which architectural novelty consisted in exceptional feats of carpentry, in curious enrichment or in extravagant use of stone. The wonder-pieces of Jacobean London were still Gresham's Exchange, the turreted Nonesuch House on London Bridge, and Holbein's Gateway at Whitehall. To put up a pure Italian building in such a setting was sensational – almost like realizing a stage-set in permanent materials. It could only be done under the immediate patronage of the Court, and it is essential to think of Jones, from first to last, as a Court architect imposing foreign formulas which were neither comprehensible nor particularly welcome to the ordinary Englishman.[1] It is not exaggerating to say that Jones's influence did not really take hold of English architecture till nearly a century after his most important works were finished.

Jones's chief building, the Whitehall Banqueting House, was begun in 1619 and finished in 1622. It was really an extension of his stage work, a growth into solid masonry of paste-board perspectives. This growth was also a growing-up. Jones's buildings, from the Banqueting House onwards, are intensely serious. In their proportions they are calculated; in their details abstracted with fastidious taste from Roman and Renaissance authority.

1. 'For they seeme like Bug-beares, or Gorgons heads, to the vulgar,' said a writer of 1642. (James Howell in *Instructions for Forreine Travell*, ed. Arber, p. 73.)

Jones was a fundamentalist – a founding father, careful and rigorous in all he did. And when the opportunity came for him to turn from the world of Court entertainment to the control of London building he seized it with single-minded earnestness.

Charles I, succeeding his father in 1625, had definite and autocratic ideas about the improvement of his rather squalid and untidy metropolis. In the very first year of his reign a Commission for Buildings was set up, its object being to enforce the application of existing laws as to the limits of development and the technical standards of construction. The operations of the Commission, which had Jones as one of its executive officers, were resented and their effect was not at first very pronounced : Charles was not to be allowed to play with his capital as if it was a Royal pleasaunce. And so it came about that the one case where Court influence did assert itself was one where circumstances played directly into the King's hands. This was at Covent Garden, where the building of the Piazza by the fourth Earl of Bedford was the first great contribution to English urbanism (Plate 1a and Fig. 2).

Now this Earl was far from being one of that inner circle of cultivated Royalists who were Inigo Jones's chief patrons. He was different politically and temperamentally. He shared neither the frigid pomposity of Arundel, the more humane and poetical qualities of Pembroke, nor the decorative exuberance of young Buckingham. He was nearly half a puritan – politically, a 'moderate'; and had even been arrested on a charge of circulating disloyal literature – a charge he was able, however, to refute. He was very intelligent in a practical, business-like way and his greatest contribution to his time was probably the reclamation of the Fens – the area still referred to as 'the Bedford Level'.

The Earl's business aptitude induced him to think of turning to account the land behind his house in the Strand. Developments along Drury Lane and Long Acre were already bringing in £500 a year when he succeeded to the property[1]; a substantial revenue was clearly obtainable by a sound development of the intervening area. There were, however, difficulties. There were the Commission on Houses and all the prohibitions it

1. G. Scott Thomson, *Life in a Noble Household, 1641–1700*, 1937.

stood for. There was the Royal prejudice against the expansion of London. Many of the existing buildings on the Bedford property were, in any case, more or less illegal; to build any more would mean getting a special dispensation from the King.

The Earl of Bedford did get a special dispensation. For a consideration of £2,000, a licence to build was made out on the King's own instructions in 1630. But the interesting thing about it is that it appears to have been granted on the condition, expressed or implied, that the Earl did his speculative building on such a scale and in such a manner as to provide a distinguished ornament and not merely an extension to the capital.[1]

Just how far the Earl was blackmailed into building architecture for the King's pleasure rather than merely houses for his own profit there is not enough evidence to make out. That Bedford was not indifferent to the new architecture is proved by his buildings at Woburn. But it is pretty clear that we owe Covent Garden to three parties: Charles I, with his fine taste and would-be autocratic control of London's architecture; Jones with his perfectly mature understanding of Italian design; and the Earl of Bedford with his business-like aptitude for speculative building.

The Piazza was laid out as a long rectangle lying east and west behind the Earl of Bedford's house and garden. The north and east sides were built up with houses; the south side was separated by a low terrace from Bedford House garden; and the west side was given up to a church flanked by gateways and two houses. This church, St Paul's, is the subject of a story, told to Horace Walpole[2] by Mr Speaker Onslow, which fits in nicely with the supposition that the Earl of Bedford was not nearly so interested in architecture as those in higher places who were in a position to force his hand. When Inigo Jones set about designing the church, the Earl is reported to have asked that it should be very plain – 'not much better than a barn'. If this was a plea for economy, Jones was not taking the hint. He replied: 'You

---

1. *Copie of a Petition to the Parliament of the comonwealth* (undated) in the Woburn archives. I should like to record here my indebtedness to the late Duke of Bedford for permission to inspect these archives in 1938.

2. *Anecdotes*, 1888 ed., vol. 2, p. 63.

shall have the handsomest barn in Europe.' And the Church he built, though certainly plain, was a noble Tuscan temple – and not cheap.[1]

The Piazza must have presented a fine picture. The big Italian scale, the total absence of ornament that was not of perfect academic propriety, the use of external stucco to give the effect of stone – all these things were new, and suggested new standards for London street architecture. There were probably eighteen houses on the north and east sides – each entered from a front door in the arcades (which by colloquial stupidity came to be called the 'piazzas', the name belonging by right to the layout as a whole) and running back to a garden, with a coach-house and stable at the far end. One original lease – that of Sir Edmund Verney, the brave standard-bearer of Edge Hill – has survived.[2] He had a house at the corner of Russell Street, of which he held a four-year lease, paying a rent of £160 a year. The house had a parlour and study on the ground floor, dining-room and drawing-room on the first floor, and bedrooms above. There was a good deal of panelling and the staircase will probably have been a piece of heavy oaken construction with turned balusters.

If you visit Covent Garden today you will find only a ghost of Inigo's original. The open space is cluttered up with the market and its buildings. The arcades have all gone, though one short series is adequately reproduced in a building of 1880 at the north-west corner. It follows the old design in modern masonry and records satisfactorily something of its scale and dignity. The Baroque house next door (43 King Street) has nothing to do with Jones: it was built early in the eighteenth century and was the first interloper to despoil the layout of its symmetry. Even the church preserves only the carcas of the original 'handsomest barn', having been burnt out in 1795. The portico survived, however, and the great roof was conscientiously replaced by Thomas Hardwick so that the giant Tuscan columns, the enormous eaves, are still as powerful and affirmative as ever.

1. It cost £4,886 5s. 8d. (compare Lincoln's Inn Chapel, about £2,000). See *A Perticular account of the Earl of Bedford's Expence in Building Covent Garden Church*, in the Woburn archives.
2. Extracts are in *Archaeologia*, vol. 35, p. 194.

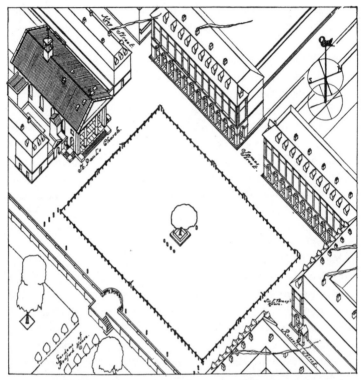

Fig. 2. The church and 'piazzas', Covent Garden. See also Plate 1.

King Charles displayed great interest in Covent Garden and visited the buildings as they were going up. But his determination to get London's suburbs fitted with a respectable Italian costume extended further, notably to Great Queen Street and the adjacent Lincoln's Inn Fields. Here another ambitious speculator turned up and had to be kept in check: not an Earl this time but plain William Newton, who had come from Bedfordshire and obtained facilities to build in the fields west of Lincoln's Inn. From 1638 till his death five years later, Newton was busy obtaining licences, marking-out plots, selling them at a profit, or building on them himself and selling house and land together. Evidently his activities were assiduously controlled by the Commissioners on Buildings, for in every case his houses

32

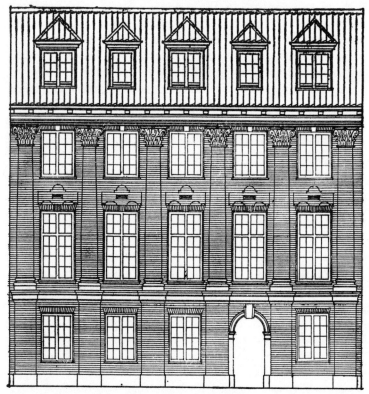

Fig. 3. Great Queen Street, 'the first regular street in London'. Compare the Lincoln's Inn Fields houses in Plate 1b.

are fronted in the Italian taste; while in almost every case tradition (but only tradition) associates Newton's buildings with the name of Inigo Jones.

The houses in Great Queen Street and Lincoln's Inn Fields[1] must be considered together, the street forming, in effect, a deflected continuation of the north side of the Fields until severed by the construction of Kingsway in 1906. All the houses have, or had, certain characteristics in common, being built of fine red brick, with heavy wooden eaves, cornices, and perfectly regular façades, ornamented – and in this is their prime importance as exemplars of taste – with pilaster orders rising from the first-floor

1. *Survey of London*, vol. 3: St Giles-in-the-Fields, part i (1912).

level to the cornice. In Great Queen Street the Corinthian
order was used, in Lincoln's Inn Fields the Ionic. In neither case
was exactitude displayed in the execution, and the introduction
of an occasional arabesque fancy suggests that a more wayward
and characteristically native hand than Jones's was on the job.

But the 'authorship' of all these houses, which has been much
debated, is an unprofitable quest; for the excellent reason that in
Jones's time the present-day conception of an architect's artistic
responsibility for a building simply did not exist. To provide a
row of houses with a proper Italian character might very well be
merely a matter of verbal instructions to a mason or bricklayer
together with the loan of an Italian engraving or two and the
correction of the 'plat-forme' or draught. Jones's part in getting
such things done was probably far more that of a Civil Servant
than a professional architect. What is perfectly clear and of real
importance is that the suggestions and instructions such as they
were for Italianizing part of Great Queen Street and Lincoln's
Inn Fields came from that Whitehall group in which Charles I,
Arundel, and Jones were the most important figures.

The Great Queen Street houses were reputed, in the eighteenth century, to constitute 'the first regular street in London'.
They laid down the canon of street design which put an end to
gabled individualism, and provided a discipline for London's
streets which was accepted for more than two hundred years.
The canon is, quite simply, the reduction of a house façade to the
terms of a classical order raised on a podium, the ground floor
representing the podium, the upper floors the column. Whether
pedestal and column are *articulated* (as pilasters, attached
columns, or in portico form) does not affect the principle. It is
a question of proportion and modulation. It places the emphasis
at first-floor level, from which the main part of the order arises.

In Lincoln's Inn Fields, Ionic pilasters were applied continuously along most of the west side. In the centre of this side, however, it was deliberately broken by the more majestic house
which still survives (Nos. 59–60) under the name of Lindsey
House. This is one of the many buildings of the kind which is
attributed (on the evidence of Colen Campbell) to Inigo Jones
himself. Faced with a combination of stone and stucco it has

34

handsome Ionic pilasters and entablature. A bust of Queen Henrietta Maria is missing from the central window. It is an instructive study in the rude expression of taste of the 1630s; and its interest as such is doubled by the presence next door (southwards, Nos. 57–58) of an imitation of the same design built nearly a century later by one of Jones's 'Palladian' admirers. There we have, side by side, a reputed Jones façade, with all its pioneer roughness and coarse craftsmanship, and the same façade copied and revised by one of the architects who picked up the threads of the Jones school in the earthly eighteenth century and established Jones and Palladio side by side as the patron saints of British architecture. The two houses form together a striking document in the history of English taste. (See Plate 1b.)

The Italianizing of Carolean London must have gone quite a long way before its progress was stopped by the Civil War. Jones was able to build a Corinthian portico at the west end of old St Paul's and encase part of the exterior in good Roman masonry; and his direct and indirect influence began to appear in quarters of the old city: one encounters, for instance, a Jones legend (it is probably nothing more) at Great St Helens, where pilastered houses like those in Great Queen Street and dating from 1647 survived to our own day.

But progressive architecture received a shock with the overthrow of Charles and his court. When the aged Inigo was bundled out of the flames of Basing House in a blanket, the Parliamentary news-sheets gloated over the capture of a prisoner whom they saw as a chief minister of Court indulgence and one of the petty tyrannizers who had lashed at them from Whitehall. Henceforward London was not to be a centre of taste. Charles's great collection of pictures was to be sold. Architecture and the arts retired to the country, where a few lords and gentlemen, who had settled up satisfactorily with the new régime, were able to experiment at their leisure with architectural fashions. Houses as fine as Wilton and Coleshill date from the years of the Commonwealth. But in London there is practically nothing. Court architecture was dead – as dead as the King who walked to his execution through an Italian casement.

The course of taste in the Restoration years and beyond will emerge in the following chapters. Here I have only sketched the foundation, as it was laid by the Court of Charles I. But before leaving the subject it will be as well to insist on one characteristic of the later history of taste in England – the continuity of its Palladian basis. I have already said that the beginnings which Jones made and which were all but severed by the Civil War, were not resumed for nearly a hundred years, thus suggesting that the enormous artistic activity after the Restoration, and particularly after the Great Fire, may be regarded as an interlude. So, in a sense, it may. Sir Christopher Wren's surveyorship was remarkable for many things, but not – except in the Surveyor's own personal work – for the extremes of elegance and refinement. The art of the Restoration was borrowed from many sources, learned and vernacular. It was an art dominated by intellectual ideas, but not of the sensitive, poetical character associated with Inigo Jones. And from the eclectic half-Baroque of Wren, taste veered for a time to the whole-Baroque of Vanbrugh and Hawksmoor and Archer. Then came the reaction, led by Burlington and his group; distressed by Baroque deviations and extremely critical of Wren, they used every device of persuasion and performance to fix a standard of architectural taste conforming exactly to that exhibited by Palladio and Jones. They succeeded. Under George II Palladianism conquered not only the high places of architecture – the great patrons, the government offices – but, through the medium of prints and books, the whole of the vernacular, finding its way ultimately into the workshop of the humblest carpenter and bricklayer.

Palladian taste represents a norm to which classical architecture in this country returned over and over again. As an educational standard it was continuously upheld and in course of time the name of Chambers was added to those of Palladio and Jones as the guiding stars in the student's firmament. Neither Adam nor Soane, nor the Greek men, nor the early Gothic men ever dislodged, or attempted to dislodge, the Palladian dogma. Adam might ridicule the heavy handling of the Burlington school; Wyatt might advertise the Gothic, Wilkins the Greek. But entirely to supersede the traditional basis provided by the

books and buildings of the sixteenth-century Vicentine probably occurred to none of them; and Palladianism still coloured
Barry's Italian revival of the forties.

Hence the importance of what has been told in this chapter of
Inigo Jones's work in giving London the first of those buildings
which could be said to be strictly and artistically Palladian in
character. They were the foundation stones of two centuries of
London taste.

CHAPTER 3

Foundation Stones: Wealth

THAT this chapter comes after, and not before the chapter on 'Taste' is a matter of chronological propriety. It happens that, for a variety of reasons, the basic principles of taste which prevailed in Georgian London became recognizable somewhat before the basic principles of speculative development. The character of the Georgian town house was fixed under Charles I. But the methods responsible for the enormous multiplication of the town house during the eighteenth and early nineteenth centuries were hardly more than embryonic till after the fire of 1666. The land-developments of the Earl of Bedford and William Newton, inhibited by the laws against building, appear elementary beside the undertakings of a landlord like Lord Southampton and a financier like Nicholas Barbon. It is the men and methods of this later period that we are now to consider.

The speculative builder, the mainspring of London's expansion for three hundred years, has always been a person of the most various characteristics. Sometimes he has been a lord, sometimes little more than a labourer; sometimes a substantial capitalist, sometimes a craftsman, with only his skill and time to adventure; sometimes an architect, sometimes a bricklayer or carpenter; sometimes a lawyer, a mechanic, a schoolmaster, a quack, an actor – indeed, almost any class, trade, or profession.

Speculative building is a very old way of making money. It must go far back into the middle ages and have grown up almost simultaneously with the notion of a rent-roll as a source of wealth. It was familiar practice in Tudor times. As the aristocrats shifted out of the walled cities their palaces were taken over and demolished or subdivided to provide accommodation for humbler people whose rents brought an income to the new landlord. It was the poorer classes – the hands flocking to the towns from an impoverished countryside – who were the speculator's first quarry; they were served with the minimum of accommodation for the trifling rents which could be extracted from them. But in course of time the speculator aimed higher. As urban life became richer and more laborate, as the professional classes expanded, as the Court and its offices drew more men into their proximity, the 'town house' which was neither a great mansion nor a hovel became an important need.

The fourth Earl of Bedford, as we saw in the last chapter, was early in the field with his great Covent Garden scheme which aimed at fulfilling the requirements of a very select category of town dwellers. William Newton was another pioneer, of a different kind, adventuring in land-purchase rather than building. During the Commonwealth, others tried their hand at speculation but without advancing either in extent or method beyond what had been done in Charles I's time. Then came the Restoration, with the aristocracy once more in the saddle and not averse to recouping or improving their fortunes by developing their urban lands. From now on the noble landlord with a greedy purse becomes a familiar type.

Two noble landlords went to work immediately after the Restoration: they were Thomas Wriothesley, fourth Earl of Southampton, and Henry Jermyn, first earl of St Albans. The first laid the foundation of modern Bloomsbury by building Bloomsbury *Square*, the first open space in London to be so designated. The second launched a new west-end offensive by the creation of St James's Square.

Lord Southampton's story is very important. He had envisaged profitable development on his Bloomsbury manor almost as early as Lord Bedford on his land at Covent Garden – that is to say, about 1636; but in spite of King Charles's inclination to consent, a licence to build was withheld. It was not till the latter years of the Commonwealth that he was able to erect a mansion (long and low; somewhat in Inigo's style) in one of his fields and to lay out a square in front of it. The first leases in this square were granted in 1661. They were *building leases*; that is to say, the plots were let at a low ground rent on the understanding that the lessee built at his own expense a house or houses of substantial character, which house or houses, at the end of the lease, became the property of the ground landlord. A building agreement was probably signed in the first instance, to be implemented by the lease when the building was in an advanced state of completion.[1]

Here we have the beginning of that system of speculation by hereditary landlords which brought half London into being. It must be remembered that most of the great London estates have been either entailed in a family or held in trust by a corporation. They could not, except under Act of Parliament, be sold, in whole or in part. In these circumstances, the building lease represents a convenient device by which the land can be rendered profitable over and over again without being alienated.

The land round Bloomsbury Square was let off in plots of greatly varying size, but in almost every case a unit of subdivision of 24-ft frontage seems to have been envisaged, and no doubt the lessees, who included a Sir Edward Mosley and a Dr Cox as well as several plain Misters, had speculative rather than residential intentions. The ground rents averaged about £6 per 24-ft unit, the price varying, however, with the depth of the sites and the number taken. The houses were plain brick structures with horizontal bands at each floor-level and heavy wooden eaves-cornices. One or two remain, but so heavily disguised under Victorian stucco as to be unrecognizable from the street.

The conditions under which Lord Southampton let his land were the basis of all future development of the sort. Important modifications, however, were introduced from time to time. The 42-year lease was superseded by the 60-, 61-, or 64-year lease in the early eighteenth century[2] and later by the 99-year lease which was practically universal before the end of the century. With the lengthening of the lease, it became necessary to offer the lessee greater indulgence during the initial years, when he was at the expense of building; hence the one, two, or more years of 'peppercorn' rent invariably found in later leases, often in conjunction with a rising scale of ground rent for the remainder of the term.

1. Gladys Scott Thomson, *The Russells in Bloomsbury*, 1940.
2. In Neve's *Builder's Dictionary* (1736 ed.) it is stated that, 'Few houses . . . last longer than the ground lease, i.e. about 50 or 60 years'.

The Earl of Southampton was a pioneer not only in his creation of the first square, properly so called, and the first unit of
the sort to be developed by a landlord through the medium of
speculative builders, but because he realized that a square was
not enough by itself : it had to be the centre of a residential unit
comprising a market or shopping-centre and a number of
smaller, less expensive, streets. In fact, the whole thing had to
have a life of its own. When Evelyn called the Bloomsbury development 'a little town' he epitomized its virtue as a piece of
town planning. The Bloomsbury unit was organic from the start
and remained one of the most charming and sought-after suburbs of London until, as part of the Bedford Estate, it grew eastwards and northwards and became lost in the criss-cross of the
Bloomsbury of the later Georgians. Today, after so many rebuildings, you can no longer feel the separateness of the Earl
of Southampton's 'little town', and it is hard to visualize a
Great Russell Street from which Wren and Kneller and Sloane
looked across fields to Highgate Hill. No. 99 Great Russell
Street, however, records something, though only a little, of the
street's character; and the decayed shop-buildings in Silver
Street and Barter Street speak of a market place long abandoned
but never quite obliterated by modern commercial development.

It was very soon after the beginning of Bloomsbury Square
that Lord St Albans launched his great scheme at St James's.[1]
St Albans was an elderly, cultivated, luxurious diplomat who
had spent most of the Civil War period very agreeably in France.
His ideas were continental. Possibly he had the Place Royale at
Paris and the Belle Cour at Lyons in mind when he projected
St James's Square. His proposals were more aristocratic than
Lord Southampton's and were in fact strongly influenced by the
proximity of St James's Palace and the natural desire of Charles
II to have respectable neighbours. He was for forming a square
consisting entirely of really large mansions – only three or four
on each side – to be built and occupied by the very best families,
including his own. He was not, like Southampton, the hereditary landlord of the ground he proposed to develop, but he obtained, as a favour, a sixty-year lease from the Crown. That was

1. *Survey of London*, vol. 29, St James, Westminster, part i, 1960.

in 1662. A few years of preliminary testing proved that on such a basis the scheme was not going to work, since great families were reluctant to build dynastic *hôtels* which might have to be relinquished by the second or third generation. St Albans, therefore, petitioned for a favour already amounting to a long loan to be turned into a gift, and in 1665 the Petition was granted. He became the freeholder of the soil.

The building of St James's Square was thus ready to go ahead just as the great plague visited London. This disaster delayed it, and within a year the great fire had changed the housing market completely. There was a rush to the west end. St Albans abandoned his grandiose policy of enticing a few select noblemen into his square, increased the number of plots to twenty-two, and let or sold them partly to his noble friends – Lord Arlington and Lord Halifax, for instance – and partly to professional speculators who proceeded to build houses for letting or re-leasing. Thus, in the end, St Albans's policy coincided exactly with Southampton's. He followed Southampton, too, in the erection of a market; and went one further in providing a site for a church on the axis of the square. The church, St James's, Piccadilly, was designed by Wren (except for the ugly steeple) and built in 1676–84.

In these two great building schemes centring round Bloomsbury Square and St James's Square three clear principles of development were laid down. First : the principle of an aristocratic lead – the presence of the landowner's own house in his square. Second : the principle of a complete unit of development, comprising square, secondary streets, market, and, perhaps, church. Third : the principle of the speculative builder, operating as a middle-man and building the houses. It is to the speculative builder that we must now turn our attention.

A speculative builder, as I said at the beginning of this chapter, might be almost anybody, from a peer to a labourer. It is difficult to define strictly the various types of speculator. Several methods of deriving profit from housing were practised, often by the same people. Perhaps the most helpful division is between those who speculated in land *plus* houses and those who speculated only in houses. The former included financiers; the latter were principally building craftsmen. The bigger type of speculator operated like this : he would acquire a piece of land, freehold or leasehold, divide it into plots, and then either build on these plots at his own expense or let them to smaller speculators on building lease, finally disposing of the whole property with the ground rents laid on. The small speculator, on the other hand, would confine himself to taking a building lease of one or more plots on somebody else's land, building a house, and selling the lease with the house. This method was adopted by building craftsmen who, as we shall see later, used to work in groups, each trade making its appropriate contribution, so that virtually no capital was required. Obviously the big and the little speculator – the financier and the craftsman – could very well work in harmony, the financier letting off his plots to the craftsman and profiting from the improved ground rent while the craftsman profited by selling the house. This is in fact what began to happen in the great building boom after the fire.

In this period we meet many speculators whose names are familiar on the map of London. Sir Thomas Bond, for instance, who held an appointment under Lord St Albans at the Queen Mother's court, was the principal in a group which speculated (and lost heavily) in the building of Bond Street and Albemarle Street; Sir Thomas Clarges, a politician of some importance, who built Clarges Street and collaborated with Lord St Albans at St James's; Abraham Storey, one of Wren's master-masons, who built Storey's Gate; Richard Frith, who adventured in St James's Square but who is better remembered as the builder of Frith Street, Soho. Then there was Sir Thomas Neale, a Master of the Mint and Groom Porter, whose enterprise was responsible for that extraordinary freak of town-planning, Seven Dials. There was Colonel Panton, whose scheme for Panton Street was recommended by Sir Christopher Wren on the ground that it would divert traffic from the Strand; and there was Gregory King, a herald, engraver, and political writer, whose principal speculation, King Square, is familiar today as Soho Square. Almost all these men, it will be observed, were 'amateurs' so far as the building industry was concerned; courtiers, soldiers, officials, their only inducement to build was a sense of financial adventure: a belief – not always well-grounded – that to build was as easy a way as any to get rich. It should be added that in most cases they were men whose position enabled them to pull the necessary strings to obtain licences to build.

From among many amateur speculators of the time there stands out one who was not an amateur, but a first-class financier, economist, and big businessman. His name was Nicholas Barbon and his career sums up decisively the building-economic tendencies of the Restoration period.

Barbon was born about 1640 and died in 1698. He was the son of Praisegod Barbon, *alias* Barebone, *alias* Burboon, known to his contemporaries as leatherseller, paedo-baptist, Member of Parliament, fanatical anti-monarchist, mob-raiser, and general nuisance. Perhaps because the temper of the Restoration was hostile to old Praisegod, Nicholas, in his early twenties, removed to Holland, studying at Leyden and taking a medical degree at Utrecht, a step which enabled him to take an honorary fellowship of the College of Physicians on his return to England in 1669. But though he made the most of being 'Doctor' Barbon he did not practise medicine. An extraordinary capacity for finance, combined with a knack of profiting from the amiability as well as the stupidity of human nature, marked him out as a formidable adventurer. He was destined to become not merely the most daring speculative builder of his day but the virtual founder of fire insurance and an economist of prophetic perspicacity. His importance in this last respect is witnessed by Marx, who right at the beginning of *Capital* uses quotations from Barbon to define the meaning of commodities and use value.

The first we hear of Barbon after his arrival in England is that about 1670 he rebuilt his father's burnt house in Crane Court, Fleet Street, apparently shifting its site to the far end of the Court and giving the new structure a façade of some distinction. Here he lived in a lordly way, directing his mysterious, complex schemes, rarely without great profit and rarely with complete honesty.

Most of what we know about Barbon comes from the autobiography of that entertaining lawyer and chatter-box, Roger

North. North summarizes Barbon's achievement like this:

He was the inventor of this new method of building by casting of ground into streets and small houses, and to augment their number with as little front as possible, and selling the ground to workmen by so much per foot front, and what he could not sell build himself. This has made ground rents high for the sake of mortgaging, and others following his steps have refined and improved upon it, and made a super foetation of houses about London.[1]

If Barbon was hardly the 'inventor' of a 'new method' he certainly developed existing methods on an unprecedented scale.

He was active all over London, building here a square, here a market, here a few streets or chambers for lawyers. When we read in a contemporary letter[2] that he laid out £200,000 in building it certainly does not sound like an exaggeration. He completely grasped the advantages accruing from standardization and mass-production in housing. 'It was not worth his while to deal little,' he said : 'That a bricklayer could do. The gain he expected was out of great undertakings, which would rise lustily in the whole.' The houses he built were all very much alike, economically planned to the point of meanness, with coarse ornaments which repeated themselves over and over again. The design of the panelling and staircases of his houses never varies, and his carpenters must have turned out thousands upon thousands of the twisted balusters whose slick modernity was calculated to engage the eye of the bumpkin in search of his first town house.

For some of his schemes, Barbon required capital to the tune of £30,000 or £40,000 and he was obliged to get loans or credit. Credit suited him best, for by dint of an odious process of delaying, deceiving, wriggling, and pleading he usually managed to evade the law and ultimately to get away with the business at about half what it would have cost to borrow.

Barbon's ability to lead his inferiors by the nose amounted to genius. Like his father, he had the trick of firing a quick

1. R. North, *Autobiography* (ed. A. Jessop; 1887), pp. 54–5.
2. Dated 1697 and quoted in Nathaniel Lloyd, *A History of the English House*, 1931.

enthusiasm, and his technique for getting people to come into his schemes rarely failed. Profit was his only argument, and if the plausibility of a scheme did not strike home at once, he would tackle his opponents one by one. A show of extreme obstinacy he countered by affecting to quarrel and then declaring that personal animosity was at the root of the opposition. On other occasions he could be as mild as milk, submitting pathetically to tirades of calumny. 'Rogue, knave, damned Barbon,' they would call him, until some warm-hearted simpleton took his part – an occasion which the outrageous impostor never failed to improve.

But his most elaborate wiles were employed to buy up properties which stood in the way of his building schemes. His method was to treat at first with the angriest and most effective of the owners, and Roger North gives a wonderful picture of Barbon handling one of these meetings.

They would certainly be early at the place, and confirm and hearten one another to stand it out, for the Doctor must come to their terms. So they would walk about and pass their time expecting the Doctor, and inquiring if he were come. At last word was brought that he was come. Then they began to get towards the long table (in a tavern dining-room for the most part) for the Doctor was come! the Doctor was come! Then he would make his entry, as fine and as richly dressed as a lord of the bedchamber on a birthday. And I must own I have often seen him so dressed, not knowing his design, and thought him a coxcomb for so doing. Then these hard-headed fellows that had prepared to give him all the affronts and opposition that their brutal way suggested, truly seeing such a brave man, pulled off their hats and knew not what to think of it. And the Doctor also being (forsooth) much of a gentleman, then with a mountebank speech to these gentlemen he proposed his terms, which, as I said, were ever plausible, and terminated in their interest. Perhaps they were, at this, all converted in a moment, or perhaps a sour clown or two did not understand his tricks, or would not trust him, or would take counsel, or some blundering opposition they gave; while the rest gaped and stared, he was all honey, and a real friend; which not doing he quarrelled or bought off, as I said, and then at the next meeting some came over, and the rest followed. It mattered not a litigious knave or two, if any such did stand out, for the first thing he did was to pull down their houses about their

46

ears, and build upon their ground, and stand it out at law till their hearts ached, and at last they would truckle and take any terms for peace and a quiet life.[1]

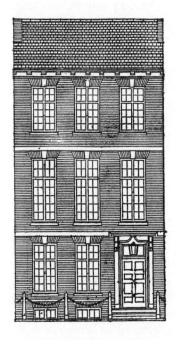

Fig. 4. A house of the type built by Nicholas Barbon between 1670 and 1700.

It is not a pleasant picture, but it is convincing. And now, having introduced the man, let us look at some of his works. Among his major adventures was the purchase and development of the Essex House estate, south of the Strand. Here stood a great Tudor mansion, with several courts, and elaborately laid-out parterres reaching down to the river. Barbon bought the whole property from the executors of the last owner. No sooner had he done so, however, than King Charles decided that it would make an excellent present for a faithful Earl who had done brave work in Ireland. An undignified scramble followed: Barbon routing up the garden and pulling down the house, while the King and Privy Council pressed vainly for repurchase. Barbon was implacable, and within a year a street of brick houses,

1. R. North, op. cit., pp. 56-7.

'for taverns, alehouses, cookshops and vaulting schools' had marred for ever the ancient pleasaunce of Earls and Bishops.

Today we know this street, finished in 1682, as Essex Street. Most of Barbon's houses have gone (Nos. 23 and 24, the least altered, were pulled down shortly before the war) but several remain in an eighteenth-century disguise. At the southern end are the remains of an arch with Corinthian pilasters, its decayed condition, even before it was burnt in the blitz, claiming a veneration which it does not deserve. Actually, it was a piece of pseudo-Roman pomp stuck up by Barbon to mask the politer houses in the street from the brewers' and woodmongers' wharves which he created on the river's edge.[1] Another relic of Barbon is in Devereux Court, near by, where a large bust of the Earl of Essex and an inscription, dated 1676, are attached to one of the houses.

From Devereux Court a rather clumsy gateway with urns, probably of Barbon's making, leads into the Temple, bringing us to another phase in the career of the great builder. Barbon's transactions with the Temple are fully explained by North. Being himself 'full of law', Barbon knew how to handle the lawyers; he knew, moreover, the sort of planning that suited them, and 'could apply to serve (says lawyer North) not only our occasions but our fancies'. It is possible that Barbon built New Court (the design is wrongly attributed to Wren) in 1675, and it is certain that he sold the ground for it. Later, when much of the Temple was destroyed by fire, Barbon built several blocks of chambers.

In 1684 Barbon started one of his biggest schemes – Red Lion Square. This got him into trouble at once. The gentlemen of Gray's Inn resented Barbon's assault on their neighbouring fields, and a hundred or more of them went to beat up the workmen as a protest. Barbon, however, mustered a powerful opposition, and building went ahead. Even when public indignation took the form of official protests by Sir Christopher Wren and warrants from the Middlesex Justices the builder could not be checked. Such was the force of private enterprise, at long last freed

1. I may as well record here that the staircase leading to the premises over the gateway had balusters of the standard profile, mentioned above.

by liberating itself from the tyranny of Royal Proclamations.

Having conquered in Red Lion Fields, Barbon moved northward, entering into negotiations, in 1684, with the Corporation of Bedford for the development of the Harpur Estate.[1] On these and on the adjoining Rugby estate he built a large number of houses, many of which he left unfinished at his death. Other schemes of his included houses in Mincing Lane (where the vaults fell in 'most scandalously', according to North), at least one in St James's Square, several streets on the site of York House, including Buckingham Street and Villiers Street, Newport Square in Soho, and Bedford Row, just east of Red Lion Square.

It is in Bedford Row (Nos. 36 to 43) that Barbon's particular brand of terrace house can best be studied today, though the mind's eye must re-establish the wooden eaves-cornice and casement windows, which have everywhere been replaced by sashes. In Red Lion Square, some Barbon interiors remain, although the brick fronts have been rebuilt in Georgian times – a criticism, this, of the quality of the original materials. There are probable Barbon houses in Great Ormond Street (Nos. 55 and 57) and Denmark Street (Nos. 7 and 10). At Osterley Park, which Barbon at one time owned and remodelled, staircases of the invariable standard type still survive and can be seen peeping through the sash windows of the great Adam mansion.

Barbon's building activities, although occupying a place of importance in the contemporary scene, represent only one aspect of his life's effort. With his work as an initiator of Fire Insurance we are not now concerned; following on the panic caused by the Great Fire, the success of this adventure was immediate, and, according to Mr Brett-James,[2] Barbon insured 5,650 houses between 1686 and 1692, the premiums being on a basis of two and a half per cent for brick houses and five per cent for timber. A Land Bank and an Orphans' Bank were two of his many other projects, and he was, besides, a Member of Parliament and a vigorous champion of debased coinage. But the work for which he is now chiefly remembered, and remembered with respect, is

1. *The Guide to the Bedford Charity* by James Wyatt, 1843.
2. *The Growth of Stuart London*, 1935, p. 344.

his extraordinarily lucid exposition of the basis of economics. The *Discourse of Trade*, published in 1690, states with real precision the relation between use and value, value and price, and defines succinctly the significance of currency, credit, and interest. The importance of building, both socially and economically, is duly emphasized. He calls building 'the most proper and visible Distinction of Riches and Greatness, because the Expenses are too Great for Mean Persons to follow'; and goes on to show that building is 'the chiefest promoter of trade' because of the large number of subsidiary trades on which it depends.

A scarcely less interesting tract had preceded this in 1685. *An Apology for the Builder*[1] is a very logically expressed attempt to overthrow the prejudice against urban expansion and to show that suburban building, far from being a menace to the public welfare, is a healthy and necessary development, which enhances existing land values near the centre of the town, provides new markets, settles the equilibrium between town and country, and creates revenue and potential cannon-fodder for the Government. The point of view is thoroughly nineteenth century, and makes one realize vividly that the mentality which we habitually associate with the Victorian epoch is merely an expansion of concepts crystallized and sanctified in the age of Charles II, Locke, Wren, and Barbon.

Perhaps the best epitaph on Barbon is North's remark that 'he never failed to satisfy everyone in treaty and discourse, and if he had performed as well he had been a truly great man'. But performance lagged far behind. When he died, many of his schemes were in utter confusion, and his debts were enormous. It was, also, characteristic of this extremely able, but far from amiable person that, when he died, instructions were found in his will that none of his debts should be paid.

The story of Barbon brings us to the threshold of the eighteenth century and closes a period of vigorous building, the like of which was not seen for many years afterwards.

1. Published anonymously, but assigned to Barbon by Mr N. G. Brett-James. There are several copies in the British Museum. It was reprinted in J. R. McCulloch, *Select Collection of Scarce and Valuable Economic Tracts*, 1859. The reprint is, however, considerably scarcer than the original pamphlet.

The circumstances with which Barbon had to deal soon ceased to be. The scramble for freehold properties within a short radius of Westminster (the magnet of the house-hunting public) could

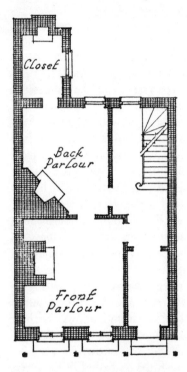

Fig. 5. Plan of a typical London house of the period after the Great Fire.

not go on for ever; and when all the eligible freeholds had gone, builders had to face up to the phalanx of entailed and trust properties in the west, properties whose owners were perfectly well aware of their probable future value. It was not till after the Treaty of Utrecht, in 1713, that this new stage in London's development was reached, and the Georgian expansion begun. It went forward from the precedents established by Lord Southampton and Lord St Albans. Its progress belongs to a future chapter. For the present we must turn from the study of outward expansion and see what changes took place in the City of London itself after the Great Fire, and what sort of a picture it presented at the opening of the Georgian period.

CHAPTER 4

The Mercantile Stronghold

WHEN one considers that, even today, the City of London is outside the jurisdiction of the London County Council, it is not difficult to realize its emphatic separateness in the adolescent London of the seventeenth and eighteenth centuries. Then the City still *was* London and the fiction of its self-sufficiency survived long into the time when London and Westminster had become an organism of which 'the City' was only a small part. A closely knit self-governing community, the City in the Middle Ages was still by no means crowded. Within its walls, houses and grounds of an aristocratic kind – not very different from the manor-houses of the landed nobility – found a conspicuous place. It was only in Tudor times that the image of the City began to be that of a counting house and industrial enclave in a larger capital. It was then that the great mansions began to be demolished or divided up, their gardens covered with tenements. Within its militarily useless walls, and for some distance beyond them, it became a mercantile stronghold. As such it entered the Civil War; and as such it emerged at the Restoration, with a social character and taste entirely its own.

This was the city which was four-fifths destroyed in the Great Fire of September 1666. As it was rebuilt, it became a component of the Greater London of Georgian times with which this book is concerned. The rebuilding of the city and the picture it presented in its rebuilt form is, therefore, a proper subject for a chapter.

The first concrete step towards the rebuilding was the Act for the Rebuilding of the City of London, 1667. This extremely comprehensive statute was compiled jointly by the City authorities and the Privy Council, presumably with the assistance of two sets of technical advisers. These would be, on the one hand, the City's Surveyors, Robert Hooke, Peter Mills, and Edward Jerman, and on the other Dr Christopher Wren, whom the Privy Council had appointed 'Principal' Architect' for the rebuilding of the City with Hugh May and Roger Pratt as his associates. It is impossible to know now to what extent Wren was effectively concerned with the Act, but his share was probably small, for, as Mr Bell[1] has shown, his contribution to the rebuilding was practically confined to St Paul's and the churches, together with a very few public buildings. His celebrated plan, sketched out while the ruins still smoked, was a hypothetical project, produced without taking into consideration the economic urgency of the situation, which demanded that the thread of City life should be resumed as soon as possible and as nearly as possible on the old lines. Wren does not come into the picture of the new London except in so far as his own particular works are concerned, and of these I shall have something to say later.

The Act covered three important aspects of the rebuilding problem: first, the re-arrangement of some of the worst features of the old plan, with its apparently wayward meanderings, jutting corners and frequent bottle-necks; second, the partial standardization of the new buildings, particularly with a view to fire-resistance; and third, the raising of money for the public (but not, of course, the private) buildings, by a tax on coal. The first category amounted to very little. The most important alteration to the old plan was the formation of King Street and the transformation of an ancient lane into Queen Street, the combined thoroughfares giving direct access from the Guild-hall to the Thames.

The second matter dealt with in the Act – the standardization of house-building – was of the greatest importance. Never before had such sweeping control of building activity been entered on the Statute-book. The houses to be built in the new City were divided into four classes, 'for better regulation, uniformity, and gracefulness'. In the 'high and principal streets' (six only were classified as such) houses were to be neither more nor less than four storeys in height; in the 'streets

1. W. G. Bell, *The Great Fire of London*, 1920. The rebuilding of the City has been described in detail by T. F. Reddaway, *The Rebuilding of London*, 1940.

and lanes of note', three storeys was the rule; while in 'by-lanes' two storeys were prescribed. A fourth class was reserved for houses 'of the greatest bigness', which did not front the street but which lay behind, with their courtyards and gardens. Their height was limited to four storeys. In practice, a good deal of freedom was exercised in the distribution of the various types, since it was obviously impossible to classify London's streets and lanes in a hard and fast manner. But that the result was satisfactory is proved by every illustration of the City streets, which shows that they achieved a reasonable orderliness without monotony.

The construction of the new houses was also standardized. That walls should be invariably of brick or stone was an obviously desirable provision, to which legislation had been tending for many years. The precise thicknesses of walls at various heights, however, were also fixed and so were the timber scantlings, and the ceiling heights of the several floors; as to the exteriors, the manner and quantity of enrichment was left to individual taste, but the larger types of houses were required to have a balcony at first-floor level and a 'pent-house' immediately below, protecting the pedestrian from the fall of rainwater from the eaves.

There was, of course, nothing new about the types of houses provided for in the Act. The provision merely crystallized the best practice of the time, as it was understood among the builders of the West End, and indeed in the City itself. And there was plenty of room for individual vagaries both of taste and construction. If the new city possessed a general uniformity of character its individual houses, especially in the main streets, did not lack variety. (Plate 2b.)

The speed at which rebuilding went on was remarkable, especially when one considers that insurance was almost unheard of and that the will to build sprang from a community of ruined or almost ruined merchants and corporations. Mr Bell tells us that in 1668 1,200 houses were begun and that in the spring and summer of 1669 about 1,600 were under scaffolding. In 1670 fourteen churches were begun, but the speed of house-building slackened. Nevertheless, the City must have been fairly thickly built up by the time that Ogilby's large-scale map was published in 1677. This map, based on survey work which its author undertook after the fire for the City authorities, gives an excellent picture of the rebuilt city, each individual house being shown. The social texture of this incredible human hive is an amusing study.

Fortunately, besides Ogilby's map and the many succeeding maps based upon it, we have the minute verbal record of John Strype, who includes in his edition of Stow's *Survey* (1720) a complete catalogue of every street, lane, alley, court and yard, and every building of importance in that packed square mile. To each item he supplies comments – curiously phrased, evading precision in a surfeit of qualifying adjectives. Through this quaintness one discerns a gradual descent from affluence to squalor, from what is 'very handsome, open and airy' and 'indifferent good' to what is downright 'small, nasty and beggarly'. The actual morphology of the city, the process of growth behind the existing complexity Strype does not attempt to analyse, but this the observant reader can supply, in a general way, for himself.

Consider the main components of the map. The streets are lined with narrow-fronted houses whose sites stretch back to twice their width or more, and which have a tiny patch of courtyard or garden – rarely more than the size of a large carpet – at the back. These houses form by far the most numerous units. But they do not cover the whole area. They are merely the breastworks of inner areas, where alleys, courts, yards, and closes meet each other in an inscrutable topographical jig-saw. These hinterlands contained both the best and the worst of mercantile London. At one extreme there was the long, broad, paved court, with a fine house fitting the end, equally good houses along the sides, and an entry to the main street wide enough for a coach or cart. At the other extreme was the miserable, unpaved alley, hastily built in the garden of a once affluent house as a means of producing rent from the labouring class which clustered around the advancing standard of capitalism. The hinterlands, in fact, belonged to the Londoner who did not require a shop-front; on the one hand, the merchant who was not a retailer, on the other, the man who had nothing to sell but the labour of his hands.

The process which brought about this pattern started right back in the Middle Ages. It can be discerned clearly in the early surveys of districts which escaped the fire and thus preserved some of their medieval groundwork overlaid with later building. Here one can distinguish the surviving halls and courtyards of medieval mansions and observe how these became fenced in by the building of small narrow-fronted houses along the street. These street houses, with no hall and consisting only of a front and a back room on each floor, multiplied to such an extent, in the later Middle Ages, that they became the chief consistency of London's plan. With the crowding of the street-fronts it was natural that advantage should be taken of the empty ground behind; and thus the houses turned inwards, here in the form of a 'court' or 'yard', there lining an 'alley' which had hitherto been nothing but a foot-path between streets. Where the halls, courts, and gardens of the greater medieval houses had been, were built the great mansions of later days, or else their sites were cut up to form courts and yards lined with tenements. By the time of the fire this process of increment and involution had reached its ultimate stage; every square yard of the City was utilized. And when the City was rebuilt this old land utilization was perpetuated in the new structures of red brick.

To visualize the anatomical structure of the City still more clearly it is worth concentrating in a small area – a sample of, say, a quarter of a mile square. Such a sample is shown in the plan (based on Ogilby) on page 57. Here we have an important commercial street, Coleman Street, which Strype characterizes as 'large and long ... very well inhabited by divers noted merchants and shopkeepers'; in other words, a typical street of three-storey houses with shops along the ground floor. Then we have the courts and alleys on either side. Most of them are very narrow, not more than eight or ten feet wide, and Strype dismisses them as 'indifferent good'. Packer's Court earns a little more because of its width, and it is 'a pretty open place', though with 'indifferent' buildings. Brickenton Court and Nun Court are distinguished as having 'a merchant's house at the

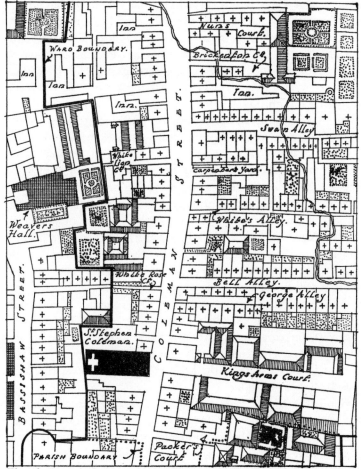

Fig. 6. A typical area of the City as rebuilt after the Great Fire.
Based on Ogilby and Morgan's map, 1677.

upper end', a circumstance clearly seen on the map. But the
only court of real quality and importance is King's Arms Yard:
'*King's Arms Yard*, or rather *Street* for the largeness and good-
ness, being graced with good large Houses, inhabited by Merchants and Persons of Repute.'

What did all these courts and alleys look like? Strype's 'indifferent' buildings were perfectly plain two-storey brick

structures of a type which survives here and there but has largely vanished, owing as much to the poor quality of its craftsmanship as to more obvious causes of rebuilding. The more important houses, built for 'Merchants, and Persons of Repute', were often very noble examples of seventeenth and early eighteenth-century vernacular. Those in King's Arms Yard we can reconstruct faithfully because an eighteenth-century survey of them has been preserved[1]; most of them comprised, on the ground floor, two big, heavily panelled parlours, a wide oak staircase and etceteras, including a closet which drained into a cess-pit under the garden. The houses were planned so as to get the maximum well-lit accommodation out of very cramped sites but, even so, it was usually found possible to find room for a toy garden, perhaps with a little fountain in it. Today King's Arms Yard survives only in name, but there were, before the blitz, places in the City where the atmosphere of these warrens of mercantile domesticity still lingered. You can just sense it still in Racquet Court and Crane Street off Fleet Street, and in Wardrobe Court off Watling Street, but not as you could before the blitz in Neville's Court (Plate 3) off Fetter Lane, where there remained patches of garden in front of the houses. Up to 1941, a great merchant's house at the end of a yard still existed in all its glory at the back of 34 Great Tower Street; it was the last of its kind.

Returning to our map, it should be observed that several of the courts are marked as Inns; these would be long galleried courts, with stabling below and bedrooms above. Strype remarks of one that it is 'pretty good for stabling and Coaches', of another that it is 'only for livery horses', and of a third that it is 'small and ordinary'. Yet another type of court is Carpenter's Court which was, in fact, a timber yard.

I have said enough, I think, to indicate the special character of the City as a medieval growth crystallized in Stuart and Georgian brick. Of its more purely architectural qualities at the opening of the Georgian era it is not so easy to speak since so little remains of it. City taste was a subject for mockery and

---

1. British Museum. *Crace Maps* (Portfolio 9, No. 168). The houses were demolished in 1881. *Builder*, 1881, i, 552.

disdain in the West End, and the men who designed the City's houses were not polite architects but bricklayers and carpenters, masons, glaziers, and plumbers, many of whom had come from the country after the fire to take advantage of the relaxations in the conditions of citizenship to which the City had been forced by the shortage of craftsmen. An amusing side-light on the varieties of architectural treatment to be found in the City is provided by a remark of Barbon's who told a friend[1] that, walking through the City during the rebuilding, he could tell at a glance the trade of the master-builder responsible for each house:

Some being set out with fine brick-work rubbed and gaged, were the Issue of a master bricklayer. If stone coyned, jamb'd, and fascia'd, of a stone mason. If full of windoe, with much glass in compass, and reliev, a Glazier's; if full of Balcone and balustrading, a Carpenter, and so others ... one may in ye face of most houses, discerne ye calling of some builder or other most conspicuously.

The high flights in City architecture were rarely of a kind to satisfy educated taste. When Lord Mayor Sir William Turner, in 1668, wished to set a brave example to the rebuilders, the house he put up in Cheapside was robustly ornamental, but hardly elegant (its stones, by the way, survive in an antique dealer's yard for anyone who cares to buy them); and the same vigorous but impolite character pervades the grand old houses which survived the blitz on Laurence Pountney Hill. The City folk prided themselves on many things which were merely vulgar to the westerners. They liked fat cornices and enormous iron-work shop-signs, just as they liked starting the day with a draught of sack, over-eating, and pinching each others' fat wives. The City contributed nothing to the art of the Stuarts and Georgians; it was content with the robust second-rate. And the only buildings there which had the stamp of real architectural excellence were those which came under the authority of the men of Whitehall and St James's.

Which brings me to the public buildings. These were of two main sorts: the halls of the Livery Companies and the Parish

1. Roger North, who records the remark in his essay on architecture, *Add.* MS. 34, 162.

Church; with the addition of certain unique buildings like St Paul's Cathedral, the Exchange, the Customs House, and the College of Arms.

The Companies' Halls were regular City architecture. They stood back from the street (a typical site is that of Weavers' Hall, shown in the plan on page 57) and were mostly provided with courtyards and gardens. Of the halls themselves, those which were not purely and simply craftsmen's work were designed by men of the type of Jerman, the City Surveyor; two (Brewers' and Tallow Chandlers', the first destroyed, the second badly damaged) were designed by a Captain Caine. In spite of all claims to the contrary none were designed by Wren. Several survive : notably Skinners' Hall and Vintners' Hall, both with interesting woodwork, and Apothecaries' Hall, whose courtyard has that trim, doll's-house charm which must have been as characteristic of the better parts of the City as it is of the Amsterdam painted by Vermeer and de Hoogh.

And now, to complete our picture of the rebuilt City, we come to St Paul's and the churches. To put them last may seem anomalous; but it is logical, because we have been considering the City as an organic urban growth, and although the churches were a vital part of the City's building-needs they necessarily came after the houses and even the halls in urgency and in point of time.

With the cathedral and the churches the name of Sir Christopher Wren is indissolubly connected. They formed the major part of his work as Principal Architect for the rebuilding and there is little doubt that he personally consulted with the churchwardens of each of the fifty-one parishes whose churches were rebuilt. That all of them, equally, represent his personal work, executed according to his precise wishes, would, however, be too much to take for granted. The City churches must be studied with discrimination. If Wren's was the great mind determining the general shape and structure of each, much of the working out was left to others; to Wren's friend and fellow research-worker, Hooke, one of the City Surveyors, who had not one ounce of sensibility in his composition, and to able masons like Kempster, Pearce, and Strong, who were not always, perhaps, alive to the *finesses* upon which an architect with half Wren's responsibilities might have insisted. Indeed, in many of the City churches you find the rather gross aldermanish vernacular which comes out so strongly in the City halls; and only occasionally does the lucid genius of Wren shine through with recognizable brilliance. One cannot seriously place in the same category, as works of art, a thing of brilliant skill and masterly refinement like the tower of St Mary-le-Bow and a quaint piece of almost vernacular expression like St Mary Aldermanbury.

The glory of the City churches is, first, in their original and daring variety of planning in which one sees Wren's keen experimental mind at work; and, second, in the lovely additions their steeples made to London's Georgian skyline. That skyline, an even horizon of tiles and parapets, rose no higher than forty feet from the streets. Above it soared Wren's fifty steeples in Portland Stone and lead. Above it, too, rose the upper part of St Paul's, the whole of the superior order clear above the roofs, so that a temple seemed to be established on the house-tops. Of St Paul's I shall say no more than to remind the reader how much of the London of which I have been describing lay in its vast shadow. St Paul's is a building into whose form the spiritual history of seventeenth-century England is as firmly built as it is into the writings of Locke and Dryden. There is the science of the Royal Society, the latinity of Restoration Oxford, the religious equivocation of the House of Stuart.[1] That such a monument should rise, not among the new streets and squares around Westminster but on the barren, unintellectual soil of the mercantile stronghold, is one of the freaks of history – that peculiarly capricious freak whose origin in a baker's house in September 1666 is commemorated by a huge Doric column conceived by Wren and erected by Hooke at Fish Street Hill.

The rebuilt City changed its character little all through the eighteenth and early part of the nineteenth century. Dickens knew and wrote about that cramped mosaic of commercial

---

1. I have attempted an analysis of these contributory influences in the designing of St Paul's in 'The Tyranny of Intellect; a study of the mind of Sir Christopher Wren', *R.I.B.A. Journal*, 20 February 1937; reprinted in *Heavenly Mansions*, 1949.

domesticity where merchants lived above their counting houses, where the high pews of fifty or sixty churches were sparsely occupied every Sunday morning, and where countless little gardens were laboriously watered by City wives. It was only a little more than a century ago that the great transformation began, when not only the wealthy but even the shopkeepers and clerks began to seek villas in Blackheath, Peckham, Dulwich, and Ealing.

The chief architectural events of the City's eighteenth-century life before 1760 were the building of a Mansion House on the old Stocks Market, the building of a new market on the covered-in Fleet River, the building of a Corn Exchange, the building or rebuilding of a few more churches and City halls, and the building of the first Bank of England.

Over most of these activities and many others, presided the able, energetic figure of George Dance, a stone-cutter by trade who was 'Clerk of the City works' from 1735 to 1767. It was this Dance who built the Mansion House, under circumstances very typical of the time.

The Mansion House was proposed in order to put an end to the inconvenient practice of lodging the Lord Mayor in one of the City Halls during the period of his Mayoralty. In 1734, a committee of City fathers set about choosing a design. Dance's appointment to his official post was just then pending and he was asked to submit drawings. At the same time, James Gibbs and Giacomo Leoni were also applied to, and a date was fixed for the submission of all three designs. A fourth, indescribably gauche design, was thrust under the Committee's nose by young Batty Langley, the publishing carpenter; while a fifth was submitted at the very last moment by Isaac Ware. There is a story of a design of Palladio's being sent in by Lord Burlington as suitable for adaptation as a Mansion House, and of its being rejected, because Palladio was not merely not a freeman of the City but a papist. It is a pretty story, but, according to Mr Perks,[1] quite without foundation. However, I suggest that it may well be a perversion of the reasons which eliminated

1. Sydney Perks, *History of the Mansion House*, 1922, in which the designs of all the architects are reproduced.

Leoni from the contest, he being the author of an edition of Palladio, an Italian, and a Catholic.

Dance's design possessed considerably less *finesse* than those of some of his rivals, but he was an agreeable and convenient choice, so Gibbs and Leoni were paid off and Dance set to work. The result of his labours may be appraised today by anyone who cares to take up one of the few points of vantage from which the Mansion House can be adequately seen. The tall pilastered façade (Plate 2a), with its ungenerously shallow portico, leaves an impression of uneasily restricted bulk; of the classical canon used without emotion, simply to harness a structure already ill-sited and too large for its site. As originally built, the Mansion House possessed two ark-like attics at front and rear which, if they did not improve the design, at least gave it an exciting touch of millionaire enormity.

The interior is as ungracious in plan as in ornament. The vast Egyptian Hall ('Egyptian' because the columnar arrangement employed is so described by Vitruvius) compels respect from its size and discipline. But, on the whole, the building is a striking reminder that good taste was not a universal attribute in the eighteenth century and that, in the City of the 1730s, there was a great deal more money than discrimination.

Dance's churches, one of which was built before the Mansion House and two after, are worthier of respect. They follow in the steps of other church-builders of the time and therefore belong to a separate chapter. But while on the subject of City taste it is impossible not to mention St Luke's, Old Street, where somebody (not Dance) hit on the truly remarkable notion of erecting an obelisk to serve as a spire. It is a fine obelisk and there is nothing much wrong with the tower below it – except that it is a ludicrous base for an obelisk.

But Palladianism was not always ridiculous beyond Temple Bar. Prints of Dance's original Corn Exchange (an overflow from Jarman's crowded central building) show a serene and sensible design with an open Doric colonnade on the ground floor. The long arcades of the Fleet Market do not seem to have been contemptible. And when the Governors of the Bank of England secured the services of a relatively unknown Mr

Sampson for their new building in Threadneedle Street, they were given a design which would not have disgraced any friend of Lord Burlington's (Plate 26). Almost, but not quite, the same might be said of the very ornamental façade by T. Holden, of Ironmongers' Hall, which stood in Fenchurch Street.

After the accession of George III one begins to lose the impression of the City as a philistine fort. The merchants begin to take West End houses and to form West End tastes. Committees are more knowledgeable, architects better educated. Dance was succeeded in office by his son; and he, significantly, was a man of taste and scholarship and a founder-member of the Royal Academy. We shall meet him in a later chapter.

CHAPTER 5

The London House and its Builders

THE size and shape of the London house have been conditioned from the first by the economic need to get as many houses as possible into one street. Economy of frontage means not only economy of site area but economy of road-making, which is equally important. The typical site of a London house is therefore a long strip of ground running back from the street. The house covers the front part of the strip, the middle part is garden or courtyard, and at the back is, in the larger type of house, a coach-house and stable served from a subsidiary road.

Georgian London was a city made up almost entirely of these long narrow plots with their tall narrow houses and long narrow gardens or courts. Practically the whole population lived in one version or another of such houses. A handful of aristocrats had their isolated palaces; and the unemployable and criminal classes had their centuries-old rookeries; but the remainder, from earls to artisans, had their narrow slices of building, now called, for no very good reason, 'terrace-houses'.

The vertical relation of the terrace-house to its site is not as simple as it seems. All houses except the poorest have basements. But the basement represents only a shallow excavation, while the roadway is partly *made up*. That is why the front basement room of a London house invariably looks into a deep 'area', whereas the back room has a door leading straight into a court and then usually up two or three steps to a yard or garden. The roadway and the garden are at different levels. The garden level is the 'natural' level, whereas the roadway represents an 'artificial' level (see Figure 7).

The custom of building vaults under houses is very ancient and the 'basement' probably perpetuates the medieval vaulted cellar which was used either for storage or as a shop and was entered by a few steps going down from the street. The basement of the Georgian house is also approachable by steps from

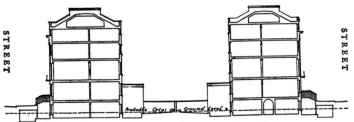

Fig. 7. Typical section through parallel streets in Bloomsbury. Compare end elevations of same houses in Fig. 26, p. 192.

the street, but there is an 'area' intervening whose outer wall forms, in effect, the retaining wall of the made-up roadway. Actually the area is usually extended under the pavement to provide fuel storage so that the real retaining wall is about in line with the kerb. The providing of storage space under the pavement gave rise to those circular openings with cast-iron covers through which coal can be delivered without entering the area – a device which appears to date from about the middle of the eighteenth century.

The diagram on this page (Fig. 7) explains the whole principle. The roadway is, as it were, the surface of a trough filled with earth, the area walls forming its two sides. This means that the roads in any given part of London are uniformly raised above the natural level, which, however, still exists, unseen, behind the houses and sometimes discloses itself by a slight change of level between an old road formed on the natural surface and a later road made up by a Georgian builder.[1]

As for the plan of the house itself, nothing could be simpler. There is one room at the back and one at the front on each floor, with a passage and staircase at one side. On a site as narrow as twenty-four feet hardly any other arrangement is possible; in broader sites it is still a perfectly satisfactory and economical arrangement. There is no escape from it. Mariners' humble cottages in the East End have this plan; and so have the great houses in Carlton House Terrace.

1. For instance, Gower Street, formed at the end of the eighteenth century, is at a higher level than Euston Road, formed without houses in 1756, and the difference is perceptible at the junction of the two thoroughfares.

Minor variations, however, are infinitely possible. The stair can be turned this way and that, made to descend into a great hall, or built in a circular well; columns and entablatures, double doors, coved recesses and niches can be introduced. As the site is increased in width, it is possible to contrive features and modulations which give the whole house a formal, architectural character which carries through from front to back. Again, it was early discovered that an annexe or addendum built out at the back could be made so as to provide additional room-space while not necessarily robbing the main back room of its necessary window area. Closets could be introduced; and when they became unfashionable (as they did) they could be left out. The story of the better-class London house is a story of ingenious variation within the inflexible limits of party-walls.

The insistent verticality of the London house is idiomatic. The French learnt at an early date to live horizontally and most, if not all, continental capitals followed the French lead. In London, only bachelor lawyers lived in 'chambers', and the block of apartments of high social standing was unknown till Henry Ashton built the flats in Victoria Street, in the 1850s. The vertical living-idiom produced many comments from foreigners, the best of which is Louis Simond's,[1] written just after Waterloo:

These narrow houses, three or four storeys high – one for eating, one for sleeping, a third for company, a fourth underground for the kitchen, a fifth perhaps at top for the servants – and the agility, the ease, the quickness with which the individuals of the family run up and down, and perch on the different storeys, give the idea of a cage with its sticks and birds.

The external details and internal fittings and finishings of the London house have changed more than its plan. They follow changes in fashion, and also the more radical shifts in the control and responsibility for design. In the course of this chapter I shall examine the marked change which occurred between the house of Queen Anne's time – still substantially seventeenth-century in character – and the Palladian house which was produced with little change during the thirties,

1. *Journal of a Tour and Residence in Great Britain*, 1817, vol. 1, p. 64.

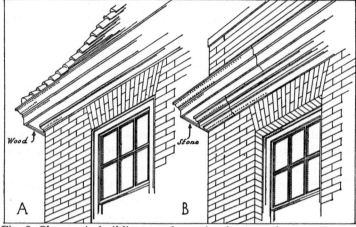

Fig. 8. Changes in building practice under the Acts of 1707 and 1709. The parapet, stone cornice, and recessed window-frame in B show the effect of the Acts.

forties, fifties, and early sixties of the century. The changes have deep and interesting origins.

First we must observe certain modifications in building technique. Between the Barbon house illustrated on page 47 and the first of the strictly Georgian houses, certain important innovations were introduced. Continued fear of conflagrations prompted a Statute of 1707, which abolished the prominent wooden eaves-cornices which were such a striking feature of the streets and squares of the Restoration. 'No mundillion or cornish of timber or wood under the eaves,' states the Act, 'shall hereafter be made or suffered'; and so the roof was half-hidden by a parapet wall, with a cornice of brick, stone, or, in later years, stucco, a few feet below the summit. Two years later, in 1709, another attack was made on exposed woodwork, this time in the window-openings. The frames, instead of being nearly in the same plane as the brick face, were to be set back four inches, leaving a naked 'reveal' of brickwork and incidentally giving a sense of solidity to the walls (Fig. 8).

It was about this time that the great change-over from casement to sash-windows took place. The sash, a Dutch invention, had been known for many years, but its popularity only dates from Queen Anne's time. Then, however, it swept the town and few of the older houses, even, were suffered long to retain their transomed and mullioned casements. Today, hardly any eighteenth-century casements exist in London, except in an occasional back-elevation or basement where it has never been thought worth while to supersede them.[1]

With the general adoption of parapet-roofs and sash-windows with recessed frames, the characteristic Georgian town house had arrived. No further legislation interfered with its externals until the great Building Act of 1774, which belongs to a later chapter. But change did not stop. The pressure of architectural discipline continued until, by the middle of the century, the craftsman's hand in design was no longer seen and the architect was in complete control.

This change, the last phase in a very long chapter in the history of taste, leads us to consider who were the people who built the houses of Georgian London.

The building trade consisted, firstly, of craftsmen trained in a variety of different crafts – carpenters, joiners, masons, brick-layers, plasterers, glaziers, plumbers, painters, carvers, and paviors. These men were apprenticed for seven years, worked as journeymen, and then perhaps set up on their own. The system was still more or less medieval, except that trades were no longer closely organized, even in the towns. Although the City of London still had its Companies which were able to control the craftsmen within the City itself, the majority of men working in the expanding districts outside were not organized in any way.

The London craftsman was, as a rule, a man of considerable skill and status – proud, conscientious, and expensive. He lived well and drank heartily. He was capable of writing a fairly good letter and could usually (if he were a mason, bricklayer, or carpenter) make a plain 'draught' of a small building.[2]

1. There are a few survivals in Middle Temple Lane and King's Bench Walk.

2. Venterus Mandey, author of *Mellificium Mensionis: or, the Marrow of Measuring*, 1682, 4th ed. 1727, was bricklayer to Lincoln's Inn. His literary accomplishments were, of course, above the average.

But his social importance did not end there. In the building trade, as in almost every other, there was, at the beginning of the eighteenth century, a strong capitalist element. The capitalist in the building trade was the 'master-builder'. Usually either a carpenter or bricklayer by training, he would undertake the construction of entire houses and build for the speculative market. He was not necessarily (for reasons which we shall see in a moment) a great employer of labour but he was of the greatest importance because he took the initiative in building; as his point of view – the point of view of the businessman rather than the craftsman – became dominant, skill and originality became of secondary account. The constructional trades – brick-laying and carpentering – became businesses, and the trades requiring taste and good workmanship – joiners and carvers, for instance – became largely dependent on these.

If the master-builder was the central figure in the building trade, he was overshadowed socially, if not financially, by the *surveyor*. The surveyor was what we should call a black-coated worker. As a type he was descended from the surveyors of Tudor times – products of the agrarian revolution; he was quali-fied not merely to survey land but to supervise building work and measure it for estimating and pricing.

Lastly there was the *architect*. But it cannot be too strongly emphasized that until about half-way through the eighteenth century there was no such thing as an 'architectural profession' in the modern sense. The high-sounding title, 'architect', was adopted by anyone who could get away with it. Architects were recruited from tradesmen, from surveyors, and from the gentry. Good posts in the Royal service were open to them, though the word 'architect' was rarely attached to these offices, which were mostly surveyorships and clerkships of works, or offices nomin-ally assigned to masons or carpenters.

Architecture was open to all. A Vanbrugh or an Archer might come to it as gentlemen with a passion for building and under an obligation to find themselves a 'place' (Archer's 'place' in-cidentally was the wholly non-technical sinecure of 'groom-porter'). On the other hand, many of the most distinguished architects were trained as craftsmen. Flitcroft was a joiner by training, Ripley a carpenter, Kent a coach-painter. A writer[1] of 1747, speaking of architects, says: 'I scarce know of any in *England* who have had an Education regularly designed for the Profession. Bricklayers, carpenters, etc., all commence [i.e. set up as] Architects; especially in and about London, where there go but Few Rules to the building of a City-House.' One often finds a man described as Mr So-and-so, carpenter, becoming in a very short time So-and-so, Esq., architect. 'A pox on these builders – architects they call themselves,' says one of Wycherley's characters, and it is, in fact, often impossible to tell whether the plan and proportions of a house were designed by an architect or a superior craftsman.

Speculative building and the architectural profession were the two goals of success for men entering the London building trade. The roles might be, and often were, combined. But the man who was temperamentally fitted for the more academic and literary parts of the business usually contrived to find himself a patron, with whose help he advanced along the road of pure professionalism as far as a country estate of his own, a carriage, a coat-of-arms, and a fortune of £10,000 or £20,000. Such cases are not rare. On the other hand, you have the men of more purely commercial bent, who amassed greater wealth than the archictects but had no particular ambitions in the social sphere. An interesting illustration offers itself in the careers of two successful men of the early part of the century – Nicholas Hawksmoor, the architect, and William Tufnell, a well-known bricklayer. They lived a few doors from each other, on Millbank, and died in 1736 and 1733 respectively. Hawksmoor was of farming stock, Tufnell of a family of building tradesmen. Hawksmoor, a senior Civil Servant, was styled Esquire at his death and had gotten a country estate as well as a good deal of London property. Tufnell, as bricklayer to the New River Company, and in other employments, is reputed to have amassed a fortune of £30,000. Both died rich. But whereas Hawksmoor's wealth took the shape of the social pyramid, Tufnell's did not. The divergence of aim is interesting. It shows the artist conforming, the capitalist laying the foundation for a new wealthy class – the class

1. R. Campbell, *The London Tradesman.*

which, by sheer wealth, was to dominate the Victorian period.

The ability of the craftsman to better himself by becoming an architect or a quasi-architect provided a strong inducement to self-education, even to the more commercially-minded man, for he could not afford to be behind in questions of taste. Self-education meant getting a hold on the artistic needs of the centres of fashion. It meant the desertion of traditional crafts-manship and the adoption of certain academic formulas. Com-petition made this necessary; for with the growth of capitalism in the building world the individual either had to make a place for himself or remain a journeyman all his days at a wage of 12s. or 15s. a week under conditions which became rapidly less tolerable as time went on.[1]

Thus we find the building industry transforming itself from a homogeneous body of independent craftsmen to a body com-prising, at the top, the speculating master-builder, at the bottom the journeyman, and between the two, but on a pedestal of his own, raising him socially above either, the architect. The loss of status to the individual craftsman is obvious. He had to go into business as a speculator or get himself a patron and become an architect, or perish. To stand on his own feet he had to become something of an architect himself. This he was able to do through the medium of books.

Books were the most important single factor in establishing the dictatorship of Palladian taste throughout the building world. The great period of book production for craftsmen began in 1715 when two important works were launched. One of these was the first volume of *Vitruvius Britannicus*, a magni-ficent record of the best classical buildings so far erected in Eng-land. The other was a sumptuous edition of Palladio, brought out in instalments by the Italian, Giacomo Leoni. In the *Vitruvius* the list of subscribers contains the names of several masons, carpenters, and joiners, though its aim was clearly to inform and please a much loftier region of society. Within ten

1. In 1783 a skilled London carpenter made 18s. 8d. in a seven-day week and looked forward to making 20s. or 21s. 'if the peace continueth' (it did, for ten years). H. G. Davis, *Memorials of the Hamlet of Knights-bridge*, 1859.

years of this event, however, an avalanche had begun of books compiled by craftsmen and exclusively *for* craftsmen, with a view to instructing them in that self-improvement which would see them on the right side of the fence. I cannot indicate the spirit in which these books were written better than by quoting the first paragraph of a book called *The City and Country Workman's Treasury of Design, or the Art of Drawing and Working the Ornamental Parts of Architecture*.[1] It runs:

The great Pleasure that Builders and Workmen of all kinds have of late years taken in the Study of Architecture; and the great Advantages that have accrued to those, for whom they have been employed; by having their works executed in a much neater and more magnificent Manner than was ever done in this Kingdom before; has been the real Motive that induced me, to the compiling of this work, for their further Improvement.

That was written in 1741, but it refers to a process which had been going on for some time. If you compare a doorway of Queen Anne's time – say one of those lovely examples in Queen Anne's Gate – with a doorway of about 1750, you will see the change which books, more than anything else, brought about. The Queen Anne doorway (Fig. 9) is uncouth, perhaps, but it is inventive and 'curious' in the good old sense and the carving is spirited and personal to the carver. The other doorway (my example, Fig. 10, is from a house in George Street, Westminster) is a standard product, simply a Doric order neatly adapted to the purpose of an ornamental porch. It is superbly executed and is in what the author I have quoted would call 'a much neater and more magnificent manner' than the other. By the standards of his time he was right, though it was already admitted by some of his contemporaries that carving, as such, was a decaying art.[2] The Queen Anne doorway is, and always was, unique, The George Street doorway was never unique; it was repeated all over London and corresponds exactly with published plates of the period. A striking instance of the correspondence between pattern-book and executed example is given in Plate 4.

1. By Batty Langley, 1741.
2. 'The carving now used is but the outlines of the art,' says Campbell in *The London Tradesman*, 1747.

Fig. 9. Doorway in Queen Anne's Gate (about 1704).

The bibliography of the building craftsman's pattern-book is enormous. I will only mention some of the more famous and prolific authors. William Halfpenny, a Twickenham carpenter, was responsible, from 1722 onwards, for a continuous stream of books of designs addressed sometimes to the gentry, sometimes to the trade. Batty Langley, a carpenter-surveyor-architect, whose bumptious personality crops up continually on the architectural scene, published, from 1726, over twenty books all containing good, workmanlike plates. Then there were Francis Price, William Pain, Abraham Swan, William Salmon, John Crunden, and, later in the century, Peter Nicholson. The main output was between 1725 and 1760; it diminished with the expansion of the architectural profession and the coincident repression of the craftsman's initiative. In the latter part of the century we get a very different wave of book-publishing, sponsored not by craftsmen but by architects, and designed not to instruct the workman, but to charm the potential client.

The larger and more academic books, such as *Vitruvius Britannicus*, were usually published by subscription. Books for

Fig. 10. Doorway
in George Street,
Westminster (about
1750).

tradesmen, however, seem to have made tolerably good business for the booksellers, since they were able to put them on the market at anything from 3s. for an octavo book to £1 1s. for a folio. One of Langley's quarto *Treasuries*, with 184 elaborate and accurately engraved plates, was sold by Harding, of St Martin's Lane, at 16s. (in sheets); it has a subscription list of over 300 names, almost all tradesmen. Halfpenny's useful *Magnum in Parvo*, a practical quarto hand-book on the orders, cost only 4s., a sum within the reach of every craftsman.

Books were the instrument with which the Palladian group unconsciously established its dictatorship, a dictatorship whose rule lasted for more than thirty years. It is an easy matter to distinguish a house of 1715 from one of 1730. But it takes a far more skilled eye to draw distinctions between one of this latter date and one built even as late as 1760. Such was the stabilizing influence of the Palladian formula and the copy-book.

We come now to the procedure followed in the building of a London house. It varied, of course, according to the class of

75

house and according to whether it was built as a speculation or for a specific individual, or, again, whether it was built under the supervision of an architect or not.

Take, first, the case of a big house built by a wealthy individual with the advice of an architect. The first step was to find a site; the second was to call in an architect. The architect produced a plan and approximate estimate. This estimate would be based not, as today, on the cubic capacity of the house, but on the number of 'squares' of building comprised in its plan. A 'square' was a hundred square feet and was priced in accordance with the quality of building intended and the proposed height of the structure. Thus, in 1734, a house (No. 10) in St James's Square[1] comprised twenty-seven squares; these, priced at £110 a square, produced an approximate estimate of £2,970. Out-buildings, door-furniture, and the architect's fee were regarded as extras.

The next thing was to procure tradesmen to undertake the work. There were two ways of doing this. Either a lump sum could be agreed with a master-builder for the whole structure, or separate sums could be agreed with separate tradesmen – bricklayer, carpenter, joiner, plumber, pavior, tiler, painter, and glazier. The first of these two methods was the commonest, but the second was considered more business-like and more conducive to good workmanship. The first method obviously meant that a great deal of what we should call 'sub-contracting' had to be done by the master-builder behind the scenes, and this might react unfavourably on the finished job. It must be remembered that the 'master-builder' was not a builder in the modern sense. He had not a comprehensive organization of skilled workmen in all the trades. He might undertake to execute complete buildings, but his own training and equipment only qualified him to ply *one* of the many necessary trades. If he was a bricklayer, he would have to sublet the carpentry; if he was a carpenter he must sublet the bricklaying; and in either case he must put all the minor trades into other hands.

Sub-contracting was an essential and striking feature of the

1. It was designed by Flitcroft for Sir William Heathcote and is now Chatham House. The relevant papers are in the R.I.B.A. library.

Georgian building industry. A very large part of the ordinary tradesman's work was done for his fellow tradesmen, while he himself was constantly employing them on the houses for which he was responsible in the capacity of master-builder. All such sub-contracting was signed and sealed in a perfectly regular way.[1] Its advantage lay, however, in the economic balance which could be achieved by continuous collaboration among a group of tradesmen working for each other – a balance which eliminated any considerable need for cash payment. It was, in effect, a remarkably efficient system of barter.[2]

In the case of a builder of good repute, a contract for the whole work could, no doubt, be confidently entered into, especially when an architect was on the job. The architects and the master-builders were not strangers to each other. Each architect knew which tradesmen he could trust, and there was no reason for him to employ any others. The system of 'competitive tendering', in which it is a point of honour for the architect to choose the lowest tender, had not yet been envisaged.

Thus, in spite of criticism, it was common and satisfactory for even the best class of houses to be undertaken by master-builders for a lump sum. A contract would be drawn up, in the form of a general specification and introducing the name of the architect from whose designs and to whose satisfaction the work had to be done. The contract, and in some cases the drawings as well, would be signed by the building-owner and the master-builder.

So much for building procedure at the top of the social scale. Less wealthy and fastidious building-owners might cut the £50

1. Stowe MS 412 in the British Museum is a document comprising models for all the legal instruments in common use in the building trade. It is entitled *The Practising Attorney or Conveyancer's Guide* and dated 1738-9.

2. Robert Morris, in *An Essay in Defence of Ancient Architecture*, 1728, pleading for the employment of surveyors, says: 'Bricklayers and Joiners, Carpenters and Masons, are so confusedly mixed, that nothing of consequence is performed but under each other.' A writer in the *Builder* in 1850 (p. 602) recalled that 'the bricklayer worked in exchange with the carpenter and the plasterer in exchange with the mason. It was a system of barter and the Surveyor was employed to measure and adjust the claims between the parties.'

or £100 incurred in the employment of an architect and do business with a master-builder direct, at considerably greater risk of getting a bad bargain. The majority of house-hunters, however, bought their houses, half-built, in the speculative market. Here, the master-builder's technique was this. He would sign a building agreement with the ground-landlord, preparatory to taking a building-lease of perhaps sixty, perhaps ninety-nine years, with a 'peppercorn' rent for the first year or two. During this initial period he would erect the carcass of a house – simply a brick shell with floors and roof – and offer it for sale. With luck, he would find a purchaser before the peppercorn period expired, so that his outlay on ground-rent was *nil*. The customer would buy the house, finished and decorated to his own taste, for a lump sum and the lease would be made out in the customer's name.

The salient feature of the speculative builder's operations is that he laid out very little cash. He carried on his building work by a species of barter and the land he built on merely passed through his hands on its way to the customer. It was reckoned that a man needed £100 capital to set up as a master-builder,[1] but in fact, any clown of a bricklayer with a guinea or two in his pocket could plunge into the speculative business. Many did, with the result that bricklayers and carpenters stand high in the bankruptcy lists of the eighteenth century. A writer of 1747, whom I have already quoted,[2] says of bricklayers that theirs is a profitable business but 'especially if they confine themselves to work for others, and do not launch out into Building-Projects of their own, which frequently ruin them'. 'It is no new thing in *London*,' he adds, 'for these Master-Builders to build themselves out of their own Houses, and fix themselves in jail with their own Materials.' Nevertheless, the temptation was great. A Foreman Bricklayer earned but 21s. a week and was employed for less than half the year. One speculative venture that turned out well would make him, relatively, a rich man.

Bricklayers and carpenters led the industry in the speculative

1. See *A General Description of All Trades*, 1747. (Guildhall Library, A.5.1.)
2. R. Campbell, op. cit.

field, since theirs were, of course, the biggest shares in the building of a house. The lighter trades – slaters, plumbers, glaziers, and so forth, grouped themselves under one or other of the principals and the more substantial bricklayers must have had tradesmen in various crafts more or less continuously at their disposal.

The materials with which all these tradesmen worked form an interesting study, and a short survey of them shall serve as a conclusion to this chapter.[1]

Georgian London's native building material was brick, made of the London clay in hundreds of suburban brick fields, whose smoking kilns marred the prospect. In quality these bricks ranged from the good hard 'stocks' of which all outer walls were constructed, to the worst 'place' bricks, whose composition included as much ash as clay but which, for cheapness' sake, were used for the unseen work in party walls and partitions, sowing the seeds of structural defects which are constantly becoming apparent today, under stress of time, traffic, and bombs.

The 'stocks' were of two colours – grey and red, the latter being a trifle more costly. The grey bricks, however, were preferred for walling in general. Red had been fashionable in Queen Anne's time but the later builders considered them not merely unfashionable but too 'hot' in colour, and ugly in combination with stone and white-painted wood. The grey stocks varied considerably in actual hue. The bricks of St Peter's, Vere Street (1724), for instance, though described as 'grey' in the specification, are a reddish-brown; other 'grey' bricks have a yellowish tinge; indeed, strictly grey bricks are uncommon except in the best work of 1740–60 and particularly in houses associated with such men as Ware and Flitcroft. In the latter part of the century London stocks were almost uniformly a pale, yellowish brown.

The red stocks were sometimes dark red, sometimes a dull pink. They were largely used for walling at the beginning of the century, for lintels and dressings to windows in the first half;

1. The main sources for this subject are I. Ware, *The Complete Body of Architecture*, 1756; Batty Langley, *The London Prices of Bricklayer's Materials and Works*, 1748; R. Neve, *Builder's Dictionary*, 1736, and building agreements and contracts of the period.

in the latter part, they were practically abandoned except for window arches.

A fourth, much more expensive type of brick, was imported from the country outside London. This was the 'cutting brick', a crimson brick of very fine sandy quality and capable of accurate cutting – hence the name. It was, and is still, known also as 'rubbing brick' or 'Windsor brick'. In the best work this was used instead of red stocks for window arches and decorative dressings. The bricks were usually laid in putty instead of mortar.

As an index of the relative preciousness of the London brickmakers' materials here are their prices (per 1,000 delivered) in 1748.

Place bricks		14s.
Grey stocks		18s.
Do.	(specially picked for uniformity of colour)	20s. or 22s.
Red Stocks		30s.
Cutting bricks		60s.

These were the standard Georgian varieties, the survivors of innumerable earlier types. All conformed in size to the Act of 1739, which laid down that bricks made within fifteen miles of London should measure 8¾ in. × 4⅛ in. × 2½ in. Carefully laid, they rose four courses to eleven inches; but four courses to the foot was common.

As to the manner of laying bricks, 'Flemish' bond with 'headers' and 'stretchers' alternating in each course, was practically universal. It is worth observing, however, that walling which showed nothing but 'headers' was sometimes considered a worth-while concession to textural uniformity, in spite of the amount of extra cutting involved.[1]

After bricks, the London builder's chief material was timber, and under this head we need only mention Baltic fir and English oak. The seventeenth-century architects had been less hidebound in their use of timber, and country builders still con-

1. The same effect, however, could be obtained by forming bastard vertical joints in ordinary bond. This may be seen at 13 St James's Square but may be later than the date of the house (*c*.1735).

tinued to develop the resources nearest at hand. But Georgian builders in London used fir for nearly everything, finding it adequate for most structural purposes and adequate, too, for ornament since they habitually painted and gilded it. (The scraped pine panelling and fireplaces one sees in museums and period-conscious houses would have been disgusting to a Georgian eye; Georgian woodwork, unlike Stuart woodwork, should nearly always be painted.) The fir logs were shipped from Danzig, Riga and Memel to the port of London and sold cheaper than oak. English oak, nevertheless, always retained its prestige and was used for the best structural work and window joinery. Mahogany, imported from the West Indies, was occasionally used for the more expensive class of joinery from about 1720, and in particular for handrailing. The sweeping handrails to the later staircases are often beautifully finished works of craftsmanship.

The roofs of early Georgian London were covered with tiles – either plain tiles or pantiles, the latter sometimes glazed. Purple English slates were used occasionally; they were considered much the handsomest kind of roof covering but were expensive. It was not till after 1765, when Lord Penrhyn began to develop the export trade from his Welsh quarries,[1] that slating became cheap and consequently common. By 1792, 12,000 tons a year were being exported from the Penrhyn quarries alone and London rapidly became a slate-roofed city.

The houses were glazed with Crown glass. Most of it was manufactured in Newcastle, whence it came down to the Thames in coal-barges. Some, however, was made at Ratcliff, in east London. Crown glass can be distinguished from the ordinary sheet glass of today by a sheen on the surface and a faint bluish tinge. Plate glass was rarely used in buildings, owing to its great cost, until the early nineteenth century.

Stone, much used in public buildings, played a relatively small part in the architecture of the London house. When stone was used it was almost invariably Portland. Porches, window dressings, cornices, and even fireplaces were often of this material.

1. Sir L. T. Davies and A. Edwards, *Welsh Life in the Eighteeenth Century*, 1939, p. 107.

Bath stone, Portland's only serious rival, was tried at rare intervals but was not found satisfactory in the London atmosphere; though, curiously, when stucco was popularized by Nash it was frescoed in imitation of Bath, not Portland, stone.

For the paving of halls and areas, Purbeck stone was often specified; it was laid in squares, often with little diamonds of black Namur marble at the crossing of the joints. Reigate stone was commonly employed for hearths.

Of the other trades in the building industry the most important were the joiner's, the plasterer's, the plumber's, the smith's, and the painter's. Plasterer's work and smith's work account for many of the most delightful accessories of Georgian houses – the gay Rococo ceilings, in which a limited freedom from Palladian rule was allowed, and the railings, lamp-holders, and link-extinguishers in wrought iron, whose fine, well-judged lines still give pleasure to the discriminating pedestrian; while the plumber's contribution is perhaps best appreciated in his cisterns, with their arabesque ornaments which the Palladian tyranny never refined away. To these cisterns, sometimes still to be found fixed in the front areas, came the water laid on by the New River Company or the Chelsea Water Works and made available at fixed hours for a small quarterly rate. There was not sufficient pressure to raise the water, but this was sometimes done by a hand-pump, with a second cistern in the roof.

Finally, drains. Georgian drainage was simple. A brick drain was laid under the house and carried to the public sewer beneath the road – or, if no public sewer were handy, to a cesspool in the garden. Rain-water was carried from the roof in lead pipes connecting with branch drains joining the main drain.

Sanitary accommodation consisted of a spacious 'bog-house'; built either at the end of the garden or attached to the back of the house. A brick-lined circular pit was constructed under it and connected to the main drain. Water was sometimes laid on to flush these receptacles, but it was not till much later in the century that the regular water-closet, fitted with a trap, was introduced, the first patent for such a device being Alexander Cumming's in 1775. Joseph Bramah's valve-closet followed in

1778; this proved a very hygienic and, in spite of its complexity, a reliable apparatus, and examples of the later versions of it are still to be found working merrily after eighty or a hundred years of use.

CHAPTER 6

'Fifty New Churches' and Some Others

AN Act of the ninth year of Queen Anne provided for a tax on coal to pay 'for Building fifty new churches ... in or near the Cities of London and Westminster or the Suburbs thereof'.[1]

If this pious ordinance, in an age not notoriously pious, needs explanation, it is to be found in the political crisis of 1710. In the General Election in the autumn of that year the Whigs, after twenty-two years' serene power, were trounced by the Tories. It was a political event of the first importance. To the Tory statesman it looked like successful counter-revolution; to the Tory churchman it was the re-entry of High Church policy and practice. The victory had to be secured and celebrated. And what more splendid affirmation of Tory High-Church principle could there be than the erection of fifty churches? – not mere tabernacles either, but 'churches of stone and other proper Materials with Towers or Steeples to each of them'.

Fifty was a good round number. It appears to have had no calculated relation to the needs of the growing metropolis and perhaps no responsible person ever believed that fifty new churches would be built. They were not. The net achievements of the Act between 1711 and 1730 amounted to twelve completely new churches, a few extra steeples, and some works provided for under 'other purposes' in the preamble, such as the aggrandisement of Westminster Abbey, the completion of Greenwich Hospital, and the payment of arrears of Sir Christopher Wren's salary as Surveyor to St Paul's, meanly withheld from him by the Whigs.

The history of the Act in operation does not suggest that it worked smoothly. Seven further Acts were placed on the Statute Book within eight years of the first to 'explain' and expand it and to acquire part of a London thoroughfare as a site

1. Howard Colvin, 'Fifty New Churches', *Architectural Review*, March 1950.

84

for one of the churches. The last of these Acts disclosed that by 1718 the Commissioners had committed themselves to an expenditure of £161,000, which was far more than the coal tax, whose funds the first Act had ear-marked, had so far yielded. The basis of expenditure was then revised, the Commissioners being doled out an annual £21,000 for their churches, the surplus going partly to the King and partly to the public funds. After 1714, Whigs once more in the saddle, the church-building movement soon ran down, but the coal-tax continued and was occasionally raided for cheap suburban churches and public improvements until it was finally repealed in late Victorian times.

The building achievements of this curiously indecisive legislation may not have been loyal to the promoter's original intention but so far as they went they were magnificent. Such lavish expenditure placed before the fortunate architects opportunities such as only Wren had met with, and it must be confessed that the architects rose nobly to the occasion. Nicholas Hawksmoor, James Gibbs, John James, Thomas Archer, and Henry Flitcroft: these are famous names in the history of London architecture and famous, one and all, because they are attached to churches which every Londoner knows. These are the churches of the Tory Act of 1711. Their white steeples and porticos are among London's most precious, as well as most conspicuous, artistic treasures.

A convenient way of studying these churches is as part of the life-work of their several architects and chronology dictates that we should begin with Hawksmoor, who was appointed one of the surveyors to the Commissioners immediately after the passing of the 1711 Act. He was then fifty and had behind him a career of thirty-two years of complete involvement in all the major architectural undertakings of his time. Of Nottinghamshire farming stock, he travelled to London as a lad and found a clerk's stool in the establishment of Sir Christopher Wren. Before long he was Sir Christopher's right hand; at twenty-six his deputy at Chelsea Hospital; subsequently in charge at Kensington and Greenwich. Just how much these later buildings of Wren owe to him there is no possible hope of discovering; but what is certain is that Hawksmoor emerged from this unique training not merely equipped with a technique which only Wren among English architects could impart but with a power quite unlike Wren's – a genius for the disposition of mass and volume unlike anything previously seen in English architecture.[1]

From 1699 he collaborated with John Vanbrugh, and this union with another man of extraordinary imaginative power has dreadfully confused the historical issue. Until recent years it has seemed that nobody was able to believe that *both* these men had genius. Either Hawksmoor was a hack and merely followed Vanbrugh; or Vanbrugh was an incapable amateur entirely dependent on Hawksmoor. Documents and drawings, carefully collated, have proved both these theories wrong. The truth is that the Vanbrugh–Hawksmoor combination was that rare thing – a fertile marriage of equally creative minds. Each could do what the other could not. Vanbrugh's gay, humane temperament leapt at the discovery of Hawksmoor's passion for serene rhythms and dour Roman grandeur. Hawksmoor, on the other hand, reacted to Vanbrugh's splendid unorthodoxy, his love of movement, of dramatic recession and silhouette. They were complementaries. Neither could have been great without the other. In the event, both were great.

Hawksmoor's London churches may perhaps owe as much, indirectly, to Vanbrugh, as does Blenheim Palace to Hawksmoor. They are part of the Vanbrugh–Hawksmoor phenomenon. There are six of them. The first to be begun was St Alphege, Greenwich, in 1712. Three more, the grandest, had their foundations laid in 1714: St Anne, Limehouse, Christ Church, Spitalfields, and St George-in-the-East. In 1716 came the beginnings of St George, Bloomsbury and St Mary Woolnoth.

These churches are so distinctly a group and so separate from the general trend of eighteenth-century architecture that it is rewarding to try to penetrate their individualities and discover, if one can, from what common attributes their beauty and force of character derive. As in any successful classical building much – almost everything – is to be learnt from a study of the plans.

1. Kerry Downes, *Hawksmoor*, 1959, is the standard work.

Simply as patterns on paper Hawksmoor's church plans are eloquent. He set his face against the indeterminately long nave, the
traditional Gothic solution which Wren, too, had discarded
whenever he could. Hawksmoor aimed at an indivisible unity,
a geometrical pattern which would suffer neither addition nor
subtraction and yet possess an intrinsically church-like form.
Once the geometry of a Hawksmoor plan is understood the
spaces above it are seen to fall into natural, inevitable order.

Most of these plans start from the notion of a square placed
within another square of such a size that four little squares are
formed at the angles. But no Hawksmoor plan is *precisely* that.
An axis is laid across this pattern (the conventional east-west of
an Anglican church) and the pattern is then modified and extended in two or four directions – sometimes in such a way that
the original square centrality is almost lost. There is thus a
conflict. It might well be called the Gothic–Classic conflict. It is
quite deliberate and although the result is something which
an antagonist might call ambiguous it is also an invitation to
feel more acutely the spaces of which the whole is composed.

The churches develop from the central idea in a variety of
different ways. At St George's and at Limehouse, a version of
Wren's four-column plan (as for instance at St Mary-at-Hill)
makes the articulate centre; all main spaces are of equal height.
At St Mary Woolnoth and Bloomsbury, on the other hand, the
central square is pushed up higher than the outer so that the
nave is lit from high clerestories (Fig. 12). At Spitalfields (Plate
8) the square seems almost lost in the oblong of the nave yet on
close inspection it is found logically articulated. In all the
churches, the square-within-square idea serves to control aisles
and vestibules; and galleries fall into place as spacious tribunes
instead of thrusting awkwardly across an arcade as in so many
town churches of the period.

The more detailed aesthetic character of Hawksmoor's church
architecture is extraordinarily hard to analyse. The deliberate
Gothic–Classic conflict persists throughout. He can paraphrase
Boston Stump (St George's) or the spire of St Mary, Stamford
(Spitalfields) and yet in the same churches provide irresistible

reminders of Rome – not only in ornaments but in a severity which recalls the aqueducts or the stripped ruins of the Via Appia; or (in the flanks of the Spitalfields church) he can produce a Roman evocation exactly equivalent to Alberti's Tempio at Rimini.

The detail is always exciting; and nowhere more so than in the trio of elaborate panels (taking the place of windows) on the north wall of St Mary Woolnoth – a piece of sheer architectural eloquence hard to match. Sometimes Hawksmoor affected a gloomy grandeur which approaches the monstrous. In the bases of the flanking towers of St George-in-the-East are tiny doors, wrought about with such complex and superabundant masonry (all pure architecture, no carving) as to suggest the imaginative enterprises of a much later age; it is close to Piranesi who, when St George's was designed, had not been born. These same towers rise into hollow domed lanterns where tier upon tier of narrow arches remind one not at all of Piranesi but rather of the romantic inventions of the Elizabethans.

Lastly, there is the archaeological element. Hawksmoor was a passionate student of the antique, a reconstructor of lost monuments; and his reconstructions often became his inspirations. If we think of the tower lantern at Limehouse as a Gothic theme (as, in relation to the whole, we must) we are also justified in seeing it as a reconstructed Tower of the Winds. At Bloomsbury, the stepped spire surmounting a miniature temple is a fantasy based on Pliny's description of the Mausoleum.

Hawksmoor's churches were all complete by 1730. In 1736 he died. Unlike some of his famous contemporaries he desired no marble monument to be built to his memory; and his body lies, as he directed, in a remote Hertfordshire churchyard, under a plain slab.

Hawksmoor was the only surveyor to the Commissioners for Churches who stayed the whole course. His first colleague, Dickinson, left in 1713 to take up another appointment and was succeeded by James Gibbs; Gibbs, in turn, was succeeded in 1715 by John James. But of these three names, that of Gibbs is by far the most important. He was an architect of very great ability, if not quite of genius, and although his opportunities under the Act were limited to one church he was able to show himself a master in another, built under another authority, but happening to be the most conspicuous parish church in London.

Gibbs came of gentle Aberdonian parentage and was a Roman Catholic, a fact which he was sufficiently ambitious to be at pains to conceal.[1] His visit to Rome in 1703 was prompted by a desire to enter the priesthood but he changed his mind and entered the studio of Carlo Fontana instead. He returned to England in 1709, when he was twenty-seven. By then, the Earl of Mar was 'very much his friend'. So were other eminent Tories, and in the four years of Tory rule after 1710 Gibbs's position became very favourable. He made the most of it. Through Lord Bingley he got Harley himself to put him in the way of becoming surveyor to the Commissioners for the new churches. He was appointed, but it is curious to record that Vanbrugh, a rabid Whig, opposed Gibbs's election on political grounds.[2]

As a result of his appointment, Gibbs became architect of St Mary-le-Strand (Plate 6), for which the site was secured in 1714. It was designed while he was still under the spell of recent Italian work and before English taste had hardened its heart against the Baroque. For St Mary's is a Baroque church. Its clusters of vertical lines, its half-domed porch, the see-saw pediments on its long sides – all these are Baroque, and all of them earned the emphatic disapproval of critics of the Walpole type, whose condemnation of Baroque was indiscriminate. Even Soane,[3] broad-minded and sensitive, felt obliged to warn his students against Gibbs's merely decorative use of pediments.

The steeple at the west end was originally intended to be a short turret and there was to have been a column with Queen Anne on top some distance from the church.[4] But the Queen died, the Hanoverians came in, and the column was abandoned in favour of a steeple. Its unusual shape – broader one way than

---

1. Bryan Little, *The Life and Work of James Gibbs*, 1955.
2. See references to Gibbs in H.M.C., *Portland III* (Vol. 5) and *Egmont II*.
3. *Lectures* (ed. A. T. Bolton), p. 67.
4. J. Gibbs, *A Book of Architecture*, 1728.

the other – may be ascribed to provision having been originally made for a turret on this plan.

Originally, St Mary's was half surrounded by the houses form-ing the north side of the Strand. Since 1910 it has been an island church, its mediterranean grace dramatically enhanced by the American cliffs of Bush House on the north. Compact, clear-cut, and decorative, it makes an immediate and delightful im-pression and is as different from Hawksmoor as it could well be.

Perhaps as a result of his success with St Mary's, Gibbs's next task was to add a steeple to Wren's barn-like church of St Clement Danes. Wren himself was still alive, though very old; he knew and respected Gibbs, who, no doubt, worked with his approval and assistance.

But this steeple at St Clement's, begun in 1719, had nothing to do with the Act for the Fifty Churches, for in 1715 Gibbs had been superseded in his office of surveyor by John James. Gibbs's removal had a political origin. The wire-pulling game was now all in Whig favour, and Gibbs was not merely a Tory, but a Scotsman and a Catholic – neither of them good things to be in the year 'fifteen. The next phase of his career we shall meet in the chapter which follows; he became one of a little group of artists who hunted with the Tory pack, designing the homes and gardens and painting the portraits of Harley and his friends, dancing attendance on the great with ever respectful and grate-ful familiarity.

If Gibbs's political affiliations cut him off from the official em-ployments which many of his contemporaries enjoyed, they did not prevent him obtaining other work from Whig hands. In 1720, he was short-listed with John James by the Commissioners for rebuilding St Martin-in-the-Fields, the Commissioners be-ing headed by a group of Whig generals whom we shall meet in the next chapter in connexion with Hanover Square. Gibbs impressed these gentlemen not only with his designs, but by walking some of them round Wren's churches to demonstrate the problems and possibilities of modern church-building. He was elected by a large majority.[1]

1. J. McMaster, *A Short History of . . . St Martin-in-the-Fields*, 1916.

St Martin's is one of the few early Georgian Churches in London not covered by the Act of 1711, having been rebuilt by the parishioners, who obtained a special Act for raising the money. It was finished in 1726, and cost £33,000 – about double the cost of Wren's most expensive City churches. Its architectural importance is best appreciated in relation to the earlier church in the Strand. St Mary's was unashamedly Baroque. St Martin's is not Baroque at all, except perhaps for a few skirmishes in the steeple. Here Gibbs conforms to the academic standards which, about this time, began to command universal loyalty among English architects. They were the standards of common sense, as opposed to the imaginative unreason of Baroque. They were felt to be true Roman – that is, Vitruvian – standards, not merely Italian, and it was probably suspected that while there was a clear correspondence between English Protestantism, Lockeian philosophy, and this kind of building, the only correspondence suggested by the Baroque was with Jesuitry and the Whore of Babylon. Suspicions of this sort crystallized in the Palladian movement, of which, broadly speaking, Gibbs's later work may be considered a part.

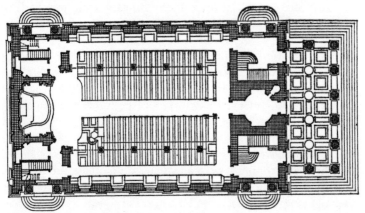

Fig. 11. Plan of St Martin-in-the-Fields. Compare Plates 7a and b.

St Martin's exhibits the more or less logical, common-sense notion of treating a church externally as if it were a temple. That is to say, the body of the church is a single rectangular mass with a continuous, pitched roof forming a pediment at either end. At the west end is a deep portico. Neither pediments nor columns are used except where the radical form of the building dictates them; the emotional 'applied architecture' of St Mary's has gone for good (Plates 7a and b).

But St Martin's is not a purist's design. The heavy rustics of the windows constitute an academic solecism in a building ruled by the essentially feminine Corinthian order. A greater impropriety is the steeple. A temple roof is, by tradition and association, a light covering on which any superstructure other than the lightest of turrets is anomalous. On the roof of St Martin's, Gibbs's enormous steeple is a monstrous apparent imposition. In placing it there, he was flouting not only the good Gothic tradition of tower-building but the invariable practice of Wren and Hawksmoor, whose steeples are always visibly planted on the ground at one side or at the west ends of their churches. This may seem a trite criticism; and most of us are sufficiently accustomed to St Martin's and its enormous brood of imitations to enjoy both the serene temple and the fancy spire without suffering aesthetic indigestion. But the fact remains that Gibbs was not quite clever enough to do these things with impunity. The placing of St Martin's steeple was an act of insensibility and remains so.

Inside St Martin's, Gibbs's ability displays itself in the adept interpretation of an aisled, galleried church in appropriate and grammatical terms. It is on the model of Wren's St Clement Danes and St James's, Piccadilly, and performs the same act, though with much superior grace and finish. Whereas Wren often allowed the galleries to swamp his churches, pitching his colonnades above and below them, so that neither the upper nor the lower columns were adequate to dominate the interior, Gibbs adopted the reverse policy of starting with a giant order and allowing the galleries to butt into the columns. Neither device is entirely satisfactory and it has to be admitted that the interior of St Martin's would be finer without the galleries. But given their necessity the handling cannot be reproached.

St Martin's, its architectural merits and defects, is an important subject because of its influence on a whole century of church

Fig. 12. Axonometric view of St Mary Woolnoth.

architecture. This influence reaches to St Pancras and the 1820s; in a geographical sense it reaches as far as America where a Gibbs tradition in church design persisted for a very long time.

And now, to return to the churches built under Queen Anne's famous Act. When Gibbs was deposed from the surveyorship, his place was taken by John James, a parson's son of some ability but no genius. James built St George's, Hanover Square (Plate 10), for the Commissioners, completing it in 1724. The Corinthian portico projecting into one of the splayed sides of George Street is as sensitively learned as are the plates in James's many books; but the rest of the church fails in all those things in which Hawksmoor succeeded; its interior is a mere paraphrase of St James's Piccadilly. James lost another opportunity when it fell to him to add a tower to Hawksmoor's Greenwich church in 1730 and he put up a weak essay in the Gibbs manner.[1]

A very different architect was Thomas Archer. Probably through Vanbrugh's influence, he designed two of the 'fifty' churches – St John, Smith Square (1713–28) and St Paul, Deptford (1712–30). These churches are worth studying, because they represent the most advanced Baroque style ever attempted in England.

Archer is a mysterious figure. He came of a distinguished Warwickshire family and is always said to have been a 'pupil' of Sir John Vanbrugh's, though there is probably no real basis for the statement, and his architectural style has little in common with Vanbrugh's except a bigness of scale and an element of fantasy which comes out strongly in his two London churches. He had a fancy for huge broken pediments – so broken that only a triangular chunk remains at each corner. He had, one supposes, spent happy hours at Frascati and Tivoli. Borromini did not appal him and was, indeed, the source of a rather perverse capital which Archer often used. In London he built a house for a Lord Mayor on the south side of Soho Square, Har-

1. To James is sometimes attributed the incredibly philistine church of St John, Horselydown (burnt in the war and now demolished), with its spire consisting of an Ionic column grotesquely distorted to give an obeliscal silhouette. Mr Downes (op. cit., pp. 196–8) seems to divide the blame between James and Hawksmoor.

court House on the west side of Cavendish Square, and (the only survivor) No. 43 King Street, Covent Garden, for Admiral Edward Russell, the date of which is about 1705.

By the time he started St John's Church in the newly formed Smith Square in 1713, his Baroque technique was well developed. The church (Plate 9b) has a nearly square plan, developed somewhat in the Hawksmoor style; and before the fire of 1741 and the consequent reconstruction without the original columns, the interior must have been extremely grand. The exterior is dramatic – an upward torrent of Baroque architecture, the vertical lines boldly carried through in four corner towers. As a blitzed ruin it was superb, stark hollowness giving intensity to the savagely hewn façades. Rebuilt, it *may* be more useful but will never look as fine.

St Paul's, Deptford (Plate 9a), the other church undertaken by Archer for the Commissioners, is equally remarkable. Again, the plan is square but there is a brilliantly original combination of semi-circular portico and steeple and the whole derives immense impressiveness from being raised on a masonry platform almost resembling a fortification.

Archer's emotional and exciting architecture was badly beaten up by all the eighteenth-century critics. To Walpole, the architect was merely 'a Mr Archer, the groom porter', and worth two lines of sour comment; and, to succeeding critics, the church in Smith Square was rarely anything but a bad joke. For Baroque architecture has always been a blind spot in English criticism. It is strange that, whereas the fantastic element in Swift was soon accepted as a golden thread in the literature of the time, the fantasy of Vanbrugh, Hawksmoor, and Archer has always been deeply suspect. Even today, the force of tradition directs more admiration to the 'safe' architecture of Gibbs than to inventors and experimenters of the deeply imaginative native school of Baroque.

Next among the architects who contributed churches under the Act comes Henry Flitcroft. 'Burlington Harry', the son of William III's gardener and a joiner by training, had been employed by Lord Burlington as a draughtsman, and became one of his principal protégés. He was engaged by the Duke of

Bedford both at Woburn and on the Duke's Bloomsbury estate. The Duke, as Lord of the Manor of St Giles and Patron of the living of St Giles-in-the-Fields, was no doubt the instigator of an Act of 1717 for rebuilding the old Gothic church, 'instead of one of the fifty new churches'. Flitcroft was appointed architect sixteen years later, and contracted to undertake the work. St Giles's is on the pattern introduced by Wren at St James's, Piccadilly, but its elliptical vault has the character of Gibbs's St Martin's. The steeple, too, owes everything to Gibbs. It is not as good as Gibbs but Flitcroft carefully avoids the solecism of making it appear to ride on a temple roof; it abuts the west wall like the Gothic tower of its predecessor on the site.

Flitcroft's other central London church, St Olave, Southwark (demolished 1930), was built under an Act of 1737, which appointed trustees to secure money in the parish. It was one of many London churches built in this way – the money being borrowed in the first instance by the trustees and interest being paid as annuities out of the rates. Such churches were mostly rebuildings, in the many cases where old Gothic churches were too small and too dilapidated to serve the purposes of a thickly populated urban parish. Practically all these churches could be described in terms of features owing their origin to Wren or Gibbs, or, to a lesser extent, Hawksmoor. Thus, the elder Dance's church at Shoreditch (1735) has a spire which paraphrases Bow Steeple; the interior and the four-column Doric portico are in a somewhat Hawksmoorean style. Dance also designed St Botolph, Aldgate.

The distribution of the new suburban churches of this time and their relative architectural quality provides a side-light on the development of the town. The wealthy suburb of Hampstead, without resorting to Act of Parliament for raising funds, approached a distinguished resident, Flitcroft, for a design to be considered in competition with others – an arrangement, however, which Flitcroft was too distinguished to accept. St John's was therefore entrusted, in 1744, to a builder-architect, John Sanderson. The most remarkable thing about it is its Vanbrughian Gothic steeple. The likewise prosperous but more commercial suburb of Islington followed in 1751–4 with a florid building designed and built under Act of Parliament by Launcelot Dowbiggin. South of the river, there was evidently sufficient increase in the population, even before the building of Westminster Bridge, for new churches to be required. The need was met by John Price's brick church of St George, 1734–6, and by the less distinguished Christ Church a year or so later. Eastwards, along the river, Wapping rebuilt its church in 1756, while the Commissioners for the 'fifty' extended their activities as far as Gravesend (Act of 1730) and Woolwich (Act of 1731).

The list could be extended to great length if one included the many chapels-of-ease on the West End estates and the churches in all the satellite villages and hamlets which were built or rebuilt. Fashionable riverside towns like Richmond and Twickenham acquired neat red-brick boxes very early in the century; so did shipbuilding Rotherhithe after a vain application to the Commissioners; and it was a poor parish indeed which did not make some attempt to get rid of its shabby old Gothic church (leaving, perhaps, the substantial and not easily replaced belltower) and substitute something more in harmony with the unsentimental, unretrospective Protestantism of the eighteenth century.

Desultory church-building went on all through the century, but in the latter part it was very desultory indeed. The younger Dance's delicate little church of Allhallows-on-the-Wall, 1765, and James Carr's belated imitation of a Wren steeple at St James's, Clerkenwell are two of the more remarkable of these stragglers. It was not until the great Act of 1818 that church-building took a prominent place, once more, in the architectural life of London. The story of this Act and its achievements belongs to a later chapter.

CHAPTER 7

Whig and Tory Landowners

WE saw in the first chapter that house-building in London was not continuously carried on but came in waves. Each wave had its origin in a period of confidence and initiative, resulting partly from political events, partly from the turn of the trade cycle and a psychological recoil in favour of expansion and enterprise. One of these phases of confidence occurred about the time of the Treaty of Utrecht in 1713. Utrecht was a Tory peace terminating a Whig war; but the death of Anne a year later brought the Whigs back to power under the dynasty whose favour they had prudently cultivated. After the fiasco of 1715 the texture of English opinion, shot through with prejudice of both kinds, was firmer than it had been for a century.

Against this background of social stability comes the great building salient in the north-west, conducted almost simultaneously on four large properties and extending from Swallow Street (roughly on the site of Regent Street) to Hyde Park. In this area there were already a few streets, coming north from Piccadilly. Dover Street, Albemarle Street, and Bond Street, with Clifford Street at right-angles to the latter, had been projected by a syndicate of 'rich bankers and mechanics', as Evelyn called them, as early as 1683. The syndicate failed, their plans were abandoned, and the streets only very gradually built up. Thirty years later came a wholly new initiative in the creation of George Street and Hanover Square. The enterprise begins with the conveyance of two acres of freehold land to Richard Lumley, first Earl of Scarborough, in 1713.[1] Lord Scarborough also took on lease a much larger area to the north, extending

1. No printed work has yet dealt with the early history of the square and I am indebted to Mr B. H. Johnson for allowing me to read his admirable study of it in typescript. Mr Johnson's *Berkeley Square to Bond Street* (1952) is also essential for the study of this area.

to Oxford Street. Over all this land was built, in 1717–19, the rectangular 'square' with two roads leading into it on the east, two on the west, one on the north, and one on the south. The latter (George Street) was planned like a funnel, widening suddenly into the square for no other reason, apparently, than to produce a striking architectural effect.

A Baroque eye for effect is very evident in the beginnings of Hanover Square, not only in the planning but, as we shall see, in the architecture. Whose eye it was is doubtful. Lord Scarborough himself was a retired general, in 1713 somewhat over seventy. He had fought for William III at the Boyne and being among those who welcomed the accession of George I he named both street and square in that monarch's honour. Early Hanover Square was decidedly Whig and most decidedly military. Among its first inhabitants were Lord Chancellor Cowper, the Duke of Roxborough, Lord Cadogan, and Generals Stewart, Evans, Carpenter, and Pepper – names conspicuously associated with episodes in Marlborough's wars or the "fifteen'.

If the names of the street and the square, the dedication of the chu·ch (St George's arrived in 1720–4), and the professions of its first inhabitants seem to unite in fervent loyalty to the throne of Hanover, so does some of the architecture. Nearly all the surviving original houses in George Street and its westward return into the square are in a style evidently intended to be German. Malton noted this in 1792 and he may have been echoing a traditionally acknowledged fact.[1] The main feature of these houses is the connexion of the windows into long vertical strips by means of 'aprons' of rusticated stone. This treatment prevailed in the south-west corner of the square (all gone, except No. 24, General Stewart's house, which is untypical), on the west side of George Street, and on the east side south of the church – the area, significantly, which was Lord Scarborough's freehold property. Nos. 12–17, on the west side of the street, still make a good group in spite of much alteration; and in spite also of the fact that No. 15 resolutely declines to look German and is, in fact, a sturdy English house in the ordinary West End style of the period. On the opposite side No. 30 (Plate 10)

1. T. Malton, *Picturesque Tour . . . through London* (1792), p. 102.

has the least spoiled German front but No. 32 is bigger and its front has been cleaned. Was it Lord Scarborough who thus attempted to float the German style on a Baroque plan in Hanoverian London? And, if so, who was his architect? Whoever he was, even Ralph, so hard to please, thought he had achieved something:

I must own this ... that the view down *George-Street*, from the upper side of the square, is one of the most entertaining in the whole city: the sides of the square, the area in the middle, the breaks of building that form the entrance of the vista, the vista itself, but, above all, the beautiful projection of the portico of *St George's-Church*, are all circumstances that unite in beauty, and make the scene perfect.[1]

Even today the charm of this perspective can be glimpsed through the post-Hanoverian chaos.

Very nearly contemporary with Hanover Square was the development by the young Earl of Burlington of land nearby to the south, behind his house in Piccadilly – one of the most architecturally interesting, though not one of the most impressive quarters of eighteenth-century London. We can date the beginnings of the development accurately, for as the land was entailed in the Burlington family it was necessary to obtain a private Act for the granting of leases. The Act is dated 1717.

Burlington's importance as an architectural patron entitles one to look for something more than ordinarily interesting in the development of his private estate. In 1717 he was twenty-two. He had been in Italy, had associated himself with the neo-Palladian movement of Colen Campbell (which was also an Inigo Jones revival), and was already transforming Burlington House into a paragon of the movement's new standards. He was only at the beginning, however, of his astonishingly influential career, during which, simply by the force of consistent patronage and example, he gave a bias to English architecture which was felt right down to the time of Barry.

The Palladian transformation of Burlington House and the

1. Ralph, *A Critical Review of the Public Buildings ... in and about London* (1734), p. 105.

laying out of street behind, went on simultaneously. It is curious, on the face of it, that Burlington did not attempt an architectonic coordination of the two, but apart from a general symmetry in the lay-out, he did not. Plots were let off on building lease and the control of elevations does not seem to have been more than usually rigorous. Nevertheless, architecture of a most distinguished kind made its appearance. In 1723, General Wade, desiring to house himself and a very large Rubens he had acquired in Flanders, took a site in old Burlington Street, stretching eastwards to Cork Street. Burlington himself designed this house[1] (which survived, buried within the Burlington Hotel, until 1935); it was a very handsome house, but uncomfortable – and there was no wall-space for the Rubens. Chesterfield (to whom Burlington's professionalism in architecture was slightly distasteful) suggested that as the General could not live in it at his ease, he had better 'take the house over against it to look at it'.[2]

Burlington also designed with his own hand the Burlington School in New Burlington Street (1725, removed 1936). Some other houses were by his dependants and associates. Leoni designed Queensberry House,[3] at the corner of Savile Row and Burlington Gardens, in 1721; it was somewhat altered later in the century by the younger Vardy and Bonomi, and is now a Bank. In 1721–3 Colen Campbell built Nos. 31–34 Old Burlington Street, taking one himself as an investment;[4] of these houses, No. 31, with its magnificent interior, is the finest to survive. William Kent, Burlington's most intimate collaborator, owned a house in Savile Row,[5] and the pedimented terminal building at the north end of it, demolished in 1937, was very much in his style. Yet another protégé, Henry Flitcroft, built at least one house in Sackville Street.[6] While an architect outside

1. Photographs in the *Architect*, 11 Oct. 1935.
2. H. Walpole, *Letters* (ed. Toynbee).
3. Documents relating to this house are in *Stowe* 412.
4. Campbell's will (P.C.C. 243 Abbott).
5. Kent's will (P.C.C. 551 Tenterden).
6. The staircase is referred to as the model for the staircase at No. 10 St James's Square, in the contract for that house in the R.I.B.A. Collection.

the strictly Palladian circle, Nicholas Hawksmoor, built a house in New Burlington Street.[1]

This galaxy of talent made the Burlington estate of special interest, in spite of its small size and indifferent lay-out. It is now being rapidly rebuilt and has lost the distinct local character it once had. But Old and New Burlington Streets and Savile Row are still worth exploring; and so is Burlington House (Plate 13), though it takes a fairly expert eye to disentangle what is left of the genuine Burlington from the coarse-grained additions made when the building was turned into a headquarters of learned societies in 1866. The great pride of the house in Burlington's day was a double quadrant of Doric columns in the courtyard facing the house; this, with the plain screen wall to Piccadilly, the low side-buildings, and the heavily rusticated entrance arch, have gone. The main building has had an upper storey and an entrance loggia added. The first floor – a *piano nobile* recalling Palladio's Palazzo Porto – is original and so are parts of the interior. Its importance as the centre, as well as a leading exemplar, of Palladian activity, makes Burlington House an important relic, in spite of its transformation into a peculiarly sombre backwater of Victorian academic life.

While Burlington's building-projects proceeded, the lessees of the City of London's Conduit Mead estate were also covering ground, but the building of New Bond Street, Conduit Street, Brook Street, Woodstock and other streets (mostly completed by 1723) was merely a work of continuation and of little organic importance in the growth of London. Nor were many exceptional houses built here.

We must now turn to the series of estates directly connected with the Hanover Square unit and orienting their lay-outs along the line of Oxford Street. Only two of them can properly be dealt with in this chapter – the Grosvenor and the Cavendish-Harley.

The Grosvenor Estate at the beginning of the eighteenth century was a group of fields in the angle between Oxford Street and Park Lane, bounded on the east by the Tyburn brook. It had come into the Grosvenor family through the marriage of

1. Specification in *Stowe* 412.

Mary Davies, heiress of the old merchant prince Audley, with Sir Thomas Grosvenor.[1] Sir Thomas was succeeded by Sir Richard who, at the time of his marriage in 1710, procured an Act to enable him to grant building leases on the property. It seems, however, that few houses were built before 1721, by which time both the Hanover Square district and some of the streets coming north from Piccadilly were sufficiently advanced to form links between the Grosvenor property and the older parts of the West End. The story of the Grosvenor estate is not easily put together, since the material which exists has never been made the subject of systematic study. It was, however, planned as a more or less complete unit, the principal feature being a very large square (twice the size of Hanover Square) with two streets entering on each side. A chapel-of-ease was provided in South Audley Street but apparently no space was reserved for a market.

The man in charge of this lay-out and of the general management of the estate seems to have been Robert Andrews, a lawyer and the agent or steward of the Grosvenor family. A manuscript notebook with his book-plate and containing records of the leasing of sites, is preserved in the Grosvenor Office. It seems that under his, or somebody else's, direction an attempt was made to constitute Grosvenor Square not only the largest square but architecturally the most imposing. No less an architect than Colen Campbell made a design for treating the whole of the east side in a strictly architectural way.[2] Although this was laid aside, all the sites here were taken by a builder called John Simmons, and made to form a symmetrical block, with tall units in the centre and at either end; it is probably the first instance of London terrace-houses being thus grouped to provide a monumental façade as though of a single building. The idea may have been Simmons's or it may have originated with Sir Richard Grosvenor or his agent, and the general design may or may not have been provided by an architect. On none of these things have we any information.

The architecture of the block, which was erected between 1725 and 1753, was massive and coarse, with rusticated quoins

1. C. T. Gatty, *Mary Davies and the Manor of Ebury*, 1921.
2. Campbell's design is in the Ashmolean Museum, Oxford.

and window-dressings and one big pedimented house in the centre.

The rest of the square was built up in a variety of different styles and Ralph[1] wrote in 1734 that the houses were 'little better than a collection of whims, and frolics in building, without anything like order or beauty'. Especially did this apply to the north side, where a group of houses with a columnar façade, off-centre, is characterized by Ralph as 'a wretched attempt at something extraordinary'. This was unjust of Ralph, because the builder-architect of these houses, Edward Shepherd, had attempted to coordinate the whole of the north side into an architectural composition but had been thwarted by other interests.[2] Several pompous Palladian houses (the last demolished in 1962) were built on the north side, but the average house in the original Grosvenor Square was modest and substantial, built of brown brick with red dressings. Two such houses, Nos. 43 and 44, survived till 1968; one certainly and probably both the work of Thomas Barlow, a master-builder whose family built and speculated considerably in this district. Thirty years after Ralph's time a less exacting critic noted that the houses in the Square were 'so far uniform as to be all sashed and all pretty near of an equal height' – which, under the conditions prevailing in the earlier part of the century, was about all that could be expected. The formal garden in the centre of the square is said to have been laid out originally by William Kent.

The chapel-of-ease in South Audley Street is, externally, an uninspiring structure of brown brick and stone; but the interior is cheerfully light. It was built in 1730 or a little later by a partnership comprising Benjamin Timbrell, carpenter, Robert Andrews, William Barlow, bricklayer, and Robert Scott.[3] They built the chapel and vested it in the parish in return for a perpetual annual payment of £20 arising from fees for burial vaults. Timbrell, 'one of the most eminent builders about town', acted

1. Ralph, op. cit., p. 108.
2. R. Morris, Preface to *Lectures in Architecture*, 1734.
3. Vestry Minutes of St George, Hanover Square. The Rev. Basil Clarke kindly drew my attention to this entry.

for the partnership and perhaps produced the design. It is very much a craftsman's work. Francis Price, who lived near by in Mount Street, engraved something like it in his *British Carpenter* (1733–5) and it resembles, more than any other surviving London church, the kind of thing which emigrant builders were putting up across the sea in New England.

From the Grosvenor Estate we pass northwards, across Oxford Street, to the Cavendish-Harley estate. Here, there are many more facts at our disposal and the method of estate development comes out very clearly.[1]

The salient fact about this estate's early history is that it was a Tory enterprise. Just as the Hanover unit was got going by a group of military Whigs, so the Cavendish-Harley estate depended for its success, from the very start, on the interest of some of the big men in the Tory party. The joint owners of the property were Edward Harley, son of the First Minister of Queen Anne's last years, and his wife Henrietta, daughter and heiress of the Duke of Newcastle. Young Harley was an ineffective man in public life but a greedy collector of books, manuscripts, and works of art. Both he and his wife were extravagant, and the Marylebone Fields offered a welcome augmentation of their already considerable income.

In 1717 the first steps were taken; Harley's uncle, another Edward Harley, was entrusted with the general supervision of the proceedings.[2]

An early list of those who signified their willingness to build in the fields consists wholly of distinguished Tory names – the names of men who had held one post or another in the great Harley administration, broken up three years earlier. There were Lord Dartmouth, a Secretary of State; Lord Carnarvon, the future Duke of Chandos; Lord Chancellor Harcourt; Lord Chancellor Bingley; Lord Castleton, a principal Secretary of

1. Many papers relating to the Cavendish-Harley estate are among the Harleian Collection in the British Museum (Add: MSS. 18,238 onwards). The writer possesses the original lease and a re-lease of No. 11 Henrietta Street (now Henrietta Place). See also a map in the Crace Maps (Portfolio 14, No. 19) giving all the original lessees.

2. See many references in H.M.C., *Portland*, Vols. 5 and 6.

Fig. 13. House characteristic of the period 1715–30. Brown brick with red dressings and stone cornice.

State; and Lord Bathurst, eminent in the Commons before entering the upper house. All these considered sites; by 1720 some of them had signed up.

The lay-out of the estate was the work of John Prince, who appears to have acted as agent for the Harleys while speculating considerably on his own account. A plan, signed by him, was engraved in 1719. It shows that this estate was quite clearly conceived, from the first, as a residential unit, with its square, its streets, its church, and its market. It shows, too, that one of the inducements to house-hunters to live on the estate was its relative nearness to Westminster, and a comparative time-table is included on the engraving showing that the Marylebone

Fig. 14. House charac-
teristic of the period
1750–65. 'Grey' brick
with stone bands and
cornice.

fields had advantages over, say, Red Lion Square or Bloomsbury
in this respect.

Prince revised his plan in 1720, in which year the market
house was begun, so as to forestall other possible adventurers.
In 1724 the church was built, and by that year Henrietta Street
and parts of Cavendish Square were inhabited. The names of
the streets were, of course, mostly family names of the noble
landlords or the names of their country estates – Welbeck and
Wimpole. Princes Street, however, probably commemorates the
industrious planner and builder, John Prince, who owned the
island site westwards of the street.[1] He liked to call himself
the 'Prince of Builders', a foible which called down a virulent

1. It has now appropriately been re-named John Princes Street.

attack in the *Morning Advertiser*[1] on his vanity, arrogance, and general hatefulness. The builders of Georgian London were rarely amiable men.

As a distinguished connoisseur and patron it was natural that Harley should see that attention was paid to the visual character and style of the developments on his land. And so we find him employing James Gibbs to supervise the architecture and Charles Bridgman to lay out the garden in Cavendish Square. Gibbs was, of course, the inevitable architect for Harley to employ. He was one of that group of writers and artists which revolved round the Harley family, and of whom Matthew Prior was the most important, Sir James Thornhill the most artistically celebrated; Dahl, the portrait painter, and Wootton, of hunting-piece fame, were of the number, as well as Gibbs and Bridgman. They were the *cognoscenti* of Prior's letters to Harley. They lived well, much in each other's company; at last three of them, Gibbs, Wootton, and Bridgman, had houses on their patron's London estate.

Gibbs's contribution to the street architecture on the estate was not very consistent. Indeed, the only documentary evidence of his participation is a building agreement of 1723 for a house in Henrietta Place (formerly Street) in which it is provided that a return elevation must conform to a design by him and that he is to approve the work. On the other hand, some of the houses in Henrietta Place, demolished in 1956, bore a stylistic resemblance to his work and of these houses three had been built by him as investments.[2] One of these (No. 11) contained an admirably decorated drawing-room, close to designs in Gibbs's *Book of Architecture*.[3] Gibbs's own house was in the same street (No. 5, demolished about 1911).

The two public buildings on the estate – the market (demolished 1880) and the church – were entirely by Gibbs. The 'Oxford Market' was a plain square building with an arcaded

1. September 1719. Quoted in T. Smith, *A Topographical and Historical Account of the Parish of St Mary-le-Bone*, 1833.

2. J. Summerson, 'Henrietta Place, Marylebone and its Associations with James Gibbs', *London Topographical Record*, XXI (1958), p. 26 ff.

3. This room is now in the Victoria and Albert Museum.

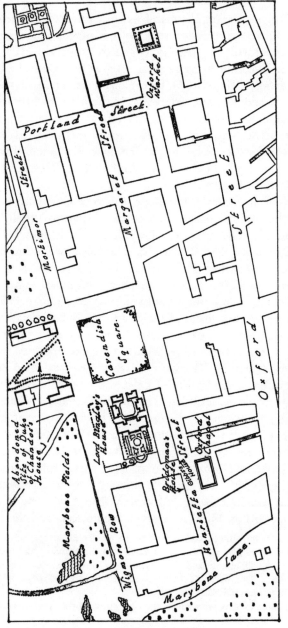

Fig. 15. The Cavendish-Harley estate, developed from 1717 onwards.

ground floor, like markets still existing in many old country towns. There was a steep roof with a cupola and a weather vane pierced with the date (1721) and the initials of Harley and his wife. The church, known for long as the 'Oxford Chapel' but in modern times as St Peter's, Vere Street, is of red and grey brick and as plain, externally, as the houses which used to surround it; the interior, surprisingly, turns out to be a miniature forecast of St Martin-in-the-Fields, exquisitely carried out. It has all the features of the larger and later church and was built by the same firm, Timbrell and Phillips, and decorated by the same plasterer, Bagutti.

The central feature of the estate was to be Cavendish Square, where the luminaries of Tory politics began to install themselves in the early twenties. The Duke of Chandos, who, as Lord Carnarvon, had dabbled in real estate at Queen Anne's Gate, took the whole of the north side, his ground running a long way back. With Edward Shepherd and others as his architects, he started to build a mansion on the scale of a really big country house. But losses in the South Sea Bubble delayed him and in 1723 the scheme was abandoned. Instead, he employed Shepherd to build two large houses at the east and west corners of the site (Plate 11). The space between them remained vacant, was acquired by the Society of Dilettanti in 1743 to build themselves an Academy, abandoned by them thirteen years later, and eventually filled, shortly before 1771, by two pairs of houses (Nos. 11–14) built as an investment by a Mr Tuffnell.[1]

The west side of the Square was taken in the first instance by the Duke of Norfolk but most of it passed subsequently to Lord Bingley. He laid the first stone of a very large house in 1722, his architect being Edward Wilcox,[2] working from a design by Archer. Hidden behind a high screen wall this house

1. These have columns and pediments so wholly inappropriate to speculative work as to give rise to the suspicion that the masonry had been prepared for the Dilettanti and was bought by Tuffnell with the site. J. Summerson, 'The Society's House: an Architectural Study' in *Royal Society of Arts Journal*, October 1954.

2. The same Wilcox who added the ugly spire (burnt in 1940) to Wren's St James's, Piccadilly.

existed, under the name (taken from a subsequent owner) of
Harcourt House, till 1903.

The rest of the square filled up slowly – so slowly that its
disorderly appearance gave rise to much criticism, until the
boom of the seventies swept over it and gave it completeness,
though not by any means uniformity.

The failure of Cavendish Square to rise to the palatial grandeur and unity hoped for by its promoters proved once more
that members of the aristocracy were not interested in their
town houses to anything like the extent that they were in their
country dwellings. As a writer[1] of 1771 put it, 'many a nobleman, whose proud seat in the country is adorned with all the
riches of architecture, porticos, and columns ... is here [i.e. in
London] content with a simple dwelling, convenient within,
and unornamental without.' 'We should be astonished at our
own riches,' wrote Gibbon on the same theme, 'if the labours
of architecture, the spoils of Italy and Greece which are now
scattered from Inverary to Wilton, were accumulated in a few
streets between Marylebone and Westminster.'[2] They were not.
Only a very few noblemen – those, for the most part, who were
wedded to French taste and manners – built great houses in
London. Chesterfield was a conspicuous example. The Duke
of Devonshire was another. For the most part, the nobility were
content with the standard product of the times, the terrace-
house.

The backwardness of builders in Cavendish Square was
equally symptomatic of the decline of the early Georgian building boom. In the 1730s expansion slowed down almost to a
standstill. A period of consolidation and gradual rebuilding in
central areas began. In 1739 Thomas Huddle, gardener, who
had been active on both the Grosvenor and the Cavendish-
Harley estates, began building along the Oxford Street frontage
of the Berners estate. About this time it was rumoured that 'at
least fifteen hundred houses now uninhabited in St Martin's,

1. J. Stuart, *Critical Observations on the Buildings and Improvements in
London*, 1771.
2. E. Gibbon, *Autobiography*.

and other adjacent Parishes, will be rebuilt'.[1] Of this activity, May's Buildings, St Martin's Lane, with Mr May's own house towards the lane (No. 43) may serve as one existing example, Meard's Buildings in Soho, where Batty Langley set up when he first came to town, is another. Many seventeenth-century houses began to be in serious need of rebuilding or refacing and, as the leases around Bloomsbury and St James's Square fell in, the landlords took the opportunity of enforcing complete or partial reconstruction.

Berkeley Square originated in this rather dim period. Some houses on the east side had been built by 1739; they were part of what was called 'Berkeley Row'. The west side was built up by 1745 and in 1747 some further sites were taken from Lord Berkeley by two carpenters, Cock and Hillyard. No regularity seems ever to have been enforced in the square, and its architectural interest never extended much beyond the few magnificent houses on the west side.[2]

The war period of 1743–8 seems to have witnessed building activity at its lowest ebb and as a result the 'fifties saw a housing shortage, and we find a nobleman[3] of 1754 complaining that 'houses are so difficult to get, and there are so many purchasers, that I am under a necessity of taking the first opportunity'. Even so, the north-western estates continued to resist further expansion till after the Seven Years War; and before we take up their story again there are other aspects of London architecture to be discussed.

1. *An Examination of the Conduct of Several Comptrollers of the City of London in relation to . . . Conduit Mead.* In the library of University College London.

2. See Christopher Hussey in *Country Life,* 26 May 1928, and E. B. Chancellor, *History of the Squares of London,* 1907.

3. Lord Waldegrave, in Add: MSS. 22, 254, f. 66.

CHAPTER 8

Public Buildings under George II

ALL through the eighteenth century, complaints were made that London's public buildings were not good enough. Shaftesbury,[1] towards the end of Queen Anne's reign, deplored the fact that Wren had spoilt all the great opportunities; which, from the sectional point of view of a rabid Palladian, was perhaps partly true. Anyway, not many more buildings of the calibre of St Paul's, Greenwich, or Hampton Court were wanted; and England under the Whig oligarchs was more interested in the construction of private fortunes than public buildings. Public architecture took a back seat. It was characteristic of the times that Vanbrugh should be jockeyed out of office to make room for Thomas Ripley, a nonentity who happened to have Walpole's ear and who immediately proved his incapacity by building the Admiralty – a work which even today is not much admired.

That was towards the end of George I's reign. Under George II the architectural scene was even emptier. Two public buildings, nevertheless, are important – Westminster Bridge and the Horse Guards: the one because it was London's first work of *engineering*, almost in the modern sense; the other, because of its prominence and its artistic pretensions.

Westminster Bridge was an engineering triumph in a capital which possessed no engineers. It was the work of a Swiss, Charles Labelye. Many English architects would have been glad to try their hands at this formidable task of spanning 1,200 feet of river; many offered their opinions; but it is doubtful if any had the experience and resource necessary to achieve what Labelye achieved, a scientific and classically designed structure, which did its job adequately until it was replaced by the present iron bridge in 1861.

Bridge-building in the 1730s was probably better understood by certain provincial masons than by anybody in London. It was

1. *A letter concerning the art or science of design*, 1712.

still conducted very much on medieval lines by bridge-building families. No bridge had been built over the Thames in London since London Bridge itself, in the twelfth century; the nearest new structure was at Fulham and this was in timber, built by John Phillips, the contracting carpenter, to a design made, not by an architect, but by a famous surgeon. It was always regarded as inconvenient and ugly.

So the idea of a new stone bridge at Westminster, put forward about 1734, was impressive. The scheme was initiated by Henry Herbert, ninth Earl of Pembroke, who was nearly as much an architect as Lord Burlington and, in addition, held influential posts at Court. With his interpreting architect, Roger Morris, he was responsible for the Palladian Bridge at Wilton and for the White Lodge in Richmond Park. In spite of vigorous protests from the City, who throughout the century consistently opposed public improvements outside their own territory and in the slightest degree liable to injure their monopolies, an Act was obtained in 1736 and the first stone laid by Lord Pembroke in January 1739.

Little is known of the skilful Charles Labelye but he had certainly been in England for some years when the Commissioners under the Act chose him as their engineer. He was an authority on land-drainage, river and harbour works, and was consulted on these subjects while engaged at Westminster. One imagines him to have belonged to that class of philosophical craftsmen and watch-makers which flourished in Switzerland and of which one gets an interesting glimpse in Jean-Jacques Rousseau's account of his early life; it is characteristic that Labelye should have borrowed his method of pile-driving (as he confesses) from a watch-maker friend. He remained in England till he had finished the bridge and was well rewarded. But his success raised clouds of jealousy and abuse. He left for Paris where he died, probably in 1781.

It was to be expected, perhaps, that English architects should be a little huffy about the alien engineer and feel it up to them to offer opinions on the new bridge, especially as they had not been asked. As soon as the work was started, pamphlets appeared. Hawksmoor, seventy-five and racked by gout, produced a short historical account of London Bridge to which he added some observations and a tentative design for the new bridge at Westminster. John Price, at work on St George's, Southwark, followed with another design and more observations. Then Batty Langley, never to be kept out of an architectural argument, butted in with a critique of both designs and a not unintelligent suggestion for the use of parabolic arches; he dropped out of the discussion when he found that 'interest' was being preferred to 'merit'. John James hastened to review all three productions and add an opinion of his own. To which Batty Langley replied. None of the pamphlets is important, or inspires confidence in the authors as potential rivals to Labelye. Anyway, nobody took much notice and Labelye got on with the job.

Westminster Bridge took nine years to build and cost the vast sum of £393,189. The builders, under Labelye, were Andrews Jelfe[1] and Captain Samuel Tuffnell, the latter mason to Westminster Abbey. It was at first proposed to build stone piers only and bridge the spans with timber, but the more ambitious conception of a complete masonry structure prevailed and Labelye went off to Portland with his masons to choose the stone.

His design involved a novelty in the use of caissons for building the piers, instead of the primitive method of piling, and then sinking a quantity of rough masonry. These caissons were enormous barge-like timber boxes, 80 ft long and 16 ft deep, each made to accommodate the masonry of the lower part of one of the piers. Shallow excavations were dug in the bed of the river at low tide and sparsely piled. The caissons were floated into position, over these excavations, the lower courses of masonry laid and cramped inside them; eventually the caissons were sunk, one by one, into the excavations, the water pumped out, and each pier built up inside the caisson to a convenient height. Then the sides of the caisson were struck, the flat bottom remaining under the pier. The merit of the system was that the piers were of accurately laid masonry from bottom to top. This did not, however, prevent an awkward subsidence of one pier, when the bridge was nearly complete, owing apparently to

1. He designed the excellent little town hall at Rye, Sussex.

sabotage, perhaps inspired from citywards. The pier and adjoining arches had to be rebuilt, delaying the bridge's completion for several years.

The arches of the bridge were built with the same handsome extravagance as the piers, the Portland stone voussoir courses being continued through from one face of the bridge to the other and backed by another continuous arch, of Purbeck stone, nicely adjusted in thickness, between haunches and crown, so as to direct the superincumbent weight to the piers without trespassing on the equilibrium of the adjoining arches.

The whole bridge was ingenious and delicate, the engineering facts simply and gracefully expressed in the pattern of the masonry. Although the bridge has gone, its grand scale and architectural quality are preserved for us in Samuel Scott's paintings and numerous engravings (Plate 14). It was real engineering. Its author was neither mason nor architect, but a man of a professional type which England had not yet learned to produce, although an aptitude for empirical engineering had already proved, and was to prove again, singularly natural to the English mind. Labelye set a standard which was recognized by Gwynn, Mylne, and Smeaton, Telford and the Rennies; and his bridge was the foundation of an English tradition in bridge-building second to none in Europe.

As Westminster Bridge was finishing, another conspicuous public work – the Horse Guards, in Whitehall – was being begun. This remains little altered, a monument to George II's passion for military order and display. It was designed to be the headquarters of the General Staff and continued as such until 1872. The Horse Guards (Plate 12a), designed by William Kent, and executed under Vardy after his death, took the place of a dilapidated brick building of Charles II's time, rather similar in general silhouette. The rebuilding was begun in 1750 and finished in 1758. Kent had already built the Treasury (the façade towards St James's Park is his) and had prepared elaborate if rather stiff designs for a new Parliament House which never got further than paper. The Horse Guards remains his principal London work and the most considerable public building to issue from the offices of the Burlington group.

The plans of the Horse Guards building make it amply clear that its architect studied the design from outside in. With its complex projections and recessions and varied skyline it is irresistibly picturesque – especially in its spacious park setting and with the linen sheen of two-centuries-old Portland stone. But as a rational building the Horse Guards is decidedly quaint. The plan is a collection of square or nearly square boxes squeezed into a predetermined composition – and a composition, at that, full of points of emphasis, which, on analysis are revealed as grotesquely out of harmony with the function of the elements of which they form part. Thus, of five imposing Venetian windows towards the Park, only one lights a room of any consequence – the Commander-in-Chief's audience room – and two are miserably squeezed in at the corners of small offices. The central drive-through has an arch so uncomfortably low that Hogarth, no lover of the Burlington gang, gleefully painted a coach emerging with a headless driver. The Horse Guards justifies Pope's inimitable lines about the architectural snob who is 'proud to catch cold at a Venetian door'. Many an unhappy War Office clerk must have taken a chill at Kent's Venetian windows.

But the point of this sort of criticism is not utilitarian but academic. And it is important, because the aim of the Palladian group itself was academic in the highest degree. One may be tempted to see in Kent's failure to conform to the best standards of his own school the impatience of an artist who, at bottom, had something in common with Vanbrughian Baroque. But Vanbrughian Baroque is far more organic, far more reasonable in its plan-elevation relationships than this building of Kent's. The truth lies, more probably, in Kent's attitude to design which was that of a decorative painter. Painting had been his first study, when his Yorkshire patrons sent him to Rome. A painter, of a slick superficial kind, he remained on his return, though he then designed the rooms on whose walls he used his brush. Burlington, his second patron and life-long friend, made him an architect, injected him with his own passion for architectural detail. But Kent never saw a building as a thing with an artistic life of its own, but only as a delightful ornamental property, a piece of full-scale scenery, developed from the kind of sophisticated scenery which spread itself over so much contemporary canvas.

The Horse Guards showed up the limitations of Palladianism, and the unhappy results of trying to fit every contemporary problem into garments copied from the gear of a sixteenth-century Italian. The building served as a ready text for the eclectics, who were preparing to supersede the Burlington theory with one based on a much broader conception of aca-demic architecture – a conception tinged with the current academicism of France. William Chambers, as early as 1757, referred to the 'general dislike' of the Horse Guards, suggested that 'Mr Kent ... was fond of puzzling his spectators', and called attention not only to the artificial complexity of the design but to the lack of a true scale relationship between the several parts – a point which Hogarth had already made with rather more verve than the future architect of Somerset House.

Westminster Bridge and the Horse Guards – these two build-ings stand out in a thirty-year desert of architectural dullness. If we comb George II's London we shall not find much else to hold our interest. The churches we have already dealt with. Four great private palaces – Devonshire House, Chesterfield House, Burlington House, and Spencer House (Plate 12b) arrive on the scene and rank almost as public buildings. Kent, Ware, Burlington, and Vardy are the inevitable architects. The houses have or (in the case of the first two) had academic merits; Burlington's, of which we have already spoken, something more. There were the smaller palaces – like Kent's enormously grand house for Lady Isabella Finch in Berkeley Square (Plate 5), and like Cambridge House (the Naval and Military Club) in Piccadilly. And as an agreeable relief from the eternal book-learned façades, there were the Baroque, Gothic, and Chinese temples of Vauxhall, and Mr Jones, the furniture designer's, clever Rococo rotunda at Ranelagh.

Of greater sociological if less artistic interest are the hospitals, some new, some reconstructions. These buildings reflect an attractive aspect of Georgian life – the rational, unsentimental humanitarianism which characterized, for instance, men like

Henry and John Fielding, the Bow Street magistrates, and some of the pioneer doctors and surgeons. Hospital building originated partly in compassion, partly, perhaps, in fear of the seething filth and contagion of working-class London, and partly in the anxiety of medical men to come to grips with the most glaring problems of disease.

Of the three ancient hospitals, Bethlehem had been rebuilt late in the seventeenth century and St Thomas's very early in the eighteenth, while St Bartholomew's was largely rebuilt by Gibbs in four distinct stages, beginning in 1730. Its ceremonial portions, the great hall and staircase, survive; they were almost the only early Georgian buildings in London to be faced with Bath stone,[1] the reason for its use being the anxiety of Ralph Allen of Bath to make his quarries known to the building world of London.

The new hospitals owed their beginnings either to private generosity or the enrolment, by a few enthusiasts, of bodies of annual subscribers. To the former class belong Guy's (built 1721-5) and the Foundling (1742-52); to the latter, the Westminster (opened 1719), St George's (1733-4), the London (1752-7), and the Middlesex (1755-75). These early hospitals, distributed for health and safety's sake over the fields of outer London, were symmetrical brick boxes, never quite without architectural features. St George's was a refitting, by Ware, of a large private residence; the London Hospital was designed by an otherwise unknown Boulton Mainwaring, Esq., and its plan, with ward wings and tiers of privies in the angles, forecasts the arrangement of the typical Victorian hospital; the Middlesex (Plate 15a) was another big symmetrical block very artificially composed by its architect, James Paine. In most cases the architects supplied the designs free, and Gibbs, Mainwaring, and Ware were governors of the hospitals for which they were responsible.

Both Guy's and the Foundling, being the product of private wealth, were handsomer than any of these. The Foundling, especially (Plate 15b), made a deliberate artistic appeal to the

1. An earlier example, however, is Burlington's dormitory at Westminster School.

public, in music and painting as well as architecture. Its build-ings were elaborately composed, somewhat in the style of Kent. Its architect was Theodore Jacobsen, a retired businessman of German extraction.

It will be seen that most of London's principal modern hos-pitals were founded and first built in the forty years between 1720 and 1760. In spite of the worlds which separate modern from Georgian clinical practice some of the old buildings are still in use. There are Georgian sash windows in some of the wards at Guy's and the centre of the London Hospital is Main-waring's original block. The Foundling has gone, but some of Jacobsen's loggias survive in what is now called 'Coram's Fields'.

CHAPTER 9

The Spirit and Practice of 'Improvement'

ONE of the most remarkable books ever written about the planning and architecture of London is John Gwynn's *London and Westminster Improved*, published by the author in 1766. We do not know exactly when Gwynn was born but he must have been about the same age as his friend Dr Johnson, whose sturdy, critical conservatism he shared. Because he knew the Doctor, we get a glimpse of him in Boswell. He was 'a fine, lively, rattling fellow'; and there is a Zoffany portrait which preserves his keen, inquisitive, rather challenging aspect.

Gwynn built little, but thought and wrote much, especially about the foundation of an Academy and the planning of London. He got hold of Wren's City plan when it was sold, with Wren's other drawings, in 1749, and published it, with some energetic observations, incidentally misleading posterity by making a wrong guess at the reasons why the plan was never executed. Then, in 1766, came *London and Westminster Improved*, accompanied by three plans. Gwynn took a very serious view of the future of London. He saw that the West End estate developments (those we described in Chapter 7) were far too loosely controlled :

Why so wretched an use has been made of so valuable and desirable an opportunity of displaying taste and elegance in this part of the town is a question that very probably would puzzle the builders themselves to answer.

The builders were the trouble – and, in a lesser degree, the landlord who, when he planned at all, planned badly. 'The finest part of the town is left to the mercy of ignorant and capricious persons'. Gwynn urged that the map of London should be considered as a whole and future activity controlled by a general plan; and in support of this he produced his scheme of improvement, with more than a hundred separate suggestions in the form of new streets and squares, widenings, clearances, and embankments. The amazing thing about this plan is its complete grip on reality. Nothing in it is Utopian, and, in fact, a very large proportion of his suggestions were carried out within a hundred years of the publication of the book; while of those which remain to be implemented, some were included in the proposals of the L.C.C.'s County of London Plan of 1943. Among the features on the modern map of London which are found in embryo in Gwynn are the Embankment, Waterloo Bridge, Trafalgar Square, Bedford Square, Finsbury Square, Moorgate Street, Cranbourn Street, and dozens of minor improvements long since carried out. He envisaged a 'Regent Street' on the line of the Haymarket and sited a Royal Palace in the Green Park. He replanned Tower Hill and Parliament Square, exposed St Martin-in-the-Fields, and foresaw the need for a great new parish church for St Marylebone.

The one conspicuous defect in this extraordinary performance is Gwynn's naïve belief that London could be called to a halt at Marylebone Road on the north and Hyde Park on the West.

Gwynn's plan inaugurates the age of *improvement*. We cannot now estimate its direct influence, though this must have been considerable, for the book is occasionally mentioned in reports and memoranda on the subject of London's development. But Gwynn crystallizes a point of view, the point of view subsequently maintained by most educated and responsible Londoners until the Reform Bill of 1832, after which social responsibility was gradually shaken out of the aristocracy without being shaken into the bourgeoisie.

What was 'improvement'? At the lowest level, it might be said that an 'improvement' occurred whenever a sufficient number of influential men were so far inconvenienced as to be induced to act in accordance with the public spirit with which they believed themselves endowed. Their own interest and that of the public being seen to coincide, they set about obtaining from Parliament powers to carry an 'improvement' into effect with the minimum of expense to themselves. But that is too cynical an interpretation. A disinterested 'spirit of improvement' did exist among a great many people in Georgian London and many individuals, from peers to company promoters (the latter, to be candid, more than the former), took a much wider view of their obligations than was necessitated by strict social or economic expediency.

The innumerable Road Acts of the middle part of the century were among the first evidences of 'improvement'. Then there were the Lighting and Paving Acts for London, the first of which, affecting Westminster and the adjacent parishes, was passed in 1761 and received high praise from Gwynn. Even the City, usually backward and all too ready to sabotage the initiative of people outside its boundaries, came to the front in the 1760s with a scheme of improvement in its own territory which requires more than a passing glance.

Improvement talk had been dormant in the City since the Great Rebuilding, but started again in the Common Council about 1753. A pamphlet appeared in the following year, suggesting the filling in of the Fleet Ditch and the building of Blackfriars Bridge. This idea and a rival scheme for rehabilitating old London Bridge both eventually took effect. In 1760, an Act was obtained for widening and improving streets in the City. In the same year, the old gates, except Newgate, were demolished. In 1761 came another Act for an improved approach to London Bridge. Then, as a result of the building of Blackfriars Bridge, an Act was obtained for additional road-making on the Surrey side, and the lines set out for a great new suburb (see Chapter 20). Finally, in 1767, the City secured an Act for finishing the bridge, rebuilding Newgate Gaol, and repairing the Royal Exchange.

Much of this legislation is associated with the name of an extremely able sculptor-architect who was in his time Alderman and Sheriff – Sir Robert Taylor. In his artistic capacity Taylor belongs to the next chapter, and so does his collaborator George Dance, the younger, a man of greater artistic achievement, who succeeded his father as Clerk of the City Works in 1767–8. Taylor and, in the later stages, Dance were the principals in all these schemes. But in the case of Blackfriars Bridge, a third name emerges, that of Robert Mylne.

Mylne was selected from sixty-nine competitors to carry out his design for Blackfriars Bridge, and commissioned in February 1760. One of the competitors was Gwynn and it is greatly to be feared that a certain 'Mr Trowel', a character invented and mocked by Gwynn as the typical upstart youngster 'just arrived from Rome', is in fact Mylne. Mylne came of a family of bridge-builders, active in Scotland since the Middle Ages. He went to Rome, carried off all the honours at St Luke's Academy, and was only twenty-five when, immediately on his return, he won the competition for Blackfriars Bridge.

Gwynn, disappointed at Blackfriars, was to prove himself an excellent bridge-builder in Shropshire a few years later and it was a pity he found it necessary to resent Mylne's success. For it was no mere paper success; the bridge, completed in less than ten years and well within the young architect's estimate, was an excellent piece of work. It curved gently across the river over nine arches of nearly elliptical form. Each pier was adorned with pairs of Ionic columns, supporting an embrasure in the parapet on each side of the roadway; an architectural device which Rennie was to borrow in the next century. The bridge was an advance on Westminster Bridge (just thirty years older) not only in point of performance (it spanned the river in nine arches instead of twelve) but in refinement of design : the rise to the centre from either bank being in a single curve – the segment of a huge circle – and not two straight lines meeting abruptly in a hump.

The repair of old London Bridge was another part of the City's improvement schemes. This was undertaken by Taylor and Dance together. They pulled down all that was left of the old houses in 1757, built a new centre arch in 1759, and refaced the piers, adorning them with Gothic panels just to show that it was still the same old bridge. Already nearly six centuries old, its survival was prolonged for another sixty years.[1]

The spirit of improvement in the City, after a quiescent inter-

1. Each pier was given a hooded alcove, and two of these alcoves were preserved and rebuilt near the eastern boundary of Victoria Park in 1860. They are interesting for their good detail and the effective tooling of the masonry.

val, manifested itself again in 1777 in the laying-out by George Dance of Finsbury Square on a tract of land north of Moorgate which the City had leased from the Prebendary of Finsbury in 1768. Dance seems to have entrusted this work to his very good assistant, James Peacock, a man rather older than Dance and of a very original turn of mind. Peacock designed the houses on the west side of the square, most of which were burnt down in 1941. The terrace was quite exceptional in the logic and decorative originality of its design, the garret roofs being frankly exposed as mansards instead of concealed behind a light-inhibiting parapet. At first the terrace stood alone in the fields, between Bedlam and St Luke's Hospital – London's two great mad-houses. 'I think,' said Dr Johnson, 'a very moral use may be made of these new buildings; I would have those who have heated imaginations live there, and take warning.' James Peacock, notably sane, to judge by his works, lived in No. 17.

The remainder of Finsbury Square (all now rebuilt) was of no special interest; the north side was erected in 1789, the east in 1790, and the south in the following year.

To this improvement was added the elliptical Finsbury Circus in about 1814, on the site of Bedlam, probably under the direction of William Mountague who in that year was taking over the City Clerkship from his master, Dance, whose retirement, after nearly fifty years of magnificent service, dated from 1815.

To return to improvement by legislation : there was on the Statute Book an accumulation of Acts controlling the manner of building in London. Some of these Acts, relating to the standardization of bricks and the restriction of woodwork on house fronts, we have already noticed. There were several more aimed chiefly at securing the more proper construction, in manner and material, of party-walls. But to crown these separate and tentative efforts to improve the standard of London building, came the great Building Act of 1774, a milestone in the history of London 'improvement'.

This Act was drafted by Sir Robert Taylor and Dance. Its main object was to consolidate and enforce the many provisions made in previous years. It aimed at stopping once and for all the slipshod construction of party-walls and evasive quibbling between adjoining owners; and it aimed, too, at making the exterior of the ordinary house as nearly incombustible as possible. In order to lay down hard and fast rules of construction it was necessary to categorize London buildings in some detail. In fact, they were coordinated into separate categories or 'rates'. Each 'rate' was confined within specific limits of value and floor area. Thus, a 'First Rate' house was one valued at over £850 and occupying more than nine 'squares of building' (i.e. 900 sq. ft). At the other extreme, a 'Fourth Rate' house was one valued at less than £150 and occupying less than three and a half 'squares of building' (i.e. 350 sq. ft). The areas excluded out-buildings.

Each 'rate' had its code of structural requirements as regards foundations, external and party-walls. But the real importance of this system was not so much that it facilitated the enforcement of a structural code but that it confirmed a degree of standardization in speculative building. This was inevitable; for the limitation of size and value set out in the rating tended to create optimum types from which there was no escape and within which very little variation was possible. Especially did the second, third, and fourth rates of houses tend to become stereotyped. This was, in many ways, an excellent thing: it gave some degree of order and dignity to the later suburbs and incidentally laid down minimum standards for working-class urban housing which would have been decent if they had been accompanied by legislation against overcrowding.

On the other hand, the Act contributed largely to what the later Georgians and early Victorians conceived to be the inexpressible monotony of the typical London street, a monotony which certainly must, at one time, have been overpowering and which can still be felt in the lonelier tracts of Islington and, to a really distressing degree, in a more or less intact Georgian capital like Dublin.

For not only did the Act tend to create standard types of houses; it saw to it that the London house should not adorn itself with any but the most exiguous and reticent kinds of ornament. All woodwork (the cheapest and most tractable

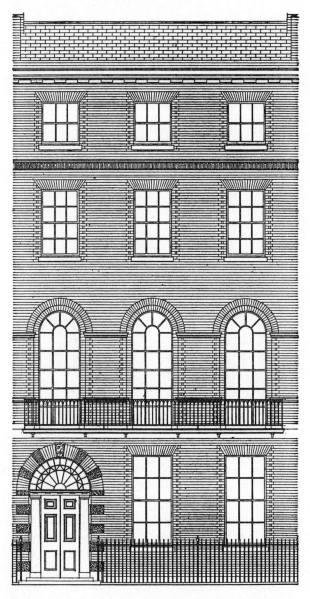

Fig. 16. A first-rate house (No. 109 Baker Street) built in 1789, in
brown stock brick, with 'Coade' ornaments.

Figs. 17 & 18. Elevations for 'second-rate' and 'fourth-rate' houses under the Building Act (adapted from R. Elsam's designs in the *Practical Builder*, 1825).

material for ornament) was banished, except in so far as it was necessary for shop-fronts and door-cases. The old generous type of bayed shop-window was made to draw in to a mere 10-inch projection – or less in a narrow street. Window joinery, which Queen Anne had caused to retreat from the wall-face, was now further concealed by being lodged in recesses *behind* the wall-face in the top and sides of the opening, so that only a tiny strip of woodwork was visible from outside (See Fig. 19).

It was fortunate that the Building Act came at a time when ornamentation could perfectly well cope with these restrictions. In 1774 thin, wiry detail was already well on the way and the feeling for restrained detail did not quarrel with the dimensional restraints imposed. Indeed, it is perfectly clear that, in drafting the Act, Dance and Taylor – excellent artists both of them, as well as shrewd draughtsmen – were thinking in terms of the most advanced types of London practice and merely crystallizing the regulations against this background. It was not their generation, but a later one, which, in bitter resentment of what they conceived to be tyranny, christened the Act 'The Black Act of 1774'.

This question of ornamentation brings us back once more to Gwynn. One of his strictures on contemporary building practice was that too many public buildings were built of brick. Failing stone, which he admitted to be expensive, he advocated stucco; he thought, for instance, that Wren should have stuccoed St James's, Piccadilly:

In fact no publick edifice ought to be built with brick unless it is afterwards stucco'd, for a mere brick-face in such buildings always makes a mean appearance. ... As the building with stone is so very expensive in this metropolis, it is to be lamented that encouragement is not given to some ingenious person to find out a stucco or composition resembling stone, more durable than the common sort, and in which exterior ornaments might be easily wrought at a very easy expense.

Whatever we may think of Gwynn's dislike of brick in important buildings, it was a dislike shared by many of his contemporaries. But when he wrote, in the 1760s, there was still no really serviceable exterior stucco on the market, nor yet a sufficiently reliable 'composition ... in which exterior ornaments might be easily wrought'. But both stucco and composition were on the way and by the time the Building Act was passed they were becoming established in the builder's armoury of materials. The Act gave them every encouragement.

It is impossible to fix a precise date for the arrival of stucco in London building practice. Inigo Jones rendered several of his buildings in lime mortar but after his time the practice lapsed and brick was always exposed. Adam used stucco – perhaps Liardet's patent – in Hanover Square about 1776; Wyatt covered the (still existing) front of 9 Conduit Street with Higgins's cement in 1779; Nash first used stucco in Bloomsbury Square in 1783, adopted Parker's Roman Cement on its introduction in 1796, and continued to use it till he changed to Hamelin's mastic or Dehl's mastic about 1819–21. More important to us than this list of dates is the general truth that various patent stuccos came in just about the time of the Building Act of 1774, and were sparingly used until Nash inaugurated the real stucco age with the building of Park Crescent in Parker's Roman Cement in 1812 (see Chapter 13).

Stucco is regarded with affection today, chiefly because it recalls the taste of a period which we happen to like. But the present-day notion of painted stucco is, according to eighteenth-century standards, inaccurate because we rarely appreciate its intention, which was, in the strictest sense, to imitate stone. All the respectable stucco buildings of the eighteenth and early nineteenth centuries were carefully scored with horizontal and vertical lines to represent stone jointing. More than that, each separate stone was 'frescoed' to imitate the weathering of the real thing. As we shall see later, Nash thought of all his London work in terms of Bath stone and when he could afford Bath stone (as at Buckingham Palace and All Souls, Langham Place) he used it. But in speculative work it was out of the question and he restorted to the *trompe-l'œil* substitute in stucco.

Our modern view of painted stucco is really more candid and sensible and offers greater possibilities; but in looking at old examples of stucco facing, it is as well to perceive the builders' intention behind the present unelaborate effect, charming as the latter often is.

Quite as important as stucco, in the 'improved' London of the 1770s, was a species of composition known as Coade Stone. The history of this astonishingly fine material, which provided the answer to the second of Gwynn's demands, has been told by Mrs Esdaile.[1] She has discovered that the manufacture of some sort of artificial stone was carried on by a man called Richard Holt, who took out a patent, in partnership with Ripley, the architect, as early as 1722. This business flourished in a dim way but had fallen on evil days when, in 1769, or shortly before, it passed

1. Two articles in *Architect and Building News*, 19 and 26 January 1940. See also S. B. Hamilton, 'Coade Stone' in *Architectural Review*, November 1954.

into the hands of Mrs Eleanor Coade, 'the daughter of the person who discovered the composition'. Mrs Coade must have been a remarkable business woman; and she had the imagination to secure the services of a young sculptor, John Bacon, who worked with her long enough to place the whole artistic output of her factory at Lambeth on a very high level, before he himself became one of the most successful sculptors of his time.

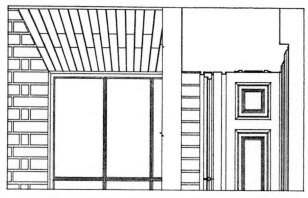

Fig. 19. Elevation and Section of typical window as prescribed in the Building Act of 1774. (Compare Fig. 8, p. 68.)

The output of the factory was amazing, both in quantity and scope. A catalogue[1] in the British Museum (Plate 17) proves that most of the architectural ornaments in the West End of 1774 onwards came from Lambeth. Many London churches, and the village churches round about, contain elegant mural monuments signed with the names of E. & W. Coade or of Coade and Seely, her later partner; and there are Coade table-tombs in the church-yards. From Buckingham Palace to Twining's tea-warehouse in the Strand, from Westminster Abbey to the chapel-of-ease in the Hampstead Road, from the Bank of England and the Royal Exchange to the impost mouldings on the doorways of Bedford Square, Coade Stone was triumphant. And time has justified its use. In many a weather-worn façade, the Coade

---

1. Not a formal publication, merely a bound set of proofs of etchings, with a MS. title page, *Etchings of Coade's Artificial Stone Manufacture, Narrow Wall, Lambeth* . . . *published only for private circulation in the years 1777, 1778 and 1779.*

sculptures stand out crisp and firm; and I have seen burnt churches where the Coade monuments are the only ones still recognizable. Its precise composition is unknown, but it was a species of terra-cotta, the mixing of the 'earth' being a jealously guarded secret.

Stucco and Coade Stone were both, in a sense, fake materials, convenient substitutes for ashlar masonry and carved stone. But, quite unconsciously, their essential character was appreciated and accepted. We shall see, in the next chapter, how the feeling for the externals of architecture changed, after the arrival of Adam, from the grimness of a mask to the delicacy of a feminine 'make-up'. Stucco and Coade Stone have a slightly cosmetic character; they suggest, faintly and agreeably, the artificiality of powder and rouge.

John Gwynn would, I am afraid, not have liked that metaphor. There must have been a good deal in the London of his later days which he did not like, including Scottish careerists (he shared Johnson's views on the Scotch), new architectural fashions from out-of-the-way places like Athens and Dalmatia, and the setting up of more than one young cub of an architect 'just arrived from Rome'. But he saw the realization of his Academy and became one of its first members; and by the time he died, in 1786, a new sense of enlightenment in public opinion and a new generation of architects were beginning to 'improve' London and Westminster in a way which he would not altogether have despised.

CHAPTER 10

Architects of the Golden Age
1763-93

IF the thirty years before the Peace of Paris were dull and limited in their architecture it must be admitted that they laid a magnificent foundation of competence for the great period which was to follow. If English architecture built itself into a Palladian prison, the process was extremely beneficial to technique both in design and construction; and the moment of escape was all the more exhilarating.

The next thirty years – between the Peace of Paris and the beginning of the French wars – is commonly, and rightly, regarded as the Golden Age of Georgian culture. It was introduced by success in arms – success amply productive of the fruits of imperialism. A young, English-spirited Hanoverian sat on the throne and his accession seemed to mark the extinction of the triple dreads of early Georgians – Jacobitism, Catholicism, and Bourbon aggression.

It was an age which combined confidence and vitality, security and adventure: solid intellectual achievement and imaginative creation. It produced on the one hand a Johnson, on the other a Sterne; a Burke – and a Fox; a Reynolds – and a Gainsborough; a Chambers – and an Adam. There was room for the conservative cast of mind, proceeding cautiously to build on the past; and for the wit, the innovator, whose brilliance is set in relief by the grey solidity of his background.

In architecture, William Chambers and Robert Adam were the pre-eminent personalities after 1763, and with their arrival on the scene it is necessary to say something about the profession of which they became, almost immediately, the chief ornaments. The fact is that an 'architectural profession', very nearly in the modern sense, did at last exist. There were men in practice, here and there, who were neither Civil Servants (like Wren), placemen (like Archer), nor dependants of the aristocracy (like Kent

133

or Gibbs), but who were something different from mere surveyors or tradesmen with a rule-of-thumb capacity for design.
The professional gentleman-artist-architect had arrived.

In 1763, most of the old Palladian group were either dead or
very old. Kent had died in 1748, Leoni in 1746, and their patron,
Burlington, in 1753; Flitcroft, Ware, and Vardy were in retirement. The principal men in practice in London were Sir Robert
Taylor and James Paine. Taylor, son of a mason, had begun as a
stone-carver; he did important sculptural work at the Bank and
the Mansion House, and City patronage was responsible for his
later success as an architect, when he built banking-houses, West
End mansions, and country villas for rich citizens, whom he
also commemorated with excellent church monuments. He was
a City notable himself, as we have seen, and was knighted for
his services as a citizen rather than as an architect.

Paine was also trained in the arts, being a student at the St
Martin's Lane Academy. He acquired a very good connexion
among north-country landowners and his London works were
limited to the Middlesex Hospital and a few big houses, including his own (No. 73 St Martin's Lane), the houses in Salisbury
Place, Strand, one in Whitehall, and one in Pall Mall for a
famous doctor. None of these exists. He, like Taylor, had civic
ambitions and became High Sheriff of Surrey.

These two celebrities are said, by Hardwick, to have 'nearly
divided the practice of the profession between them ... till Mr
Robert Adam entered the lists'.[1] They were the first big, independent practitioners. Both founded their styles on the older
Palladianism but refined it to a remarkable degree. Taylor's
halls at the Bank of England gracefully imitated Gibbs's vaulted
nave at St Martin's, and his many London houses all reach a
high technical level. The best of them, No. 35 Lincoln's Inn
Fields, was completely destroyed in 1941.[2] No. 37 (The Bishop
of Ely's)[3] in Dover Street and some houses in Grafton Street

1. W. Chambers, *Treatise . . . of Civil Architecture* (ed. Gwilt; 1825),
p. xlix.

2. Well recorded in *Survey of London* (St Giles-in-the-Fields, Part I).

3. The excellent front survives; the interior was wholly remodelled for
the Albemarle Club by Messrs Smith and Brewer, some Taylor details
being retained.

survive. The handsome Stone Buildings in Lincoln's Inn are also mostly Taylor's work. Such buildings as these – competently and broadly handled – indicate the kind of architecture with which the great period of Chambers and Adam opened.

Both Chambers and Adam exercised enormous influence as soon as they appeared on the scene. But they were as different as possible. Both had the initial advantages of breeding, education, and financial security; both had the support of Court influence right at the beginning of the new reign. Yet temperamentally they were as unlike as Reynolds and Gainsborough (the parallel is a significant one), Chambers setting a policy of sensitive, eclectic conservatism, Adam initiating what was at once recognized as a revolution in taste and in the whole approach to domestic design.

William Chambers was the elder by two years. The son of a Scottish merchant, trading at Göteborg, he saw much of the world before devoting himself seriously to architecture; he studied under Blondel in Paris and had been praised for his draughtsmanship in Rome as a preliminary to descending upon the rather dim and stolid world of London building. At thirty he was teaching the politer elements of architecture to the Prince of Wales, and at the same time he published a book of Chinese buildings, furniture, costume, and decorations, based on notes he had made in Canton during his travels. Dr Johnson praised it. At Kew, he laid out the gardens and built the Pagoda and other ornaments. The year before his Royal patron's accession, he produced the book for which he is chiefly remembered, the *Treatise of Civil Archicture*. This is a work parallel in many respects to Reynolds' *Discourses*. Chambers had neither Reynolds' scope nor his eloquence, but within limits his criticism is as finely-tempered. Like Reynolds, he formed an eclectic taste, including sixteenth- and seventeeth-century Italian and French work among his models. He could allude familiarly to works by Sangallo and Bernini, Lescot and Delorme. His critique of the Roman orders and their application is fastidious and lucid.

Chambers was the complete academician, by temperament and in the pattern of his career. From the first, he was a heavyweight, full of learning and authority, and it is not surprising to find him taking a leading part in the founding of the Royal Academy. When he became Surveyor-General of Works he was the first professional to occupy the office since Wren. His was the model architectural career and he gave architecture a new social standing.

With Robert Adam the outcome was rather different, though his early career and that of Chambers were parallel. The son of a successful Scottish architect, he started with much the same advantage as Chambers and was already conscious of rivalry with him before either had begun to practise. He spent four years in Italy with Clérisseau as his tutor and Piranesi as an inspiration. He crossed the Adriatic and surveyed Diocletian's Palace at Spalato. When he returned to London he was, like Chambers, at once besieged by clients. Publishing his folio of Diocletian's Palace in 1764 he was able to designate himself on the title page, *Architect to the King*. He was then thirty-six.

But Adam was not an academic. Impatient of English tradition, set forms, and official procedure, he aspired to be an innovator. Such, indeed, he at once became. He revolutionized the use of ornament; and the revolution was felt not only throughout the building trade but in furniture, and even in textiles and pottery. In architecture the change can best be expressed as the substitution of a 'make-up' for a mask. The Palladians had ruled that the only proper adornments for buildings, both inside and out, were the grammatical elements comprised in the five orders and the somewhat limited number of expansions and variations exemplified in the works of Palladio and Inigo Jones. Thus, an exterior had to conform with the theoretic apparatus of a rusticated basement surmounted by columns, entablature, and attic; an interior had to be worked out so as to fit an equivalent apparatus on a smaller scale, with entablatures over the main doors and columns beside them, beamed ceilings developing from cornices strictly proportioned to the heights of rooms. Everything was to be masked, as it were, in the cold mask of a grammarian's Rome.

Adam, to use his own expression, 'exploded' all this. While ready enough to accept the traditional symmetries and mass-relationships, he began to treat ornament freely. Arguing, very reasonably, that the Romans themselves did not introduce temple architecture in their houses, he developed a technique of ornament which appealed immediately to over-Palladianized London of the gay, rich, and optimistic 1760s. 'We have adopted,' he says in one of the prefaces to his *Works in Architecture*, 'a beautiful variety of the light mouldings, gracefully formed, delicately enriched and arranged with propriety and skill.' The 'old tabernacle frames', copied out of Kent's *Inigo Jones*, and the heavy ceilings, were to go; and in the place of these masks came the sparkling modelled ornament, the delicate swags and ribbons, the slim, enriched pilasters – in short, the exquisite 'make-up' – of the Adam style (Plates 18 and 19).

It took few years for the Adam revolution to take effect. When London architects, surveyors, and carpenters had seen Lord Mansfield's pilastered front at Kenwood and Garrick's airy portico at Hampton, when the Adelphi rose up on Thames-side with its thin embroideries, and, above all, when the *Works in Architecture of Robert and James Adam* began to come out in instalments in 1773, the building trade responded rapidly. How rapidly and how sympathetically, one may judge by comparing a carpenter's copy-book of the seventies with those of previous decades. Take for instance William Pain's popular *Practical Builder* which first came out in 1774. Not only does the carpenter-author speak of the 'very great Revolution' which has taken place in 'the ornamental Department' of architecture, but many of the designs, including what he calls a 'modern composed capital', are derived quite obviously from Adam work. In practice, the change is equally apparent, and after 1775 it is rare to find any London houses, at least in the West End, which do not betray some debt to Robert Adam's invention and daring.

The Adam revoltuion was, however, not approved by everybody and most emphatically not by Sir William Chambers. Adam had nothing to do with Chambers and was, in turn, ignored by the Royal Academy, in whose exhibitions the only 'Adam' designs to be seen were by Robert's innumerable imitators. The story that Chambers influenced the King to prevent

Adam receiving a knighthood may be apocryphal, but that such a tale should be spread about illustrates the antipathy between these two artists. Chambers, in the later editions of his Civil Architecture, hinted broadly at his dislike of Adam 'affectations', and his buildings are protests in themselves.

Chambers and Adam presided over London architecture for thirty years, and all questions of taste in that period must be resolved in relation to them. All too few of their buildings remain. By Chambers, there are only Somerset House and Melbourne House (incorporated in the Albany). By Adam and his brothers, there are still a few expressive fragments of the Adelphi, as well as three fine houses, scraps of Portland Place,[1] two façades in Fitzroy Square (Plate 31a), and the Admiralty screen. For sheer contrast, no two buildings by this formidable pair were as telling, in their day, as Adam's Adelphi and Chambers' Somerset House, the one begun in 1768, the other in 1776. In every respect these were characteristic of their authors – in inception, construction, and design. Both had Thames-side sites and rose up out of the sodden margins of the river on arcades of Palatine grandeur.

Somerset House survives, but the main blocks of the Adelphi have been destroyed. There is little need for regret, however, because their destruction had, in effect, already taken place in 1872 when the exterior was remodelled in a style calculated to bring to the purlieus of the Strand some of the stucco amenity of the Cromwell Road. The interiors had good ceilings and fireplaces but little else of value except their memories and even these had, perhaps, been somewhat too richly overlaid. An unspoiled and representative fragment of Adam's design survives in Adam Street as the Lancet Office. This ought to be preserved (Plate 18).

The story of the Adelphi is of a gallant and imaginative enterprise, a bid to realize a big architectural idea with no more backing than a modest professional fortune and a sanguine

1. No. 37 Portland Place was hit by a bomb in 1940, but the fine stucco façade remained. In 1943, however, movement in one of the badly-built party walls caused a partial collapse, and half the façade was taken down (see Plate 16).

anticipation that a living-quarter of such unique splendour could not want tenants. Robert Adam and his brothers (James, the fellow-artist, and the businesslike William) took a ninety-nine-year lease from the Duke of St Albans of the site of Durham House in 1768. They cleared the site and petitioned, in 1771, for an Act of Parliament to enable them to reclaim a shallow 'bay' formed by the river at this point, and erect a wharf and other buildings to a certain height. In spite of the City's inevitable bone-headed opposition they got their Act, and by 1772 the substructure of tunnels was complete and many of the houses built.

The idea had taken concrete shape. For the first time, the Thames was architecturally embanked. Brick catacombs supported blocks of houses, level with the Strand, a 'Royal Terrace' (Plate 19b) in the centre and streets at the sides terminating in pedimented and pilastered ends. And these houses were conceived as architectural masses with the natural splendour of size and symmetry. There was no attempt to give them a Roman dress; their siting and disposition were already as Roman as Spalato. But they were humanized and rendered expressive by gay strips of honeysuckle embroidery, adroitly distributed at the centre and sides.

The idea had taken shape, but at great cost to its inventors. Financially, everything had gone wrong. The Ordnance Department failed to come up to Adam's expectation that it would rent all the vaults for storage. The level of the wharf turned out to be too low by about two feet. And the houses did not sell, even though the friendly and enterprising Garrick had given the best lead that any house-agent could desire. Bankruptcy faced the adventuring brothers, and to save their scheme and themselves they resorted to the expedient of a lottery. This was not a wholly original idea; John Simmons had disposed of the centre house on the east side of Grosvenor Square in the same way about fifty years before. The gamble was widely advertised, there were 4,370 tickets at £50 apiece, with 108 prizes; and the upshot was that the Adams remained solvent – though they had to dispose of their collections of works of art, and the speculation hung like a millstone round their necks for many years.

As a feat of architecture, the Adelphi was a success. It brought the new style right into the centre of the town where everybody could see, admire, and criticize it. Opinions differed vastly as to its merits. Walpole's smart, unjust verdict was that it was 'like a soldier's trull in a regimental old coat'.[1] Sir William Chambers and his academic friends naturally found it affected and meretricious; and their criticism was somehow mixed up with a profound dislike of the way in which the Adams had made the whole thing a personal advertisement, even christening it with a name betokening their brotherhood.

It was Sir William Chambers's turn next. The conditions for the siting of Somerset House were very like those for the Adelphi. Once again an ancient palace was cleared away from Thames Bank, and once again an arcaded terrace rose from the water. But in nothing else did the great new administrative centre resemble the Adelphi. Far from being speculative, it was a national building paid for out of the public funds. Far from being the work of an individual out to realize his own private architectural dream, it was a building of a kind which educated opinion had long advocated and whose erection was felt to be overdue. And far from being a dashing, original gesture in design, it was eclectic, conservative, and if anything, over-studied.

Somerset House (Plates 20 and 21) was built under an Act of Parliament of 1775. Behind this Act is a long tale of proposals and counter-proposals for a building of the sort, a central rendezvous for official and academic bodies. Apart from churches, the Banqueting House, and the Horse Guards, London had no Great Public Building in its midst. The Government departments were housed in a motley collection of structures around Whitehall. The Royal Academy, the Royal Society, and the Society of Antiquaries were lodged in buildings grotesquely out of keeping with their standing. The Government buildings and Academies of the peoples of the Continent were a reproach.

Edmund Burke, aesthetician as well as political philosopher, had a big hand in the passing of the Act, and it was inevitable

1. H. Walpole, *Letters*, ed. Toynbee (1903–5), viii, 313.

that Sir William Chambers, as Surveyor-General, as well as Treasurer of the Royal Academy and personal friend of the King and Burke, should preside over its architecture. The site was cleared of the many curious and beautiful buildings with which Protector Somerset, James I, and Charles I had adorned it and as Chambers marched for the last time through the long-locked state-rooms of Tudors and Stuarts, he paused to regret the passing of a little domed breakfast-room from the hand of Inigo Jones. But the ground was remorselessly cleared and the first stone of the new building was laid during 1776.

After several preliminary trials, Chambers pitched on a plan consisting of a great central courtyard, flanked by narrower courtyards; but only the main courtyard was to be tackled in the first instance. It was to be approached from the Strand through a block of narrow frontage compared with the width of the building as a whole, and this narrower block was to contain the headquarters of the learned societies.

This block, with its frontage to the busy Strand, was the first to be built, and was complete by 1780, when the learned societies moved in. Chambers took enormous pains with this building, both because of its conspicuous position in London's main street and because of the intellectual status of its tenants. In general composition, the columns and arches imitate Inigo Jones's posthumously executed river façade of the old Somerset House, but there are French and Italian influences as well. The vestibule (Plate 21) is a technically perfect Doric loggia. The symbolic sculpture, of which there is much, is almost all from the hands of Chambers's fellow academicians, Wilton, Carlini, and Bacon, and all the figure sculpture was carved from cartoons provided by Cipriani.

Rarely has so much care been expended, so much thoughtful collaboration undertaken, on a London building. And yet, all things considered, the result is not overwhelmingly effective. Today, the Strand façade of Somerset House is almost unnoticed. There is an admirable view of it from between two blocks of Bush House, but even from there it requires concentrated attention before its many admirable qualities can be evaluated. It is singularly uncommunicative and the truth is that the design shares the failing of some of Reynolds's canvases – it is over-worked, and the freshness of the basic idea is polished away. All eclectic art, perhaps, is subject to this kind of anaemia and the Strand front of Somerset House is a typical case. It is a work of technical virtuosity, but an education rather than a delight. Compare its effect with the surviving Adam front in John Street, where the slick, decorative pilasters in artificial stone catch and hold the attention unfailingly (Plate 18).

The main buildings of Somerset House, designed to house the Navy Office, the Ordnance Office, the Stamp, Salt, and Tax Offices, and a variety of others, suffer less from the shortcomings of Chambers's academic temperament. His use of rustication makes a delightful linear pattern; the sculpture is always adroitly placed and well executed; there are many subtleties of finish in the façades, and the fireplaces and ceilings within are as decorative, though not as gay, as anything that Adams did. In short, Somerset House is a delightful, civilized, accomplished building; but one must not look to it for grandeur of effect or depth of imagination.

Today, of course, allowance must be made for the intervention of the Victoria Embankment between the river and Chambers's arcades and water-gates, forming, in effect, a secondary terrace which dwarfs the architecture behind and above it. The river front today is longer than it was in Chambers's time; the scheme having been completed during the first half of the nineteenth century, first by the building of King's College on the east and later by the building of the Inland Revenue Office on the west.

The Adelphi and Somerset House – *magna opera* of the two architectural giants of mid-Georgian London – epitomize the situation in the contemporary arts. But the picture must be elaborated. Both Adam and Chambers contributed other things to London – private houses, for instance, on the generous scale and with the modest externals demanded by the richest Londoners. Chambers built a house off Piccadilly for Lord Melbourne. It survives as the central block of Albany. He also built a house in Whitehall Gardens for another great Whig, Lord

Gower (Plate 22). It was demolished in the eighties of last century. And he built several houses, including one for himself, in Berners Street. All are stamped with Chambersian dignity. Their details are extremely delicate but avoid the least suggestion of the elongations and lawless omissions and embellishments of Adam. The façade of Albany, for instance – brown brick, with stone dressings – is Palladian in general design, though the ornaments have the elegance of French work and are placed with a fine feeling for the whole effect. The rusticated stone doorways which survived until recently in Berners Street formed an even more decisive contrast with anything emanating from the Adam office. They might have been borrowed from Somerset House and were as solemn as the doors of a senate-house.

Adam's houses – glamorous, gay, original, full of affectations which, nevertheless, are rarely tedious – tell a very different story. The earliest of them, Lansdowne House (mauled in 1936), was begun for Lord Bute in 1762, six years before the Adelphi was begun. It is an instructive contrast to Chambers's Albany, building at the same time. But the finer Adam houses were still to come. There were four of capital importance: Chandos House, Chandos Street, Cavendish Square, for the Duke of Buckingham, 1770–1 (in good preservation); No. 20 St James's Square, for Sir W. Williams Wynn, 1772–4 (well preserved, but the façade has unfortunately been extended by three identical units and an attic added); No. 23 Grosvenor Square ('Derby House') for Lord Stanley, 1773–4 (demolished); No. 20 Portman Square ('Home House') for the Countess of Home (exists, in good preservation, as the Courtauld Institute), 1775–7.

These last four houses represent, perhaps, the highest point of imagination and artistry in the handling of the London house. They are not mere repositories of delicious ornament; the basis of their splendour is their minutely considered arrangement. The rooms in an Adam house are not a simple aggregate of well-proportioned and convenient boxes, but a harmony of spaces – a harmony in which many contrasts reside. The hall, the staircase, each room, each closet, fits into a counterpoint of living-space; every wall of every room has been caressed in

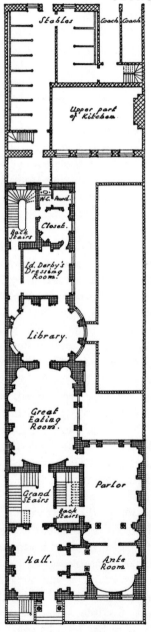

the architect's mind and persuaded into some delicate discipline mutually enhancing that of the rooms before and beyond it.

It is all devised for the conduct of an elaborate social parade, a parade which was felt to be the necessary accompaniment of active and responsible living. These houses of Adam's were not pleasure pavilions or settings for Vanity Fair; they were built by people with a certainty of their own importance and of the paramount justice of whichever political cause they espoused. They were not built for domestic but for public life – a life of continual entertaining in drawing-rooms and ante-rooms and 'eating-rooms' where conversation would not be wholly ephemeral, where a sentence might be delivered which would echo round political England, where an introduction might mean the beginning of a career or a deft criticism the dethronement of a policy.

Adam's letters and sketches show how fully he appreciated for what kind of life he was planning. He ponders the assembly of guests, the conversation before dinner, the procession to the dining-room; he considers

Fig. 20. Ground-floor plan of Lord Derby's house in Grosvenor Square.

where the upper servants shall stand, how the under servants shall perform their duties without being noticed; and behind the parade he plans for the dignified, easy privacy of lord and lady, with study, dressing-rooms, closets, and bed-chambers.

The real glory of the Adam houses died with the life for which they were built. When they become 'mixed' clubs, council rooms for distillers, and seminaries for the University of London, it is no longer easy to see what underlies the Pompeian lace and the Etruscan colouring or to give back to each room the measure of emphasis or reticence which it had when the regulated tide of eighteenth-century society flowed through it. Adam houses are always pretty but in their origin they were something more.

Chambers and Adam left their marks on London, both directly, and also indirectly through their imitators. The Adams, being fairly easy to imitate, especially in their exterior 'make-up' of thin pilasters, balconies, and pretty door-frames, scored the most hits. James Adam's façades in Portland Place (Plate 16) hardly preceded the accomplished quasi-Adam of Stratford Place and Bedford Square and Sir Joseph Banks's beautiful house in Soho Square (No. 32; its demolition in 1937 was a sad loss). Moreover, the tradesmen went mad over the Adam 'revolution' and brought it into every little street and every shop-front of later Georgian London.

Chambers had little popular appeal, and his academic gospel was spread rather among his fellow-academicians and pupils than in the building-world at large. Thomas Sandby, William Tyler, and the younger Dance shared, to some extent, his conservative viewpoint, and it appears in the set of churches built by his pupil, Thomas Hardwick. But if Chambers was not much imitated he was always greatly respected and critics who wearied of the 'frippery' of Adam fell back comfortably on his solid merits.

Although it is correct enough to present Chambers and Adam as the mightiest figures in the architecture of their time, it would be wrong to give the impression that the whole of London architecture in the 'Golden Age' can be accounted for in terms of their work and influence. The scene is more complex than that, especially after 1775, when a generation fifteen to twenty years younger than the two giants began to make its reactions felt. The architects of that generation are an attractive and interesting group, but before introducing them we must break off for a moment to glance at a very singular figure, who belongs to no group at all but whose importance was considerable for several reasons.

James Stuart was born in 1713 and was thus an almost exact contemporary of Sir Robert Taylor. But his entry into architecture was delayed. He started as a painter of fans, employed by Louis Goupy; in 1742 he was in Rome but it was not till nine years later that he joined Nicholas Revett in an expedition to Athens, hitherto practically unexplored as a source of architectural inspiration. He returned to England in 1755, and the first volume of Stuart and Revett's *Antiquities of Athens* was published in 1762. With Wood's *Ruins of Palmyra* (1753) and Adam's *Palace of Diocletian at Spalatro* (1764) it ranks as one of the three most important architectural travel books of the century, though its immediate influence was small. He found a patron in Admiral Lord Anson and was employed to design several large London houses, including Mrs Montagu's (later Portman House; completely destroyed 1941; Plate 23) in Portman Square, Lord Anson's in St James's Square (No. 15), and parts of Spencer House. In the first two of these he introduced the Athenian orders, disposing them precisely as a Palladian would have disposed the ordinary Vitruvian elements. This was a revolution in the letter rather than the spirit. But there is another side to Stuart's work. He was a painter before he was an architect and he seems to have studied the Raphael *loggie* and Giulio Romano's work; for at Spencer House the painted room (*c.* 1760) is an interesting and beautiful example of this kind of decoration. Later he used Adam detail of the most elaborate kind as in the drawing-rooms at Montagu House but there is evidence that much of this was the work of Joseph Bonomi.

Stuart's most remarkable work is the interior of the Chapel at Greenwich Hospital, reconstructed after a fire in 1779; but here again there is some doubt as to his real authorship in the face of claims made by William Newton. Irresponsible and intemperate in his later years, Stuart's career hardly did justice to his talents. His book opened up a great new field of interest for the future and the next generation benefited richly from it. He died in 1788, an isolated, enigmatic figure in Georgian history.[1]

Stuart was admitted to be a rival – occasional and uncertain – to his juniors, the Adam brothers. More real and formidable to them, however, was the assault from the younger men who, having grown up with the Adam style, were fully armed to overthrow it. The most important of these were the younger George Dance, Henry Holland, and James Wyatt.

Each of these three architects had a clearly marked field of work. Thus, George Dance inherited his father's valuable office of Clerk of Works of the Corporation of the City of London. Henry Holland was exclusively at the disposal of the inner circle of great Whigs. Wyatt, it is true, practised at large but in 1796 he suceeded Chambers in the office of Surveyor-General and was thus the chief architect to the Government till his death in 1813.

George Dance was a very much more remarkable architect than has ever been fully realized. Only his masterpiece, Newgate Prison, has been admitted to be a great work; but when the records of the whole of his output are assembled it will, I think, be seen that his power as a designer places him among the few really outstanding architects of the century.

His first work as City Surveyor, All Hallows, London Wall (badly damaged 1940–1, and rebuilt 1961–2) is remarkable enough (Plate 25). It was built immediately after his return from Italy, at the age of twenty-four. Its exterior is nothing much, but internally the barrel vault, pierced by semi-circular lunettes and supported on an Ionic order with the cornice and frieze suppressed, has that acute feeling for simple geometrical forms which is the hall-mark of what we now call Neoclassicism. There is a sharpness in the detail which probably derives

1. There is a valuable paper on Stuart and his fellow-traveller, Revett, by Miss Lesley Lawrence in *Journal of the Warburg Institute*, ii, 2. 1938.

from an acquaintance with Piranesi. With its raised apsidal end, it reminds one of another London church built by a young architect fresh from Italy – Gibbs's St Mary-le-Strand. At its date (1765–7) All Hallows was probably the most advanced move towards the simplification which was later realized and justified by Soane (who knew and acknowledged his indebtedness).

Newgate Prison (Plate 24a) followed in 1770–8. Built at the joint expense of City and Government, it superseded the old gatehouse jail, a fever-incubator which had been known to kill not only the prisoners but judge and jury as well. The City provided the Old Bailey site and Dance devised a plan with three courtyards, a long elevation to the Old Bailey, and a shorter elevation to Newgate Street. Unfortunately the prison was built too early by a few years to benefit from the movement towards prison reform started by John Howard, whose work on English prisons appeared in the year of the building's completion. Hence, Dance's plan was out of date within a decade of its execution. It has, in any case, little architectural interest and need not detain us.

But the composition as a whole was magnificent. Towards the Old Bailey, there were two great masses of unwindowed wall, rusticated from plinth to cornice. Their ends were brought slightly forward and marked off as pavilions, with arched openings filled in again with rusticated columns and pediment as though to frame a window but in which were set instead symbolic figures. Between the two great masses was placed the many-windowed keeper's house with entrance lodges to left and right. The composition is doubly remarkable. First, because of its Piranesian sense of the drama of rustication, and the deft accentuation of mass by recession at certain points. And second, because of its vivid articulation. The keeper's house and the entrance lodges are separate entities, declaiming their purpose, contrary to – almost in the teeth of – academic propriety. Here was no mere 'centre and wings' Academy picture, but a forceful expression of purpose, cruelly eloquent in all its parts.

The prison was burnt out by the Gordon rioters in 1780 and rebuilt with minor variations. It survived till 1902 when it gave place to the present Central Criminal Courts.

Dance built St Luke's Hospital (which survived till about 1965 as the Bank of England's printing works), and re-fronted the Guildhall (1789) with a Gothic fantasy. The spirit in which this last work was designed is difficult to recapture; it is a deliberate modernization of Gothic but with a strong feeling for the Islamic architecture of India as recorded in the paintings and engravings of William Hodges. Inside the Guildhall, Dance built a domed top-lit hall for the Court of Common Council, which anticipated Soane's similar inventions at the Bank. It was destroyed in 1906.

To form a true estimate of Dance we must take into account his work at Lansdowne House (the ball-room, completed by Smirke, still exists) as well as the demolished Shakespeare Gallery built for Alderman Boydell in Pall Mall, and his country houses, which, of course, fall outside our present scope. There is no English architect whose life and work has been so undeservedly neglected by historians, and of whom a fully documented and illustrated memoir is so much needed in the library of English art-history.

Five years younger than Dance was Henry Holland, a builder's son who seems to have introduced himself into practice by marrying the daughter of 'Capability' Brown, the landscape-gardener. All Holland's London works were for the Whig hierarchy – the Grand Whiggery as it has been called – and the period of his success coincides neatly with the career of the greatest of Whigs, Charles James Fox, which is to say, from 1774, when Fox joined the opposition in the Commons, till 1806, the year in which both Fox and Holland died.

An early product of Holland's association with Whiggery was Brooks's Club in St James's Street, built in 1776–8. It shows him as a conscious corrector of the Adam manner. On the street front the Corinthian pilasters and cornice are unaffectedly bookish; there are no elisions and no embroideries. We find the same restraint in the interior, where even in the drawing-room the only concessions to Adam ornamentalism are some carefully placed medallions and swags. Holland was interested in shapely and appropriate expression unelaborated by any decorative overlay. It was a healthy and intelligent reaction, sacrificing none of the essential benefit which the Adam revolution had engendered, but returning to the fountain of scholarship with fresh vision.

Holland's next work in London was the vestibule and portico of Dover House, Whitehall (1786), for the Duke of York. Here he set off a Greek Ionic portico flanked by attached columns against a delicately rusticated front. It is a charming, gentle piece of work, even if, as one critic observed, 'its diminutiveness is more striking than its beauty'.[1] The building (the rear part of which is by Paine) survives as the Scottish Office.

Holland's greatest opportunity arrived when the Prince of Wales came of age in 1783 and immediately moved into Carlton House, an old-fashioned *hôtel* in Pall Mall, built in 1709 for Lord Carlton. He proceeded to have it converted into a palace and employed the man whom his friends of the Fox circle all employed, Henry Holland.

Carlton House was destroyed in 1826, but we can still enjoy its architecture in the pages of Pyne's *Royal Residences*, in Pugin's *Microcosm* and Britton's *Public Buildings*. The Palace was strictly classical and perfectly free from Adam influence. It seems possible that Holland had been to Paris and seen some of the latest *hôtels* by Gondoin, Peyre, Rousseau, and others, with their feeling for 'archaeological' integrity and exceedingly fine and unaffected detail. Rousseau's Hôtel de Salm, in particular, with its six-column Corinthian portico and Ionic screen is a possible source of inspiration for Carlton House. It was finished the year before Holland's building was begun.

The Pall Mall façade of Carlton House (Plate 27a) was long and low and lightly rusticated from top to bottom. In the centre was an admirable Corinthian portico, generous enough to serve both as porch and *porte cochère* and richly detailed. Immediately inside was an oblong hall, with two Ionic columns *in antis* on all four sides and open segmental arches over each pair. This hall led to an octagon, with an open well, admitting light from the first floor, while to the right of the octagon was the double

1. W. H. Leeds in J. Britton and A. Pugin, *Public Buildings of London* (1828), vii, 194.

staircase, planned within a large oval and covered by two semi-domes meeting a coffered barrel in the centre.

Screening the Palace from the street was a colonnade of coupled Ionic columns, with arched entries at either end; a Parisian idea, which Londoners found slightly ridiculous. Architecturally, it formed a nice preliminary to the porticoed part beyond.

Horace Walpole was immensely impressed by the new Palace. There was an 'august simplicity' which astonished him. 'You cannot call it magnificent; it is the taste and propriety that strike.' A very just comment: taste and propriety are precisely what one enjoys in all Holland's work. And he added: 'How sick one shall be after this chaste palace of Mr Adam's gingerbread and sippets of embroidery !'[1] This last remark is interesting because Walpole was old enough to remember the Palladian dictatorship and as an old man of seventy was perhaps rather glad to see again an architecture which, however, un-Palladian, showed a strong inclination to scholarship and discipline.

Among Holland's last works were East India House and the formation of Albany, to front and rear of the house which Chambers designed for Lord Melbourne. The residential suites survive, but the houses towards Piccadilly, with galleries supported by eagles, were demolished in the ten years before 1939.

The third major architect in the generation which took up a position independent both of Adam and Chambers, was James Wyatt. Although he was employed to an enormous extent and was Surveyor-General for seventeen years after 1796, he left a very slight impression on the architecture of the capital. Today he is represented only by the narrow façade of No. 9 Conduit Street. His Gothic House of Lords, which was unhappily preferred to Soane's splendid designs of 1794, was, from all accounts, perfectly uninteresting; his own house in Foley Place (demolished) was good but not extraordinary; and Samuel Rogers's house in St James's Place had been so much altered, before being finally burnt in 1941, that little is known of what it may have contained.

1. H. Walpole, *Letters*, ed. Toynbee (1903–5), xiii, 321.

James Wyatt's only important London building was his first – the Oxford Street Pantheon (Plate 27b). It was built in 1770–2 as 'a winter Ranelagh', Wyatt's brother being a principal promoter. There were several different rooms, but its chief glory was a domed cathedral-like hall with double-storied aisles and rounded ends. The shape was like a compressed version of Santa Sophia, Constantinople. Justinian's church was, of course, hardly known, still less admired, in Georgian London, but drawings of it were in circulation and Wyatt brilliantly adapted the plan to the current Adam style which he nevertheless modified in his own way.

No interior so gorgeous had been built in London since Wren finished St Paul's, and Wyatt, whose timber-framed dome involved no statical difficulties, produced what Walpole enthusiastically called 'the most beautiful edifice in England'.[1] The Byzantine body, mantled in Hellenistic embroideries, must have been wonderfully surprising in 1772. The artificial lighting played up to the architecture; candle-light quickened the chiaroscuro paintings into glimpses of Valhalla, while friezes and niches were accented with green and purple lamps and the dome swam in a heathen twilight, reflected from gilt vases.

The success of the Pantheon was tremendous. But the novelty passed; and though its architect's reputation soared it did so on the afflatus of a Gothic revival. Wyatt became the Gothic master, and although his little church at Dodington once again (and perhaps involuntarily) strikes a Byzantine chord, that side of his genius had cooled. The Pantheon was destroyed by fire in 1792, rebuilt in less brilliant fashion, taken down and again rebuilt by Cundy as a theatre in 1812. It was remodelled by Sydney Smirke in 1834 as a bazaar and picture gallery, but converted into Messrs Gilbey's warehouse and offices in 1867. All this time, Wyatt's little Oxford Street façade survived, though a Doric porch had been added to it by Smirke. In 1937, all that was left of the Pantheon was finally demolished.

Wyatt was an extraordinary character. Apparently destitute of any convictions whatever, moral or artistic, drink and women were his habitual employments, though he indulged at intervals

1. H. Walpole, *Letters*, ed. Toynbee (1903–5), viii, 313.

in orgies of architectural designing. He told Farington that his real inclination was for the sober classicism of Sir William Chambers, but that he was obliged to bow to the public's taste for the Adam style and the Gothic. A man so irresponsible was unlikely to make much impression on English architecture. When he met his death in a coach accident in 1813, and was buried in Westminster Abbey, only his wickednesses were remembered.

Dance, Holland, and Wyatt are the three great names which succeed the greater names of Chambers and Adam. With them should be mentioned the slightly older Robert Mylne, whose first and greatest work – Blackfriars Bridge – has been described. Mylne was an excellent designer, almost comparable to Dance, but hardly any of his work was in London. An exception was the City Lying-in Hospital, long ago destroyed; another exception, badly singed in the blitz, is the lovely east elevation of Stationers' Hall. To the same generation as Holland and Wyatt belonged lesser men like Thomas Leverton, whom we shall meet in Chapter 12, and John Crunden. The latter was a prolific author of books of designs, but London is indebted to him for the façade of Boodle's Club, in St James's Street, built in 1775, a witty re-hash of Adam's façade of the Royal Society of Arts in the Adelphi. Brooks's and Boodle's are two most delightful London buildings; and perhaps, in this chapter, it would be inexcusable not to mention White's, the Tory counterpart of Brooks's during the 'Golden Age'. White's ought, to fit the story, to be the work of the government architect, Wyatt, and he certainly did some work there, though whether any of the present façade, remodelled in 1850, is his it is hard to say.

The golden age lasted till 1793 and then showed not the least symptom of decline. The outbreak of war applied a brake to building activity, but standards of taste remained high, higher perhaps than they had ever been, and the buildings which were built in London during the following twenty years were almost all extremely good. This remains to be shown in the next chapter.

CHAPTER II

Building during the French Wars
1793-1815

THIS chapter will be short because there is little to put into it. Revolutionary France declared war on Britain on 1 February 1793, and except for the two years' respite after the Treaty of Amiens, 1801, the war continued till Napoleon's abdication in 1814; the escape from Elba and the final 'hundred days' bringing the war period down to 18 June 1815. Thus, for more than twenty-two years Britain had been in a state of war. It would be untrue to say that the arts of peace did not flourish. They did. In many directions, the war brought prosperity – especially to farmers, landowners, and manufacturers. Painting and literature were unhindered; patronage was plentiful. But with architecture it was different. State expenditure on building was absolutely withdrawn, except for buildings of military or naval purpose. And an acute shortage of Baltic timber, combined with high taxation of building materials, made building a difficult and expensive adventure for any private person.

Buildings in London dating from between 1793 and 1815 are therefore relatively scarce. And it is a tragic scarcity, because never had standards of taste and execution stood higher. It was, as we have seen, the period of reaction from Adam 'fripperies', the period when the purified elegance of Holland and the younger Dance came into its own, the period which produced that most exquisite stylism which, inaccurately, we call 'Regency', but which really belongs to the earlier war period and was quickly dissipated after the Regency had begun.

The tragedy extended to a whole generation of architects – the generation born round about 1770–80, which, when it grew up, found the hope of practising sadly remote. It was the generation which, in literature, produced Wordsworth and Coleridge and Sir Walter Scott, in painting, Constable and Turner. Where are their counterparts in architecture? They are hardly to be

found. Joseph Gandy had, perhaps, in his lowly way, a Cole-
ridgean imagination, but his works are few and slight, and he
exhausted his genius pathetically in huge watercolours of bale-
fully lit architecture. Charles Heathcote Tatham had wonderful
taste and skill, but he is remembered only for his books of
designs; his opportunities for building were trifling. John
Linnell Bond might have given London some superlative public
buildings; but one remembers him only for his too monumental
hotel at Stamford. John Sanders built two fine buildings for
military purposes and then disappeared from the scene. Many
men must, like J. M. W. Turner, have left architecture. Many
must have been discouraged from entering the profession at all.

One building and one architect stand out most prominently
against the dull war-time background. The building was the
Bank of England and the architect was John Soane.

The Bank of England was founded to help finance a war and
it is during wars that it has played its most critical part in the
national economy. So there is nothing extraordinary in the fact
that building-work at the Bank proceeded during almost the
whole of the French wars of 1793-1815. The work was not
necessitated in the first instance, however, by anything connected with Pitt's novel and vigorous financial policy; merely
by obsolescence and inconvenience. But it is obvious that when
the National Debt[1] increased from 230 millions to over 500
millions between 1793 and 1802, and again to nearly 800 millions
by 1815 the business of the Bank was very considerably increased
and the increase is reflected in great additions made to the site
and the rapid multiplication of halls and courts.

John Soane was appointed architect to the Bank in the year
that his predecessor, Sir Robert Taylor, died: 1788. He was
then thirty-five, but although his work as an architect amounted
only to a handful of small country-houses he was marked for
success. He was the son of a small Berkshire builder, and had
come to London as a boy and found a place with George Dance,
apparently as a servant. Later, he worked for Henry Holland.
He was a student at the Royal Academy, won the Silver and

1. See the Table in C. Grant Robertson, *England under the Hanoverians*,
10th ed., 1930.

Gold Medals, and in 1778-9 was in Italy as the Royal Academy's travelling student. He returned on the strength of a promise of employment in Ireland by the Bishop of Derry but was cruelly used in the affair, and ploughed a rather difficult furrow till, as Pitt's own nominee, he obtained the Bank appointment.

Soane was a curious, thorny, intricate personality. The leading trait in his character was, without the least doubt, a consuming ambition. He had been a poor boy; by his own endeavours he climbed out of poverty into the ranks of a respectable profession. But his ambition was unslaked by moderate success, nor did it ever become ambition of a less strictly professional kind. He did not marry much above his original social rank; nor did he move in society as anything but a professional member of it. He was always strictly and simply an architect: a furiously ambitious, wholly self-centred architect.

The story of Soane is, therefore, the story of the construction of a career: a career as integral, as precise in detail, and as deftly planned as any of his buildings. Whether in design, in construction, in professional conduct, or in social relations he was fanatical in his attention to detail, painfully anxious to perfect the role he had set himself. It was a very lonely role. Self-perfection is a lonely course, and Soane's architecture is lonely not merely in its singularity but a certain emaciated melancholy, rarely absent.

This architecture was the one transcendental thing in Soane's museum – has a desiccated correctitude which is admirable relations, his social intercourse, his assiduous collecting for his museum, have a desiccated correctitude which is admirable rather than attractive and is sometimes stained with the petulant, selfish jealousy of a schoolboy. But his architecture sings. In relation to his life, one feels that it was the precious, mercurial marrow, protected by layers and layers of complicated professional existence. His early designs are exquisitely finished essays in the kind of classicism understood by Adam and by Dance. The keenly felt geometry, the volumes and surface values in these designs are the beginning of his own manner, which constantly strips away the non-essential expressions of academism and leaves an abstract achievement, balanced on the knife-edge of sensibility.

The Bank of England was the first building in which the Soane manner fully discovered itself. Up to 1791 he was concerned with little more than a thorough survey of the existing buildings of his predecessors, Sampson and Taylor (see Chapter 4), and some minor alterations. But in 1792 he rebuilt Taylor's Bank Stock Office and in doing so produced the first of the Soane Halls. Its shape was that of a Greek-cross Byzantine church,[1] but with flat segmental arches instead of round arches, and a continuous ring of windows carrying a flat ceiling instead of a drum and dome. Two of the 'aisles' were covered by cross-vaults, two by vaults following the segmental line of the arch. No academic units (i.e. columns, cornices, architraves, etc.) were admitted to the design. Instead, the surfaces were modelled with grooves and panels of extreme subtlety and occasional sharp accents in the way of medallions and paterae. What is so daring, so extraordinarily novel and independent in the design is the degree of *contraction* manifested. Not only does Soane discard the conventional expressions of academic design but he exhausts and whittles what is left, squeezing the volume out of the solid parts so that the volume of the space contained is the more sharply felt. This contradiction is most dramatic and surprising where the soffits of the very thin arches meet the faces of the very thin piers *at a point*. From this point the architecture seems to fly into space, to be self-poised; it is the Gothic miracle rediscovered at the heart of the Roman tradition.

Soane built four other halls at the Bank, all on much the same plan and all lit from shallow window-rings. They vary considerably in date, and in the later halls (1818–23) he is more suave, more confident in his own idiom, perhaps, but no less exciting (Plate 28a).

The Bank as a whole was completed in three phases. The first (1788–1800) included, besides the Bank Stock Office, the first

1. A convenient illustration, not a suggestion that Soane had the slightest knowledge of, or interest in, Byzantine work. In many respects, Soane was a Byzantine *malgré lui*.

part of the (still existing) screen wall which eventually enveloped the whole site and in which the curiously stylized order from the Temple of Vesta at Tivoli was used – to the horror of men of the Chambers School. This phase also saw the erection of the Lothbury Court with its triumphal arch and Corinthian screens; also of the Consols Transfer Office and a new Rotunda on the site of Taylor's.

The second phase (1800–18) saw the continuation of the screen wall round the whole of the site and the erection of the 'Tivoli Corner', in which the order was expressed on a segment of a circle, suggesting the character of the circular temple to which it belongs. The Governor's Court also belongs to this time and the open loggia, with its piers formed of detached *antae* in pairs, was one of Soane's most effective experiments. Adjoining the Governor's Court was the Five Pound Note Office and on the opposite side a whole nest of exquisite little rooms associated with the Court Room suite.

The third, post-war, phase (1818–33) saw the final reconstruction of Taylor's halls and the completion of the screen wall.

The Bank, before its rebuilding, 1925–39, was Soane's greatest monument and, tragically, one of the least accessible in London. In the rebuilding, several of Soane's halls were preserved, as well as the screen wall; but, unhappily, the architect of the new building was antipathetic to his predecessor in such a degree that wherever respect has been intended the result has been a grotesque insult. The Tivoli corner has been massacred and the relation of the new work to the old is a tragi-comedy of incompatibles.

Soane built one other important building during the war period – the Art Gallery and Mausoleum at Dulwich College (Plate 29). These were built from a bequest of Sir Francis Bourgeois, R.A., to contain the collection of pictures which Bourgeois inherited from his friend Desenfans, and, further, to house the coffins of Mr and Mrs Desenfans and of Bourgeois himself. Desenfans had, it seems, expressed a strong objection to being buried; and Bourgeois had already obliged his corpse to the extent of building a mortuary chapel at the back of his own house in Charlotte Street. In his will, therefore, he stipulated for a mausoleum to be attached to the picture gallery.

Bourgeois died in 1811. The scheme was put in hand at once and the buildings finished in 1814. Both gallery and mausoleum were blown to pieces by a flying-bomb in 1944, but were rebuilt immediately after the war.

In many ways, the Dulwich building is one of Soane's most able and revealing designs and is worth considering in detail. Look first at the plan. The main element is the sequence of five galleries, three square and two oblong. Joined to this, at right angles, are two wings with lower buildings between them, while in the centre of these is the mausoleum. Observe how carefully each element is given *quasi-independence* of its neighbour, chiefly by the device of making slight recessions in the plan where small entrance lobbies are introduced. This produces a curious 'tension' throughout the design, each part bearing a distinct and intense relationship to the whole. The mausoleum is inset in the plan but retains its identity entire. The low fore-buildings are lodged between mausoleum and wings without making direct contact with either. And yet by all these contrivances unity is never destroyed, but, on the contrary made more real.

In the handling of the mausoleum (Plate 29)[1], the same quasi-detachment is noticeable. The portals in the open arches do not touch the jambs; and the frieze is recessed so that the cornice seems suspended over the piers instead of resting on them.

The resulting composition is a quintessence. Inertia has been drained away from it; and yet further to increase the feeling of tension, the masonry of the lantern is delicately grooved – a 'cat's cradle' of lines in tension. The interior of the mausoleum is a wonderful study of intersection and the building as a whole reaches a level of emotional eloquence and technical performance rare in English, or indeed in European architecture.

To the Bank of England and the Dulwich Gallery we can add few important buildings during the twenty-two years of war.

1. The very strange plan of the mausoleum was probably inspired by that of an Alexandrian catacomb, engraved in the *Description de l'Égypte*, published 1809.

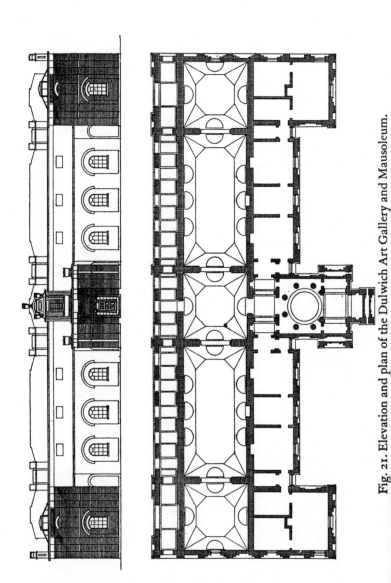

Fig. 21. Elevation and plan of the Dulwich Art Gallery and Mausoleum.

160

As I have said, government expenditure on building was reduced to an essential minimum. There is, however, one government building of great merit whose erection coincided exactly with the Peace of Amiens, 1801-3. This is the Royal Military Asylum, which still stands in the King's Road, Chelsea, and is known today as the Duke of York's Headquarters. Designed as a school for orphans of men killed in the first phase of the war, it is a noble brown-brick mass with a stone portico of four Roman Doric columns. The architect was John Sanders, one of Soane's early pupils and one of that ill-fated 1770 generation whose abilities were obscured and thwarted by the times. The building is robust and well-proportioned, a fit companion for Wren's Royal Hospital, to which it forms an appropriate satellite. The Soane-like chapel near the entrance is a beautiful example of what can be made out of stock-bricks arranged in the simplest arcuated pattern. Sanders became architect to the Barrack Department after his success at Chelsea and was responsible for the excellent buildings at Sandhurst. But he had no other opportunities worthy of him and he retired early from practice and died in 1826.

Soane himself was much employed at the Royal Hospital, where he was Clerk of Works from 1807. He built the Infirmary (destroyed by bombing 1941), the offices, and other small works, including that miracle of abstract design, the entrance to the stableyard.

Among the younger architects of the war period one was outstandingly fortunate. He was Robert Smirke, a son of the R.A. painter of the same name. His career will be discussed more fully in later chapters, but he must be introduced here as one of the few young men whose prospects were not blanketed by the war. Although in 1803 he momentarily saw himself leaving architecture for soldiering, within a few years he was full of work. Sir George Beaumont recommended him to Lord Lonsdale, who not only commissioned him to rebuild Lowther Castle, but secured his appointment as architect to the Mint, where, in 1808, he was handling £80,000 worth of work. In the same year Covent Garden Theatre was burnt down and had to be rebuilt, war or no war; this prodigious windfall went to

Smirke, and his competent handling of it placed him right at the top of the profession, so that in 1815 he took his place with Nash and Soane, his seniors by nearly thirty years, at the Board of Works.

Drury Lane was another case of fire providing an unexpected war-time opportunity and this again fell to a young architect. Both theatres will be described at the appropriate place (Chapter 18).

The building of the Docks, a limited amount of speculative housing, a couple of church towers, and the erection of quite a number of private houses for the very rich complete the war-time building scene – the Docks belong to Chapter 19, the churches to Chapter 16, the speculations to Chapter 12. Among the houses, two were very special creations. The fabulously rich Thomas Hope designed for himself in 1800 a house in Duchess Street which was also an exquisite museum. It had a short life but inspired another museum-residence, that of Sir John Soane in Lincoln's Inn Fields. Begun in 1812 and conceived from the first both as residence and gallery it survives today as the architect's principal memorial and the repository of his life's work as designer, connoisseur, and man of letters.

The war period came effectively to an end in 1814 and a few years earlier the return to peace had appeared sufficiently imminent for a few post-war schemes to be amply considered and even put in hand. In the next chapters we shall return on our tracks to consider building adventures which originated before the war, which struggled through the difficult years with practical results of varying magnitude and finally blossomed after 1815 and in the great building period which coincided with the reigns of the last two Hanoverians.

CHAPTER 12

Great Estates: I

IN Chapter 7 we brought the story of London's westward expansion to the point where the Grosvenor and Cavendish-Harley estates, south and north of 'the Oxford Road', had become large urban units with tolerably well-built-up squares and streets. We observed, however, that the building up of these estates slackened considerably during the 1730s and was not resumed for about thirty years. A revival was foreshadowed during the fifties but did not really gather strength till after the Peace of Paris, in 1763. Then, when everything in the building world was on the up-turn, expansion started again.

Westward of Marylebone Lane lay the lands of the Portman family. Henry William Portman, Esq., of Orchard Portman and Bryanston, succeeding to the estate in 1761, caused a square and streets to be laid out forthwith. They were securely tied to the neighbouring lay-outs by the main streets being extensions from those existing to the south and east; the size and position of the square were determined by the crossings of these borrowed lines. Portman Square does not appear to have been conceived on grand lines architecturally: the Cavendish fiasco having, perhaps, sufficiently enforced the lesson that the square wholly dedicated to noblemen's palaces was, for London, an impracticable affair. The frontages were offered in the speculative market.[1] They were built up slowly, and it was not until 1768 that houses on the south side began to be occupied. Most, if not all these houses, as well as those on the east and west sides, were built by Abraham and Samuel Adams (no relation to the Adam brothers). The north side only got started about 1774 when the uniform block (Nos. 20 and 21), comprising Robert

1. Articles of agreement relating to a house in Portman Square, dated 1765, are mentioned in *The Locks of Norbury* by the Duchess of Sermoneta (1940).

Adam's 'Home House' and another, were begun. James Wyatt designed some houses on this north side.

It is remarkable how 1774 stands out as a key year in the history of London building. It was the year of the great Building Act; it also marks very definitely the start of a phase of rapid estate development – some of it by Adam, much of it in the Adam manner. The north side of Portman Square comes into this phase, and in 1776 the Duke of Manchester was building himself a house on the Portman land and forming a square before it to be called Manchester Square. 1774 saw the building of Stratford Place, Oxford Street, by the Hon. Edward Stratford on a triangle of land bought from the City. His surveyor, Richard Edwin, accurately imitated the Adam style and many of the houses have admirable interiors.

Another great scheme of around 1774 was Portland Place. This was not designed as a thoroughfare but as what one might call a 'close' of great houses, terminated by the fifty-year-old Foley House on the south and opening into the Marylebone fields on the north. In 1773 Robert Adam appears to have had some hope of making this a veritable street of palaces, but like every idea of the sort it failed, and rows of normal, if more than usually spacious, houses were built, James Adam being, for once, the avowed designer (Plate 16). The speculation appears to have been supervised by Adam on the instructions of the wildly eccentric old miser John Elwes who must have had a lease from the Duke of Portland. The width of the street is said to have been conditioned by the Duke's obligations to his tenant, Lord Foley, whose northward view from Foley House could not be interfered with. The width of Foley House, therefore, dictated the width of the street.[1] The Adams took a large number of building plots in Portland Place and the adjoining streets, and the interiors of some of the houses have characteristic ceilings and fireplaces. Chandos House, with its stone façade and beautiful porch, at the end of Chandos Street, is the best example.

A still greater beginning witnessed in these years was Bed-

1. C. H. Smith in *Builder*, 3 October 1863, p. 703.

ford Square, the first move in a great new offensive on the Bedford estate. Here, as on the Portman Estate, there had been talk of building soon after the Peace of 1763. In 1766 the old fourth Duke, a heavy-weight of Whig politics and a great frequenter of Bath, proposed the erection of a 'Bedford Square' planned on the model of the King's Circus in the spa city.[1] Nothing came of this and the Duke died in 1771. His heir was an infant, but the Dowager, an able, businesslike lady, was not one to let things slow down. And her executive was somebody as energetic – Robert Palmer, principal agent to the estate. Palmer was responsible for the conduct of this great speculation and appears to have invested some of his private fortune in mortgages to the builders, who were William Scott and Robert Crews. Building agreements were signed in 1776.

The sense of prosperity and optimism which grew to a peak in 1774, received a blow when the war with America began in 1775. Prices began to rise and the building world suffered. Palmer gambled boldly, however, and saw the thing through to his own very great ultimate advantage.

Bedford Square much resembles James Adam's work in Portland Place; but the handling is looser, and the critical eye[2] of a later period was able to detect the 'spirit of speculation' at work. No designer's name can be confidently given, though Thomas Leverton probably had a hand in it. He was a builder's son from Essex, where Palmer had property interests, and it may be that Palmer got him in to do the technical side of the business. He certainly designed the interiors of several houses and, probably, the whole of No. 1, which is a particularly fine house, not forming part of the general pattern of the square.[3]

A still greater beginning witnessed in these years was Bed-Square generally are in Coade Stone and of a type not necessarily

1. See a note by G. Scott-Thomson, on p. 76 of *The University Site, Bloomsbury* by E. Jeffries Davis (*London Topographical Society's Record*, vol. 69); *A further appeal to the Governors of the Foundling Hospital* (1788), p. 17; *Gents. Mag.*, vol. 57, p. 94.

2. Sir John Soane's *Lectures*, ed. Bolton, p.179.

3. For plans and interior photographs of Bedford Square houses see *Survey of London*, vol. 5: St Giles-in-the-Fields, part ii (1914).

designed for the square;[1] they occur in other parts of London –
notably No. 39 Conduit Street, No. 7 Devonshire Street, and
many houses in Baker Street and Harley Street. The capitals and
mouldings are also probably stock patterns. Thus the façades

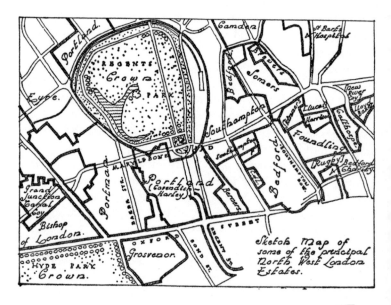

of the square may be said to have been 'collated' as well as
designed – hence the absence of any specific designer's
name.

Bedford Square is a good example of the urbanism of its time
and survives, fortunately, intact except that the upper part of
Nos. 6 and 6a (once the Lord Chancellor's official residence)
has been raised and many windows lack their original bars.
These are trifling defects in a composition whose homogeneity
alone makes it one of the most valuable relics of Georgian
London.

After Bedford Square and the beginnings of the adjoining
streets, the Bedford salient slackened and the initiative passed to

1. A doorway of this type is engraved in the Coade catalogue in the
British Museum. See Plate 17.

the Governors of the Foundling Hospital[1], which, like so many institutions of the 1740–60 period, stood out in the fields. Unlike other hospitals, however, the Foundling possessed the freehold of much of the land surrounding it and it was seen that, as London expanded northwards, this could be made a considerable source of wealth. When the Governors talked of building in 1788 there was an immediate outcry[2] against the invasion of more open country; it was also considered that the children's health might suffer. Two years later, however, the Hospital architect was instructed to make a report. This architect was Samuel Pepys Cockerell, a pupil of Sir Robert Taylor and a man who, like Taylor, combined artistic ability and scholarship with a real grasp of practical affairs and an unimpeachable professional character.

In his Report[3] to the Governors of the Foundling, Cockerell recommended the formation of the open spaces which we now know as Mecklenburgh and Brunswick Squares. In this he had the support of Thomas Bernard, one of the Governors, whose name became much associated with public improvements in the Regency. The objects of the squares were, first, to retain for the hospital 'the advantages of its present open situation' and, second, to provide an architectural setting so 'as rather to raise than depress the Character of this Hospital itself as an Object of National Munificence'.

The Report sets out that cardinal principle of Georgian town-planning, the creation of urban units containing accommodation *for all classes*. Cockerell proposes:

That there shall be such principal features of attraction in the Plan as shall not be too great for a due proportion to the whole but yet sufficient to draw Adventurers to the subordinate parts and that these subordinate parts be so calculated as to comprise all Classes of Building from the first Class down to Houses of Twenty-five

1. The ensuing particulars of the Foundling Estate are derived from documents in the Hospital archives which I was privileged to inspect in 1938.
2. *An appeal to the Governors of the Foundling Hospital., etc.* in the British Museum.
3. Printed in 1790; there is a copy in the British Museum.

pound pr. annum without the lower Classes interfering with and diminishing the Character of those above them, and particularly that the Stile of the Buildings at the several Boundaries, be (in order to ensure success to the intermediate parts) as respectable as possible consistent with their situations and with prudence in the Adventurers.

The 'principal features of attraction' were, of course, to be the squares, with their planted gardens – just as Bloomsbury and Cavendish Squares had been the attracting features of estates developed long before. To this principle Cockerell added the rather obvious one that the edges of the plan should be wedded to the built up areas adjoining. Lastly, he suggested that the plan should be capable of gradual execution so 'that each part may be complete in itself and not depend for its success, and a return of profit to the undertakers upon the execution of the others'. The condition was fulfilled by the provision of two squares with subsidiary streets around each.

Cockerell envisaged a rather more imposing architectural scheme than was to prove practicable in the years which followed – years in which, as we have seen, the first phase of the struggle with revolutionary France overshadowed the economic life of the capital. He did, however, rigorously control the elevations of each speculator's houses, making them submit sketches which were subject to alteration in the interests of a respectable and uniform standard of design.

Cockerell was also responsible for watching the quality of the materials, and in the difficult circumstances produced by a rapid rise in prices it was a tricky business. He used to visit the sites every Tuesday and this proved not quite enough. There was a row, and Cockerell was dismissed – not, it seems without some heart-burning among the Governors.[1] An unsatisfactory interlude with two other surveyors followed, the breach was patched up, and Cockerell's influence returned with the appointment in 1807–8 of his clever pupil Joseph Kay, with Cockerell as honorary consultant in the background. It was Kay who laid out the Mecklenburgh Square gardens and who provided the pretty

1. The story is told in a highly libellous, unpublished pamphlet by J. Spiller in the Soane Museum.

stucco architecture of the east side (Plate 31b). The Governors liked his work so much that they paid him eight times the modest sum he asked for it.

The builders on this estate were of many types, ranging from the small bricklayer or carpenter who applied, cap in hand, for a few plots at a ground rent of five shillings a foot, in a back street, to big men prepared to tackle one or more sides of a square and pay as much as fifteen shillings or a pound. The limitations of the speculative builder as regards quality of work are explained in a Report supplied to the Governors after the development had been proceeding for eight years, by George Dance and John Lewis, who were called in to give an independent opinion on the work in progress:

The State and general conduct of the Buildings are much upon a par with the state and general conduct of Buildings erected by speculators in various parts of the metropolis and its vicinity. Those who build for their own occupation may reasonably expect such Buildings as we fear is not practicable to obtain from speculative Builders for however prudent or desirable it may be to restrain and regulate the conduct of the work by Agreements founded on the most minute description of the dimensions and quality of every part of the Building yet experience has shewn that such restrictions would materially impede the letting of the ground.

It was at first the policy of the Governors not to allow any one speculator to undertake more than a moderate proportion of the ground; but in spite of this, the development of the Foundling estate saw the rise of a builder who soon towered above all his fellows in the building world and became the monopolist of a great part of Bloomsbury. His name was James Burton.

James Burton, the most important London builder since Nicholas Barbon, was a Scotsman, christened Haliburton. When he made his first proposition to build on the Foundling estate he was twenty-eight or twenty-nine and practising as architect and builder in Southwark, where he had designed and built the Leverian Museum in Blackfriars Road (later the Surrey Institution, now demolished).[1] In 1792 he asked the Foundling Governors for an option on the whole of Brunswick Square, but

1. *A.P.S., Dict.*, s.v. Parkinson, J.

they, not knowing the capacity of the man they were dealing with, cautiously refused, allotting him only the south side and part of Guildford Street. Soon, however, Burton was adding site to site until most of the western part of the property was in his hands. By 1802, he had built nearly 600 houses on the estate.[1]

That, however, was only the beginning of Burton's London adventures. From the Foundling Estate he passed to the Bedford, from the Bedford to the Skinners', from the Skinners' to the Lucas, from the Lucas to the Crown (in Regent's Park), and beyond to the Eyre. The gross value of the houses he built was reliably computed to be getting on for £2,000,000. It was he, as we shall see in the next chapter, who saved Regent Street from financial collapse, in return for which his friend John Nash opened the gates of professional success to his son Decimus, the architect, who does not deserve to be so *very* much more famous than his extraordinary father.

Burton's first work on the Bedford Estate was a continuation of the seventeenth century Lord Southampton's 'little town' in and around Bloomsbury Square. The Duke of Bedford obtained two Acts of Parliament in 1800 for developing his estate and in the same year Burton began pulling down Bedford (originally Southampton) House and building, at the back of it, two rows of houses which were to form the south side of Russell Square. A view of these houses appeared in the Royal Academy exhibition of the same year over Burton's name – it was his first and last exhibit.

As soon as Bedford House was razed, Burton built the houses (Nos. 18–27) which today form the north side of Bloomsbury Square. That done, he deserted London for a few years to start a big housing estate at Tunbridge Wells, but returned to Bloomsbury in 1807 to build over the whole of a piece of land leased from the Skinners' Company and adjoining both the Foundling and the Bedford Estates. Here he built Burton Street

1. Particulars of Burton and his work are derived from R. Dobie, *History of the United Parishes of St Giles-in-the-Fields and St George, Bloomsbury* (1829), p. 148. *Gents. Mag.*, 1837, vol. 1, p. 174. *D.N.B.*, s.v. Haliburton, James (J. B.'s son).

and Burton (now Cartwright) Crescent, together with a villa for himself, in its own grounds, on the site of the present British Medical Association headquarters. This he probably occupied until he moved to the Holme, in Regent's Park, designed for him by his son.

The plan of the Russell Square area, of which an engraving was issued, for the benefit of potential speculators, in 1800 may be assumed to be the work of James Gubbins, the Duke of Bedford's surveyor; but the house façades were probably initiated by Burton. In Russell Square itself (1800–14), he treated the western block with thin Ionic pilasters and pediment, echoing Bedford Square, but a good deal more perfunctory in execution. In Tavistock Square, of which he built only the east side (about 1803; demolished 1938), Ionic pilasters appeared again, surmounted this time by a curious arrangement of terms and sarcophagi. The Ionic theme was introduced in the same form, about this time, by the designer of Euston Square. But Burton was no great architect. His Russell Institution, a kind of social centre, in Coram Street, combined Greek Doric columns and Roman arches in a peculiarly graceless fashion and was justifiably sat on by the critics.

The details of Burton's houses cannot, of course, be assigned to any particular designer, least of all to Burton himself. Most of his sites he re-leased to smaller builders who, no doubt, worked in groups in the manner I have described in an earlier chapter. Most of the joinery and iron-work was, to all intents and purposes, mass-produced and an individual Bloomsbury house would be a matter of assembly rather than design.[1] In planning, the only curiosity I have ever discovered in Bloomsbury was in the demolished houses on the east side of Tavistock Square, where, for some odd reason, the staircases were made to rise towards, instead of away from, the front door, so that one of the first-floor front windows in each house became a landing window and the largest and best first-floor room was at the back – towards the garden instead of the street.

1. The normal extent of an architect's control over the details of London houses remained slight till well into the nineteenth century. See the example in T. L. Donaldson, *Specifications* (1859), p. 670.

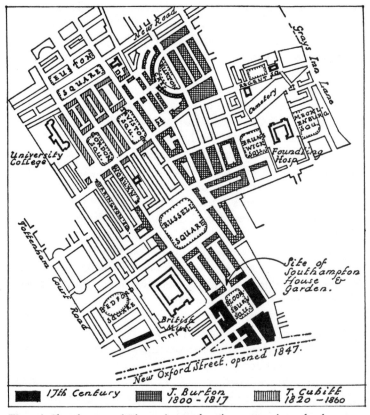

Fig. 23. Sketch-map of Bloomsbury, showing approximately the areas developed by Burton and Cubitt.

Burton was not the only builder to take sites in and around Russell Square but he was certainly the most ambitious and he may be said to have dominated Bloomsbury till 1817. The fortune he made there he appears to have lost in creating St Leonards-on-Sea, whose generous parade of stucco architecture owes its origin to him. He was a man of considerable vision, and two existing portraits of him suggest a personality not without charm and wit. In 1804, when invasion was expected, we find him figuring as Colonel Burton, raising a regiment of building operatives, 1,000 strong, officered by architects and proudly named the 'Loyal British Artificers'.[1] He died at St Leonards in 1837.

On Burton's departure, there was a pause in the development of the Bedford lands. As things stood in 1817, open fields still lay between Russell Square and the New Road; but north of this line, on the adjoining Southampton Estate, half of Euston Square had been built, obviously with the intention of eventually joining hands with the northward-moving Bedford layout.

The Southampton Estate was, at that time, of very great extent. It belonged to the Fitzroy family and had nothing to do with the earlier Southampton dynasty whose lands had all long since passed to the Bedfords. In 1790, Fitzroy Square had been laid out, and two sides – south and east – built behind decorative elevations supplied by the Adams (Plate 31a). This square, whose other two sides were not completed till about 1828, was built in anticipation of the growth of the town northwards from Oxford Street. Acting on the by then familiar principle, Colonel Fitzroy leased land for a market, eastwards of the square (off Whitfield Street; the Fitzroy Baths occupied the site till their demolition in 1940), and a chapel-of-ease, to the north. Originally intended, perhaps, to be in the square, it was eventually built – a wide brick box with few ornaments and a blunt bellcote – in Grafton Street. It became a parish hall and was destroyed in the blitz.

Euston Square (called so from the Fitzroys' seat in Suffolk) appears, from the leases,[2] to have been in progress in 1811. The main terraces, east and west of Euston Grove, were built by two small tradesmen, one of whom had already been speculating in a small way on the Bedford Estate. Who provided the elevations it seems now impossible to determine; but they were remarkable. The Ionic theme suggests a conscious allegiance to Burton's Russell Square and Tavistock Square (east side), but the arrangement of the pilasters, in conjunction with segmental

1. G. L. Taylor, *Autobiography of an Octogenarian Architect*, 1870.
2. In the possession of British Railways. The freehold was sold in 1879 but most of the Southampton estate appears to have been dispersed before that time.

arches in the attic storey, was original, while the joinery – especially the verandas at first-floor level – was fanciful and lovely. To the west of this terrace stood the plain stucco houses of Euston Crescent.

It is now time to go west again, where the Portman Estate seems to have been moving gradually throughout most of the war period. A circus or double crescent was proposed, on the axis of Great Cumberland Place, but only the west segment was completed (in 1789) and the opposite side was built straight. The houses on the straight side have thin Ionic pilasters and the details suggest that William Porden, who took a lease of No. 38, may have been responsible for the design. The lamp-irons here are some of the best in London.

Between 1810 and 1815 the axis of Great Cumberland Place was produced northwards to form the centre-line of an oblong inappropriately christened Bryanston Square. This and the even narrower Montagu Square to the east of it were leased to David Porter, who is reputed to have been 'chimney-sweeper to the village' of Marylebone.[1] Montagu Square is a plain, uniform regiment of brown brick houses, but Bryanston Square is more ambitious, with three-quarter Ionic columns in stucco adorning the centre and ends of each side. The architect for the lay-out and façades (1811) was Joseph Parkinson, a young man who had been secretary to the Emigrant Office for French refugees during the earlier part of the war and an officer in Burton's 'Loyal Artificers'. Bryanston Square was later continued northwards by Wyndham Place, at the north end of which the Church Commissioners acquired a site for St Mary's church whose portico and steeple would close the long vista from Cumberland Gate most effectively, were it not for the excessive luxuriance of the trees.

Part of the Portman Estate lies to the north of the Marylebone Road; all this northern appendage was built up in the plainest possible style, round Dorset Square, after Waterloo. Northwards lies the Eyre Estate. This again, was built up at a late period,

---

1. Clinch, J., *Marylebone and St Pancras*, p. 65. 'David Porter, Esq.', died in Marylebone in 1819. (*Gents. Mag.*, vol. 1, p. 587, 1819).

but its antecedent history is of extraordinary interest and importance.

There are copies in existence[1] of an engraved map of the Eyre
Estate showing a complete scheme of development, dated 1794.
It bears the names of Spurrier and Phipps, whom the *London
Directory* identifies as auctioneers, of Copthall Court, City. The
plan includes the usual elements: square, circus, crescent,
streets, market, church. But the remarkable thing about it is that
the whole development consists of *pairs of semi-detached houses*.
So far as I know, this is the first recorded scheme of the kind –
a kind which was to become almost universal for surburban
development in the later nineteenth century and which remains
almost universal today.

Whose can have been the initiative in this revolutionary
departure? The answer might seem, at first sight, to be provided
by entries in the Royal Academy catalogues of 1802 and 1803.
They are under the name of John Shaw, an architect we shall
meet again as the author of St Dunstan's-in-the-West and parts
of Christ's Hospital. The fullest entry is that of 1803, which
reads as follows:

An elevated view of the British Circus, proposed to be built by subscription between the Paddington-road and Hampstead, on the
freehold estate of H. S. Eyre, Esq., the inner circle consists of 36
detached houses, with appropriate offices; the outer circle of 66
houses. There will be about one acre and a quarter of land to each
house, besides the enjoyment of the central pleasure-ground which
contains 42 acres. The road between the two circles is about one mile
in circumference.

This obviously relates to a revised version of the large circus
(whose circumference is exactly a mile) in the Spurrier and
Phipps plan. But it is hardly possible to assign the *plan* to Shaw,
because at the date of its publication he was only eighteen. The
credit must remain, for the present, with an unknown innovator.
Shaw may have been employed merely to interpret the plan in
an architectural way so as to secure the valuable publicity of a
showing on the walls of Somerset House.

Neither the British Circus nor any part of the plan was ever

1. In R.I.B.A. and Soane Museum.

carried out. Probably the war put an end to the adventure. Nash borrowed the idea of the double circus for his Regent's Park proposal of 1812, though it is only fair to say that this idea, like so many others, goes back to John Gwynn. When the Eyre Estate did come to be developed, a quite different lay-out was adopted, though the name of Circus Road and the fact that part of it is curved may conceivably represent a vestige of the original plan, begun and almost immediately abandoned.

The Eyre Estate was, however, built up with detached and

Fig. 24. Typical St John's Wood villas (Nos. 107 and 109 Clifton Hill) of the 1820–30 period.

semi-detached houses and not in closed-up rows, so that the most striking characteristic of the plan of 1794 was adopted. A large number of different builders took sites.[1] James Burton was one of them : builders named Chapple, and May & Morritt were others. Today, many of these houses still exist, marking distinctly the character of St John's Wood. It was the first part of London, and indeed of any other town, to abandon the terrace house for the semi-detached villa – a revolution of striking significance and far-reaching effect.

Two more important estates remain to be described, but their character was so profoundly affected by the boldest estate development of all – that of the Crown, under John Nash – that at this point we must break off to devote a whole chapter to that great adventure and its author.

1. There is a plan of part of the estate in the British Museum (Crace Maps).

176

CHAPTER 13

The Plans and Elevations of John Nash

ONCE, and only once, has a great plan for London, affecting the development of the capital as a whole, been projected and carried to completion. This was the plan which constituted the 'metropolitan improvements' of the Regency, the plan which embraced the Regent's Park layout in the north, St James's Park in the south, the Regent Street artery connecting the two, the formation of Trafalgar Square and the reconstruction of the West End of the Strand, and the Suffolk Street area; as well as the cutting of the Regent's Canal, with its branch and basin to serve Regent's Park. The whole of this immense plan, which gave a 'spine' to London's inchoate West End and had a far-reaching effect on subsequent northward and southward expansion, was carried out under the presiding genius of John Nash.[1]

It was Nash's achievement to seize and combine a number of opportunities which presented themselves with felicitous promptitude at the beginning of the Regency. The main opportunity, which brought all the others within reach, was the reversion to the Crown of Marylebone Park in 1811. This event had been the subject of discussion and preparation for some years. As early as 1793 John Fordyce, an intelligent border Scot, had been appointed to the then newly-created office of Surveyor-General of His Majesty's Land Revenues. He had drawn up a plan of the whole property and produced four reports, in the last of which (1809) he set out a liberal and enticing programme for the development of the Park, relating the project to the need for a new street extending from the Park to Carlton House. This new street was a necessary corollary; for if the nobility and professional classes were to be expected to live north of the

1. For the whole of this chapter see the writer's *John Nash: Architect to King George IV*, 1935, 2nd ed., 1949.

New Road (hitherto the uttermost northward boundary of fashion), they would have to be provided with adequate access to Westminster, where Parliament, the Law Courts, and the Public Offices in Whitehall employed many of their daylight hours.

John Fordyce's programme of 1809 was set before two pairs of official architects. Messrs Leverton and Chawner, of the Land Revenue Office, were one pair; Messrs Nash and Morgan, of the Woods and Forests Department, were the other. Leverton and Chawner sent in a rather dull-witted scheme, merely extending the Bloomsbury pattern of streets and squares over most of the Park. Nash and Morgan presented something new – a daring and highly picturesque conception of a garden city for an aristo-cracy, supported by charming panoramas showing a composition of alluring groves and elegant architecture of a somewhat Parisian character. The Nash–Morgan plan was immediately accepted by the Treasury. But first, a word about Nash.

The true story of Nash's success is obscure, but there was cer-tainly a great deal more behind it than meets the eye in the official documents. This man Nash was no ordinary Civil Servant, as everybody well knew. Already fifty-seven, he had an odd career behind him. He was born, probably in London, in 1752, and was in service with Sir Robert Taylor. A legacy from a merchant uncle enabled him to set up as a speculating builder, but he became bankrupt and retired to Wales. Here he acquired a connexion as a country-house architect and mixed in county society. He met Humphrey Repton, the rising landscape gardener, formed a partnership with him, and was influenced by him, abruptly returning to London about 1795. It was very likely through Repton that Nash met the Prince of Wales, for whom he was designing as early as 1798, soon after which year he and Repton quarrelled and separated. Also in 1798 Nash married.

Nash's marriage, at the age of forty-six, to an ambitious young woman who is supposed to have engaged in dangerous liaisons at Carlton House, is surrounded by mystery. There is a tradition that Nash was in a certain respect unfitted for marriage and was merely the official husband of this girl, who subsequently appeared before the world with a considerable family of children incubated in a remote hinterland of the Isle of Wight, bearing the name of Pennethorne and of whom she was supposed to be a remote relation acting *in loco parentis*. The whole story bristles with scandal, and there is evidence that, for some reason or other, Nash and his wife participated in an elaborate social fake, presumably in collusion with the Prince; there is not enough evidence, on the other hand, to assert definitely either that Mrs Nash was the Prince's mistress or that the Pennethornes were her children by the Prince.

Anyway, from the year of his marriage, Nash suddenly became a man of considerable wealth and influence with a princely house in London and an estate in the Isle of Wight. He became one of the Carlton House set and contemplated a political career as one of the Prince's parliamentary pawns. However, he was not, as it turned out, to be diverted from architecture and in 1806 this opulent lackey, this big-wig of back-stair intrigue accepted, together with his draughtsman Morgan, the post of Architect to the Woods and Forests, at the ludicrous joint salary of £200 a year. Morgan, of course, was wholly unimportant, a man of straw introduced to satisfy official insistence on a partnership.

It was all very well arranged. One suspects that Nash had a hand in Fordyce's last report and that the way was paved, from the beginning, for the acceptance of his great design in preference to Leverton and Chawner's who were probably used merely as a check.

It was singularly fortunate that the elevation of the Prince of Wales to the Regency should chime in exactly with the reversion of Marylebone Park. It was fortunate too that these events should occur at a marked turn in the economic tide. There was a severe trade crisis in 1810, when house-property stood out as almost the only form of capital investment which continued to rise in value,[1] the chief reason being the virtual cessation of speculative building owing to the difficulty of importing timber in war-time. In the summer of 1811, however, there was a revival of credit and improved prospects all round

1. Tooke, T., *History of Prices*, 1838–57, vol. 1, p. 312.

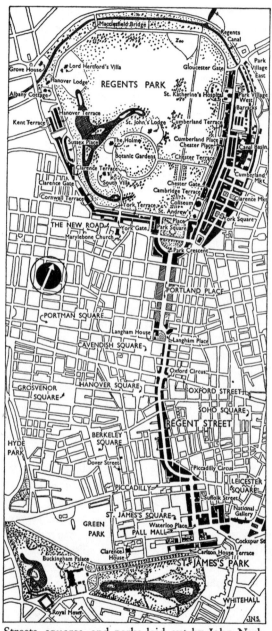

Fig. 25. Streets, squares, and parks laid out by John Nash, 1811–35.

and naturally the building trade led the way in the revival, a boom period setting in which lasted through the final war years and well into the post-Waterloo peace.

From 1811, the Prince and Nash were clearly the moving powers in the planning scheme. The Prince talked enthusiastically about eclipsing Napoleon's Paris, while Nash designed a *guinguette,* or Royal pleasaunce, for Regent's Park and planned Regent Street as a 'Royal mile' from Carlton House to the *guinguette*; he also consulted with the promoters of a canal scheme and introduced a stretch of it picturesquely into the Park.

The design for the Park published in 1812 is elaborate and dramatic. Villas are dotted everywhere in woody grooves. The *guinguette* has a strip of formal water in front of it, while the arms of a serpentine lake embrace the centre of the area where, on rising ground, is a great double circus with a 'National Valhalla' in the middle of it. Round the margins are terraces and in the south-east corner is the marketing and working-class quarter. Where the southward road crosses the New Road is another vast circus, with a church in the middle.

This plan was approved by the Treasury and planting was begun at once; the Canal Company obtained an Act and excavation was started; and half the Circus on the New Road was leased. However, as time went on many modifications had to be made. Nash was instructed by the Treasury to thin out the villas, an operation which he regretted, since it spoiled the decided 'garden city' character of his design. The great double circus, with its Valhalla, was abandoned and so ultimately was the *guinguette,* while the canal was made to run round the Park, not through it. The lessee of the Circus became bankrupt and the northern half of it was eliminated. Indeed, all that was to remain of the design were the plantations and water, eight villas, half a circus (now Park Crescent), and the ring of terraces; and these latter did not begin to materialize until Cornwall Terrace was begun in 1820.

So the Regent's Park of today is merely a shadow of what Nash envisaged in 1812. As a piece of planting it is bald and uninteresting, lacking as it does the rich gardens and groves of the forty or fifty intended villas. Its architectural beauties are confined to the margins with their noble approaches and the belt of terraces, interrupted across the north, so that the view of Hampstead and Highgate should be preserved.

The Regent's Park terraces are greatly loved today – more so than ever they were when they were new, when their short-comings in detail and finish grated on the susceptibilities of critics bred in an exacting school. The truth is that these build-ings, careless and clumsy though they are in many ways, have an extravagant scenic character which, perceived through nos-talgic mists of time, makes them irresistible. They are dream palaces, full of grandiose, romantic ideas such as an architect might scribble in a holiday sketch-book. Seen at a distance, framed in green tracery, perhaps in the kind light of late autumn, they suggest architectural glories which make Green-wich tame and Hampton Court provincial. Carved pediments, rich in allegory, top the trees; massive pavilions, standing for-ward like the *corps de garde* of Baroque chateaux, are linked to the main structures by triumphal arches or columnar screens; each terrace stretches its length in all the pride of unconfined symmetry. It is magnificent. And behind it all – behind it are rows and rows of identical houses, identical in their narrow-ness, their thin pretentiousness, their poverty of design. Where the eye apprehends a mansion of great distinction, supported by lesser mansions and service quarters, the mind must inter-pret it as a block of thin houses, with other blocks of thin houses carrying less ornament or none at all. The sham is flag-rant and absurd. The terraces are architectural jokes; and though Nash was serious enough in his intention, the effect is an odd combination of fantasy and bathos which only the re-trospect of a century can forgive.

Nash was over seventy when he designed most of the ter-races. He made tiny diagrammatic sketches which he handed to his draughtsmen for working out. Scale drawings, with mould-ings to half full size, were given to the speculating builder, who carried them out without very exacting supervision; and Nash never seems to have worried if the proportions came out a bit different from what he expected. They often did.

The earliest architectural feature of Regent's Park is the very lovely, unpretentious, neatly detailed Park Crescent (1812, the southern half of the projected circus; Plate 32b). It opens out at either end to the New Road (Marylebone Road of today) and is continued northwards by Park Square (1823–5). The design of the square is less happy, the façades being crowded and coarse in design, but the arrangement as a whole, considered as a formal approach from a thoroughfare to a landscaped park, is admirable, and the simple appropriateness of Park Crescent with its Ionic colonnades is beyond criticism.[1]

Along the south of the Park run the two blocks of York Terrace (1822 onwards), and between them is another masterpiece of town planning, York Gate (Plate 32a), devised to enclose the new Marylebone Church in a vista. Here again is a really fine piece of architectural scenery, as appropriate and effective as Park Crescent.

York Terrace and the two terraces immediately to the west, Cornwall and Clarence, were built by James Burton, of Bloomsbury fame (see Chapter 12) and the designs for the last two are by his young son, Decimus, working of course, under the general direction of Nash.[2] Both are wholly inadequate realizations of extremely ambitious architectural conceptions, but both, at a distance, do realize some of the effect which they set out to achieve. Next door, westwards, Sussex Place (1822) with its pointed roofs and curved wings is one of Nash's major outrages on the taste of his time. Regarded indulgently as a large-scale joke (the houses are the biggest in the Park), it becomes more acceptable as the years pass. It was designed, one imagines, with even greater celerity than the other terraces. Next to it is Hanover Terrace (1822–3) where Nash perversely returns to coarse copy-book Roman and introduces a pleasant arcaded feature along the ground floor. Kent Terrace, behind Hanover,

1. In recent years the whole of Park Crescent has been rebuilt, the new façades, however, being scrupulous copies of the old.

2. Decimus stated before the Select Committee on the Office of Works, etc., 1828, that he 'merely gave the designs'.

turns from Roman to Greek and pays doubtful compliments to Sir John Soane.

For sheer architectural frolic, the terraces along the east side of the Park are the most striking. Cumberland Terrace (1827) with its seven porticos, its courtyards and arches, is the crowning glory, the back-cloth as it were to Act III, and easily the most breath-taking architectural panorama in London. With its sketchy detail, its stylistic solecisms, and its pretty-pretty sculpture by Bubb, it is a marvellous, adorable extravagance. Chester Terrace (1825) with two gimcrack 'triumphal' arches superscribed with the name of the terrace, is more moderate in its pretensions. Gloucester Gate (1827) and Cambridge Terrace (1825) are almost conventional by comparison.

Regent's Park is full of amusing and effective detail. Nash's lodges at Hanover and Gloucester Gates and Park Crescent, the cast-iron railings and street lamps where they survive, James Morgan's bridge over the canal; all these are lively and inventive products of their period. And there still survive most of the eight villas, including the Holme, built for himself by James Burton and designed by Decimus, and several built by other architects.

Eastwards of the Park is the area of the Crown's Marylebone Estate reserved by Nash for three purposes; first, for a working-class quarter with markets and shops; second, for a large barracks; and third (this was an afterthought) for a miniature 'garden suburb'. The area is divided from the Park by Albany Street. The working-class district, now entirely replanned and rebuilt, comprised Cumberland Market, Clarence Market (later Gardens), York Square (later Munster Square), and the streets adjoining them. Directly north of Cumberland Market was the canal basin, served by a branch (now filled up) from the Regent's Canal and designed to facilitate the daily supply of fresh vegetables from the Middlesex market gardens to the 'shopping centre' of Regent's Park. Since 1945 all this has vanished. The squares were ordinary enough as architecture but one remembers them for their singular combination of largeness of lay-out and smallness of scale. Munster Square, in particular consists of mere stucco cottages, yet its size and regularity made it strikingly beautiful.[1]

The barracks lie to the north, between Albany Street and the branch canal, and have been rebuilt. Northward again are the Park Villages, East and West. These were among Nash's very last works and are full of interest. The houses are very small and often charmingly planned. Some are 'Italian', some 'Gothic', some affect a kind of Châlet style. Building this essay in the Picturesque compensated him for having to leave out the clusters of villas he planned for the Park itself. Trees, water, fanciful gables and balconies – all the properties of the romantic village scene as illustrated in the almanacs and keepsakes are here (except, now, the water). During the last years of Nash's life and after his death the villages were completed by his pupil and succssor James Pennethorne. Today, Park Village West survives and half of Park Village East, the other half having been erased by the railway. They are, in a sense, ancestors of all picturesque suburbia. Up to the war, housing estates were still being laid out very much on these lines with 'no two houses alike'. It would be difficult to find a prototype for these much earlier than Nash's Park Villages.

With the development of Regent's Park proceeded the cutting of Regent Street. This great thoroughfare is unique in the history of town-planning. Its amazingly successful blend of formality and picturesque opportunism could have happened nowhere and at no time but in England of the period of the Picturesque. It might be said of Regent Street, as Rasmussen[2] has said of the Adelphi, that it was 'not only a dream of antique architecture' but 'just as much a finance-fantasia over risk and profit'; the financier was an artist and the artist a financier. To

1. I recall a comment made to me in 1946 by a Polish officer who had lived near by and watched the bombing and dereliction of the square. 'It gives the peculiar feeling,' he wrote, 'of an immense room, with the skies as the roof: the same feeling you have in evenings on the Piazza San Marco in Venice: a ballroom.'
2. *London, the Unique City*, 1937. Published in Penguin Books 1960.

some extent it was a masterly, calculated solution; but also to some extent it was a no less masterly improvisation.

In the plan published with the Regent's Park report of 1812 Nash determined the fundament of his scheme. He placed the line of the proposed street exactly where the close, untidy development of Soho stopped and the open texture of the West End estates began. This was the only logical and 'biologically' correct line, for two reasons. It involved the acquisition only of an inexpensive margin of Soho property; but at the same time it enabled one side of the new thoroughfare to open into all the good east-west streets issuing from in and around the great squares. It was obviously the only right answer, but it took Nash to find it. Other planners had proposed to plough streets through Soho, leaving an obstinate strip of poor property between the new street and the West End; such plans would infallibly have failed commercially and only half resolved London's traffic problem. Nash's plan took advantage of the cheapness of the Soho area but 'hugged' (his own metaphor) the coast of the West End.

From the first, there was no attempt to make Regent Street straight. At the north end it took its direction from Portland Place; Oxford Circus was introduced as a 'pivot' on which the main part of the street turned slightly to the east; while at Piccadilly another change of direction was introduced so as to bring the southernmost section of the street exactly normal to the façade of Carlton House. But if the street was not to be straight, it certainly was to be formal. The early plan suggests that Nash was thinking of something as strictly disciplined as the Rue de Rivoli, as chaste as Park Crescent. However, he was to change his mind.

Certain modifications were made in the plan before the Bill went before Parliament, the most substantial being the introduction of the quarter-circle or Quadrant as a device of swinging the street from one axis to another.

The New Street Act was passed in 1813. Finance was obtained from an Insurance Company and later, the Bank of England; a sewer was constructed, demolition and the letting of sites begun. There was a very awkward phase when nobody would come in on the project and everybody abused it, but largely thanks to James Burton's unquenchable initiative and Nash's own colossal resourcefulness and courage Regent Street was completed.

It was during the early stages of the street's construction that improvisation developed. To get the street built Nash had to find moneyed men who would take sites, and, of course, the people willing to do this did not all want to do it for the same reason. For instance, in the lower part of the street we find a Mr Warren taking a site for a hotel, a Mr Blicke anxious to erect a large private house, Messrs Hopkinson a site for a Bank, the Church Commissioners a site for one of their new churches, and Mr James Burton a block of sites as a speculation in chambers and shops. Now, if Nash had tried to marshal all these excellent people behind one continuous façade it is not hard to imagine that most of them would have lost interest. Mr Warren wanted a distinctive façade for his hotel, the church had to have a portico and steeple. Mr Blicke wanted a drive-in for his carriage, and so on. So Nash had to extemporize and contrive an architectural grouping which had a sort of picturesque unity without being strictly balanced. In this he succeeded remarkably well, not only here but throughout the street. Starting in Waterloo Place with blocks of houses on a strictly symmetrical plan, he abandoned symmetry at the opening of Regent Street and improvized till he reached Piccadilly Circus. Meanwhile, the upper part of the street was proceeding in the same way, big speculative blocks of twenty or thirty sites being leased wherever possible and the interstices filled in with individual ventures – a concert hall, two churches, a public house, and so on. By very adroit adjustment and persuasion behind the scenes Nash managed not merely to preserve the decencies of street architecture but to produce an effective and, in parts, really admirable panorama.

But there was one part of the street where improvisation would not work – the Quadrant. A curved structure like that cannot, for aesthetic reasons, be designed with the episodic informality of a long straight stretch; nor, for technical reasons, can a uniform curved structure be built in arbitrary sections, by different builders. The whole of the Quadrant had to be undertaken by one man. The bold spendthrift Burton, who had already overspent himself to save other parts of the street, would not tackle it. So Nash did. He took the whole of the Quadrant in his own name, collected a group of building tradesmen who were willing to invest in the speculation in lieu of cash payment, and got the thing done. It was a masterly undertaking, as masterly as the proud unbroken sweep of stucco which seemed to lead out of Piccadilly to nowhere but which, with the true whimsicality of the Picturesque, landed the traveller in the bright vista of Regent Street itself with its gay assortment of architectural ideas, like a naughty version of Oxford's venerable High Street.

The irregularity of Regent Street gave Nash opportunities which he seized unfailingly. On the north of Piccadilly Circus he managed to let a site to an Insurance Company promoter who was keen on architecture to the extent of paying for a full-size replica of Inigo Jones's river façade to old Somerset House – hence the old County Fire Office (Plate 33). At Langham Place, where the opening to Portland Place fell too far west to line up with Upper Regent Street, he let a site to the Church Commissioners and built them a church (All Souls) whose nave swings erratically to the north-east, but whose circular vestibule, crowned by a quaint colonnaded spike, makes a lovely terminal feature to the northward stretch of Regent Street.[1] Again, there is the case of the Haymarket Theatre, whose Corinthian portico, thanks to Nash's succcessful wangling, still closes the cross-vista at the end of Charles II Street.

The bulk of Regent Street was built up between 1817 and 1823; the formal Waterloo Place, parading its Ionic colonnades in front of Carlton House, was rather earlier. It is characteristic of the whole story of Regent Street that Carlton House, which had virtually provided the point of departure for the whole scheme, was itself to be swept away as the scheme developed into its last stages. It happened like this. In 1821, Nash and the King managed to trick Parliament into providing funds for

1. Or did till 1960, when a yellow brick block of offices erected by the B.B.C. behind the church finally obliterated its effect.

the conversion of old Buckingham House into Buckingham Palace; their excuse being that Carlton House, on which thousands had been lavished in the previous ten years, was shabby, inconvenient, and unsafe. Anyway, the King abandoned it, and to offset the vast expenditure on the Palace it was determined to pull Carlton House down and to develop the site of house and garden as a building scheme. This led directly to the idea of making St James's Park a southern counterpart of Regent's Park, with houses along the north and south and the Palace on the west. The idea matured. St James's Park was planted on Picturesque principles and its straight canal made into a curly lake. To the north, the vast blocks of Carlton House Terrace and Carlton Gardens reared themselves on the site and grounds of Carlton House; and to the south, after a long interval, appeared – not houses, but the Wellington Barracks.

The two Corinthian ranges of Carlton House Terrace are evidently inspired by Gabriel's buildings in the Place de la Concorde. The general conception of these two great blocks, supported by a terrace formed by the projection of the service quarters towards the park, is exceedingly grand. In detail, of course, one may agree with the late Sir Reginald Blomfield's view that they are defective in scholarship. The central pediments are a somewhat too contrived means of preventing an apparent sag in a very long façade and the attics on the end pavilions may be over-emphatic. Subtlety of modelling there is none. In fact, Carlton House Terrace is thoroughly slap-dash, thoroughly typical of the extraordinary old man who designed it, but whose only contribution to the work was probably the provision of a few small sketches, done either in the glorious painted gallery of his Regent Street mansion or the flower-scented luxury of his castle in the Isle of Wight.

The development of the St James's Park area is not the last chapter in the story of John Nash's metropolitan improvements. He was full of projects and, whatever one may think of his later architecture, his genius for town-planning was at its height when he was seventy. About 1825–6 he prepared plans for a new artery to link up Whitehall with the British Museum and the Bloomsbury residential area, then on the point of renewed

expansion under Thomas Cubitt. This scheme was linked to the
Regent Street scheme by the cutting of Pall Mall East and the
formation of a square at the top of Whitehall from which a
road was to run in a direct line to Bloomsbury. The square
(occupying the site of the Old Royal Mews) was formed, and
in 1830 was christened Trafalgar Square. In the process, St
Martin-in-the-Fields was disencumbered of its shabby purlieus
and surrounded by orderly stucco buildings, some of which still
stand. Its magnificent portico was seen to advantage for the
first time. Eastward of St Martin's, part of the north side of
the Strand was entirely remodelled and the clever arrangement
of circular towers to disguise the conflicting angles was introduced. Nash designed none of the buildings in this area. He
entered a limited competition for the National Gallery, but
Wilkins won it. On the west of Trafalgar Square, Smirke designed the College of Physicians and the Union Club. On the
east, George Ledwell Taylor undertook a building speculation,
with a façade by himself. The Golden Cross Inn was rebuilt
by Tite.

Trafalgar Square proved a great success, but the northward
road was abandoned until 1887, when Charing Cross Road was
formed on a different line. A more creditable sequel to Nash's
Metropolitan Improvements is provided by the work of his successor James Pennethorne, to whom we shall return in our final
chapter.

John Nash was the central figure in the grand era of Metropolitan Improvements, the great manager, the politician with
the long-term policy. But around him were other architects
carrying out other building-schemes of narrower extent but
often of some artistic importance. To these buildings and to
Nash's one great public building – Buckingham Palace – we
shall, in due course, return.

CHAPTER 14

Great Estates: II

ALMOST coincident with the building of the first terraces around Regent's Park, came a new building offensive in Bloomsbury. With Euston Square marking a northward goal for the Bedford lay-out, it remained for some ambitious builder to take up Burton's work where he had left it and fill in the intervening gap. In 1820, such a man appeared; his name was Thomas Cubitt.[1] He was thirty-two and already famous in the building world for his great workshops in Gray's Inn Road, where he was doing what had never been done before – employing all the trades on a permanent wage basis. This daring step forward from the slow, elaborate cross-contracting methods bequeathed by the eighteenth century demanded, as a condition of success, a continuous stream of work to keep the organization moving. Thus, Cubitt was constantly leasing land and building on it. He had already done considerable things at Highbury, Stoke Newington,[2] and Barnsbury Park[3] before he came on the Bloomsbury scene.

Burton, it will be remembered, had built only the east side of Tavistock Square. In 1820, a Mr Benjamin Oakley,[4] a literary stockbroker, decided to undertake the south side as an investment for his unmarried daughters. Cubitt, however, leased the sites in the first instance and presumably assigned them to Oakley. The houses let well (£150 a year), which perhaps induced Cubitt to adventure further. In the years around 1824, he completed Tavistock Square, with the imposing columned west side,

1. Inst, Civil Eng. *Annual Report* 1856–7 gives the best account of his career.
2. In Albion Road. A contemporary, undated, plan showing the plots taken by Cubitt is in the writer's possession. Most of the houses survive, though badly blitzed.
3. See p. 283.
4. He was a friend of Burton, Britton, and Soane. His monument is in St Marylebone church.

whose façade the University of London has wisely preserved while converting the whole to a hostel and other uses. He also built Woburn Place, part of Gordon Square, and some of the neighbouring streets, all in a style and quality of building superior to anything which had been seen before in the speculative market.

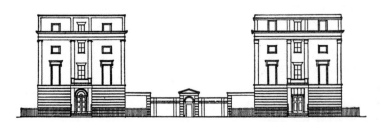

Fig. 26. End elevations of houses in Tavistock and Gordon Squares (T. Cubitt, about 1824).

The lay-out on which these houses were built was a substantially revised version of Burton's, incorporating more squares. The houses themselves made Burton's look like jerry-building, which, of course, many of them were (indeed, one of Cubitt's first independent employments had been to repair the defective roof of Burton's Russell Institution). Their design is refined and their execution so admirable that today there is hardly a wall out of straight or a sagging lintel. The designer may have been Cubitt's younger brother, Lewis,[1] who had a regular architectural training and who, at a much later date, designed King's Cross Station. The blocks of houses are arrayed in a semi-Grecian stucco dress, as neat in design as in execution; the end elevations, which Burton usually botched or ignored, are deftly ornamented so as to make a pleasant perspective; and the parallel blocks are gracefully linked (Fig. 26). A characteristic set of Cubitt houses, which it would have been pleasant to keep, were Nos. 1-6 and 55-59 on the south side of Gordon Square, but the first has been eaten up by the University and the second

1. 'Lewis . . . was always regarded by the family as the laziest and least satisfactory brother of the three.' Sir Stephen Tallents, *Man and Boy* (1943) p. 32.

is likely to follow. No. 1, the residence of Charles Fowler, the architect of Covent Garden and Hungerford markets, retained the back office with its separate entrance and a relief panel of the Nine Muses.[1] The generally restrained treatment of the blocks of houses breaks into columnar architecture in Woburn Place, where a well-executed version of the Tivoli order rises through the first and second floors.

To the east of Woburn Place, Cubitt created a little shopping centre called Woburn Buildings (now Woburn Walk), the leases of which are dated 1822, so that they were among the earliest of his Bloomsbury undertakings. These buildings are small three-storey stuccoed houses with shop-fronts on the ground floor and are designed with great skill and refinement. There is now nothing else like them in London and it is satisfactory that the St Pancras Borough Council has acquired the southern terrace for preservation. (See Fig. 35, p. 265.)

Gordon Street, Endsleigh Street, and Endsleigh Place are all Thomas Cubitt's work, but it took many years for the whole area to be completed and, moreover, another builder made a substantial contribution. He was James Sim who, in partnership with James Sim, junior, and Robert Sim, built Torrington Square in 1821–5 and Woburn Square in 1829 – two pleasantly proportioned works which, however, lack that extra finish and character which the Cubitts achieved. Sim was just a competent builder working to elevations provided by the estate.

In Byng Place, Cubitt built Coward College[2] (later converted into three houses) in 1832; the stucco elevation is one of his more monumental excursions. He was still building in Bloomsbury at the time of his death, and houses in Euston Square and Taviton Street were being built by his executors as late as 1856–8. Gordon Square was finished in 1860.

Cubitt speculations are scattered far and wide in north London, from Camden Town to Stoke Newington. East of the Gray's Inn Road, a part of the Calthorpe estate was built on

1. The panel is preserved in the Warburg Institute which stands on the site.
2. Contract and plans in R.I.B.A. Stripped of the front balcony and otherwise mutilated in 1946.

by Cubitt (he took a lease soon after 1815) and the three houses numbered 48–52 in Frederick Street make a particularly good group. But his greatest undertaking was in the south-west – nothing less than the creation of Belgravia and Pimlico.

It had been realized for a long time that the land behind Grosvenor Place had possibilities. William Porden, the architect of Eaton Hall, proposed a square for Lord Grosvenor in 1795,[1] but what gave the district a totally new importance was the conversion, from 1821 onwards, of Buckingham House into Buckingham Palace. Within three or four years of that date Thomas Cubitt took a lease of the 'five fields', belonging to Lord Grosvenor. Either this lease excluded the site of Belgrave Square or (more probably) the site immediately changed hands, for the square was undertaken as a separate speculation by a syndicate in which two financiers, George and William Haldimand, were the principals. It was they and not Cubitt who employed Soane's brilliant pupil, George Basevi, as architect, though Cubitt evidently participated in the syndicate and executed the buildings.[2]

Belgrave Square consists of four extremely handsome Graeco-Roman blocks, while across three corners of the square are large single mansions standing in their own grounds. Only the blocks of houses are by Basevi; they have Corinthian centres and ends, with ornate attics and balustrades, and porches derived from the Tower of the Winds. The end elevations of the blocks are very grandly treated so that the perspectives in the square are always interesting and architecturally replete.

Of the isolated mansions, the one at the south corner was built for T. R. Kemp, the man who, a few years previously, had begun to create Kemp Town at Brighton. Now much altered, it is still a beautiful house. Kemp's architect was Henry E. Kendall, who has an additional importance in this context because Lewis Cubitt, whom one suspects of having been the designing partner in the great firm, had been one of his pupils

In the east corner, the enormous square mass of Seaford

1. R.A. *Catalogue.*
2. In the Grosvenor Office is an Ionic design for the Square, signed by and presumably designed by Cubitt.

House, now shorn of its portico, is the work of Philip Hardwick. In the north corner is a house by Smirke.

Belgrave Square was only one unit in the plan for Belgravia as a whole – a plan remarkable for its architectural character, completeness, and generosity. For this plan we are perhaps indebted to Lord Grosvenor's architect, Thomas Cundy the younger. Apart from Belgrave Square, much of the architecture, in the early years of development, was provided by the Cubitts, who began the first block of that great 'park-way', Eaton Square, in 1827. This block (Nos. 103–118) is in the style of their Bloomsbury work[1]; most of the rest of Eaton Square is more pretentious in treatment and lacks the modest Georgian discipline of these earlier houses.

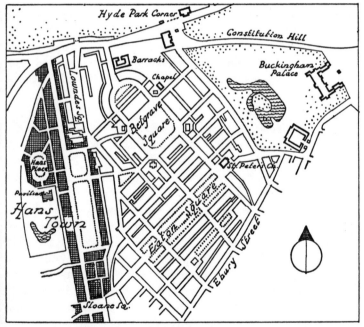

Fig. 27. Sketch-map of Hans Town and Belgravia. Hans Town is discussed in Chapter 20.

1. It is attributed to T. and L. Cubitt on the engraving of Eaton Square in Britton and Pugin, *Public Buildings of London* (1827).

But whatever the Cubitts did was done in magnificent style. The land-drainage, the sewerage, the road-surfaces, the lighting, the planting, as well as the construction of the houses and mews – everything was accurately thought out and superbly construct- ed. The tongues which wagged disapproval of the 'shoddiness' of Regent Street and the Park were bound to praise, in contrast, the conscientious solidity, both in design and construction, of the Cubitts' buildings in Belgravia. Professor Donaldson, re- viewing the architecture of the period in his inaugural lecture at University College in 1842, held up Belgravia as the most honourable specimen of speculative building and awarded it a special encomium.

Cubitt's remarkable career continued well into the Victorian period. After Belgravia, he laid out Pimlico and a great part of Clapham. He built Osborne for the Queen and was conspicuous in every movement to abate the atrocities which London's accel- erated growth was bringing with it. He was a great man; but never greater than in the fine combination of initiative and taste which mark the achievements of his early days. He died in 1855.

One more great building adventure was begun before the Georgian period closed. This was the Bishop of London's Pad- dington Estate, westward of Edgware Road. S. P. Cockerell, as surveyor to the See, provided the original plan and supervised the erection of several rows of plain brick houses.[1] But in 1827 he died. His successor was George Gutch, and it is probably to this little-known architect that we owe much of the sensational architectural scenery of the district. He remodelled the plan several times and laid out the proud stucco vistas of Southwick Crescent, Gloucester Square, and Sussex Square, mostly built between 1830 and 1836, in course of redevelopment before 1939 and now vanished. They are un-Georgian in character as well as date and announce the last, weary, ponderous phase of

1. Crace Maps (Portfolio 14, No. 4). In the Victoria and Albert Museum is an Ionic design for 'Connaught Chapel', by S. P. Cockerell, 1827, with a manuscript note stating that it was not executed owing to Cockerell's death. See W. Robins, *Paddington: Past and Present*, 1853.

'metropolitan improvements' – the phase which ended in the gloomy twilight of North Kensington and Gloucester Road.

Very many more London estates were developed after Waterloo and it is difficult to draw a line between those which are outward-growing limbs from the main body of the London organism and those which were developed separately in the rural perimeter and in a more suburban spirit. Certain estates to the east of Gray's Inn Road are strictly metropolitan in the sense that they emerge from the existing street pattern. Such, for instance, is the New River Company's Estate which includes Claremont Square, Myddelton Square, and Percy Circus, all laid out by the Company's surveyor, William Chadwell Mylne. Such also is the Lloyd-Baker Estate : here, the excellent semi-detached houses of Lloyd Square and Wharton Street are ambiguously ascribed to an unknown J. Booth, on the strength of a signed drawing in the estate office. Again, the Northampton Estate ties itself, spider-like, to the metropolitan structure with six streets radiating from Northampton Square. Eastwards, beyond the Goswell Road, lies the equally humble estate of St Bartholomew's Hospital, laid out round King Square by Thomas Hardwick, the Hospital Surveyor; the houses are all of the artisan class (probably 'fourth rate' under the Act) and their lowness makes King Square admirably light and spacious.

Eastwards of King Square, the map becomes inextricably confused in small and tentative developments, the back-wash of the great westward drive. Ambition pointed westward, as it had done ever since the magnet of Sovereignty placed itself at Westminster, and the westward flow of wealth and fashion has never been reversed. In the west, the speculator played for big stakes, and thither went capital and the planner's skill. In the east, the rewards were unimposing. Nobody thought of planning the great manors of Hackney and Stepney when the East End began to seep and creep towards them. All comers were served with their cuts from those two great territorial joints. The resulting jig-saw is a monument to the economic assiduity of the little man. That is why the East End is like it is.

CHAPTER 15

Public Works after Waterloo

IN 1827 was published a book called *Metropolitan Improvements: or, London in the 19th Century*, with engravings from drawings by Thomas Hosmer Shepherd and a text (regrettably in the style of the facetious cicerone) by James Elmes. The book is a useful, and nearly complete, guide to the new buildings of George IV's London; for it interprets its title broadly, 'improvements' meaning anything from the formation of Regent Street by John Nash to the erection of the School for the Indigent Blind by a Mr Tappen. Behind the book is the apprehension that London, within a matter of fifteen or twenty years, had taken on a new character. And so it had. Nash's operations had given it a new sense of 'circulation'. Old buildings, like St Martin-in-the-Fields and Buckingham House, had been brought into relation to the great plan. New buildings, arriving on all sides, were being sited effectively and with enormously increased respect for urbanity. Theatres, clubs, institutions, and churches rarely failed to find a site where they were well seen. Thus, the Haymarket portico effectively closed the vista from St James's Square; the United Service and Athenaeum Clubs faced each other across Waterloo Place, the London Institution commanded Finsbury Circus. While the Church Commissioners, as we shall see, displayed the greatest acumen in purchasing sites at key-points on estate development plans or else at road junctions or terminals.

John Nash must, of course, be given full credit for the good siting on the Crown Lands. He did it all by suggestion, persuasion, and bargaining, piloting the various building owners to their appropriate stations. And his influence extended further than his own official sphere. The only really badly sited buildings of the time are those which, like the British Museum, were obliged to rebuild on an old site. And Nash had shown that even the British Museum could logically have been brought within the grand framework of 'improved' London.

The quality of the new buildings varied – but within certain narrow limits. Indeed, after a century and a quarter of absolute chaos it is difficult to see that they varied at all and the amateur of classic architecture may be forgiven for not discovering any great superiority in a Greek façade by Smirke over one by, say, the above-mentioned Mr Tappen. The profession of architecture had attained a very remarkable coherence, having advanced a stage further since Sir William Chambers had given it respectability in the 1760s. It was now a fairly numerous body of men and they were *trained* men – trained in the offices of other architects.

A cross-section taken in 1820 proves this. At the top of the section we find the eminent over-sixties – Hardwick, Soane, Nash, and S. P. Cockerell – pupils respectively of Chambers, Dance, and (in the last two cases) Taylor. Then, in the fifty to sixty age-group, Charles Beazley (another Taylor pupil) and Sanders (a pupil of Soane); in the forty to fifty group, Benjamin Dean Wyatt, George Gwilt, William Wilkins, and William Chadwell Mylne, all pupils of their architect-fathers, together with Abraham (pupil of Bowen, a surveyor), Montague (Dance), Hakewill (Yenn), Savage (Alexander), Smirke (Soane), and Joseph Kay (Cockerell). The younger London architects had mostly come from the offices of Nash, Soane, Hardwick, or Cockerell. Thus, the profession had opacity and a strong sense of continuity – a continuity all the more effective because its sources were relatively few; it was the subsequent overwhelming dilution which rendered the profession as a whole so hopelessly ineffective in the Victorian period.

These architects and a few others were responsible for a large proportion of London's new buildings between 1815 and 1830. The only buildings for which they were not responsible were the ordinary houses, built in streets, terraces, and squares, and even here they often lent a guiding hand in their capacity as estate surveyors. Some of them exercised considerable influence as district surveyors under the Building Act.

The three most eminent men of the period were John Nash, John Soane, and the much younger Robert Smirke. They were the 'attached architects' to the Board of Works, a department which, since Wyatt's death and as a result of his grotesque irresponsibility, had been ruled by a Civil Servant with the title of Surveyor-General, the architects being allocated their portions of work and advising, in committee, on all architectural matters of a public nature. They received retaining fees of £500 a year, plus a three per cent commission (instead of the usual five per cent) on executed work. In theory their spheres were not delimited; in practice they worked out something like this : Nash, as the King's personal architect, conducted the King's building operations – chiefly at Brighton and Buckingham Palace; Soane was concerned with Westminster Palace and the Law Courts; Smirke, much the youngest of the three, took any other Government commissions he could lay hands on. All the commissions entrusted to this trinity were of the first importance; minor buildings erected at the public expense were usually the work of the clerks-of-works to the department concerned, or else of architects who had managed to enlist sufficient influence to secure appointment, with or without the farcical preliminary of a 'public competition'. But in reviewing the public buildings of 1815–30, the names of Nash, Soane, and Smirke are continuously paramount.

Now as to the motives for building and the sources of the necessary funds. The State was easily and by far the greatest initiator of building in London after Waterloo; so great a proportion of public wealth can rarely have been spent on architecture in the capital in so short a time. The State paid for churches. It paid for the Law Courts. It paid for revenue buildings like the Customs House and the Post Office and the Treasury's own home in Whitehall. It paid – very reluctantly – for a Royal Palace, and, more cheerfully, for laying-out and adorning the Royal Parks. And it paid in handsome style for the accommodation of the two supreme national collections – the British Museum and the National Gallery. But to whom must this policy of generous building be ascribed? Unquestionably, in the first instance, to the Sovereign. That formidable and eccentric personage had a profound desire to make London a magnificent capital and from the day that he assumed the

Regency to the day of his death, nineteen years later, he pressed continually to achieve this object. Without him, no doubt, the age of 'improvements' would still have flourished; but it was George IV's superb breadth of view, his intolerance of projects of less than regal scale, that fortified the initiative of others and lent propriety to extravagance. Below the King were the lords and gentlemen whose duty it was to see the great projects crystallized and carried into effect, and here there was no lack of sympathy with the Royal ideal. Ministers like Spencer Perceval and, later, Lord Liverpool abetted by Lord Farnborough and Lord Goderich and J. W. Croker, presided effectively over the proceedings, obtaining the grants and instructing and appointing the architects. Public opinion was, on the whole, gladly acquiescent. Especially after Waterloo, there was a widespread feeling for building adventures, a feeling copiously witnessed by the newspapers and magazines of the time. It is curious that after all this came a sense of disappointment and at the end of the period a sudden and universal revulsion against all that had been achieved. We shall see that there were some grounds for this, here and there. But the real cause was far removed from mere questions of architectural criticism or of the wisdom of expenditure on public works. The whole rule of taste was in process of being dethroned; and the last and not least effective phase in that long dominion was irrationally condemned.

To the buildings due to Royal or governmental initiative we must give our attention in this chapter and the next; other buildings, deriving their existence from corporate and private wealth, following in due course.

By all the rules of precedence, the chief public building of the period should have been the Royal Palace. Such, from time to time, was George IV's intention, and had he come to the throne ten years sooner it might well have taken effect, war or no war. As it was, he went about the business in a curious way, first talking about a remodelled Buckingham House as a *pied-à-terre* ('I am too old to build a Palace') and later, as the building advanced, insisting that it was, after all, a Palace. The project was ill-starred. Soane had been led to believe that any Palace commission would be his and had a magnificent design ready in 1821 for a site in the Green Park. But an excuse was made to snatch the work from him and give it to Nash. Four years elapsed before Nash's design for a reconstructed Buckingham House was produced. Then it was begun in great haste and when half-built looked so awkward that parts of it were pulled down and rebuilt. Still unfinished at the King's death in 1830, the work was taken out of Nash's hands and a Select Committee set up to inquire into his conduct. It was not found possible to prove him guilty of negligence, but he was never reinstated and another architect, Edward Blore, was instructed to complete the work. Blore eventually masked almost the whole of Nash's building with a new frontispiece and this, never admired, in turn gave place, in 1913, to the present Baroque front by Sir Aston Webb.

It is a melancholy story, especially as what is left of Nash's work and the records of what has gone show that much effort and invention went into the design. Clearly, he meant to give London something on the scale of the Palais Royal which, with Perrault's Louvre, was reflected in the design. Between the projecting wings he placed a triumphal arch – the arch we know today as Marble Arch; it was moved to its present site after Blore swept it away to build his frontispiece. The cheerful delicacy of the arch, with the pleasant carved panels by Westmacott and Bailey, and the rich ironwork, show the standard at which Nash aimed; and the same excellences occur in parts of the palace. But, alas! the architect was old, he was surrounded by enemies, and he was in the service of the most temperamental as well as the most spendthrift patron in Europe. He certainly failed to visualize the Palace as a coherent and satisfactory composition. So much he admitted. But his plan was admirable and so were some of his details. It was partly, but not entirely, his fault that the greatest 'metropolitan improvement' of all was the most notorious architectural failure of its time.

The building of Buckingham Palace had many repercussions, the most immediate being the improvement and architectural furnishing of Hyde Park. Here, the Office of Woods and

Forests was in command, under the guidance of Lord Goderich; their architect was a very young man called Decimus Burton.

Burton was born in 1800 and died in 1881. The son of James Burton, the great builder whom we met in Chapter 12, he was rocketed to success by the joint influence of his father and his father's friend, Nash; and it is infinitely to his credit that he stood the test of premature promotion and became a worthy and conscientious artist. Before he was twenty he had designed his father's Regent's Park villa, 'The Holme', and when he was twenty-one Cornwall Terrace was being built from his designs. At twenty-five he was commissioned to design the two works by which he will always be remembered – the screen and arch at Hyde Park Corner (Plate 34).

These handsome ornaments, together with the smaller gates and lodges, were decided upon by an informal committee of peers and commoners[1] from whom Burton received his instructions. The intent was to bring Hyde Park within the monumental orbit of the Palace. First, Burton provided a plan for the drives and pathways. Then he built the lodge at Grosvenor Gate. Then the two, most original, semi-Italian lodges at Stanhope Gate. Then Cumberland Lodge. Then the lodge at Hyde Park Corner, and finally the Ionic screen ('the façade', as it was called at the time) and the 'Pimlico' arch.

The screen and the arch belong to each other and the arch was originally on the same axis as the screen so that the graceful Ionic of the latter made a formal preface to the rich Corinthian (or, rather, Composite) mass of the arch. The whole point of the composition was to make a monumental crossing from Hyde Park to the Green Park, the road through the arch sweeping immediately to the left, down Constitution Hill into the forecourt of the Palace. In 1888, the arch was rebuilt normal to the axis of Constitution Hill and the relation between the two buildings destroyed.

Both screen and arch are effective designs and show how much Burton was able to derive from the education supplied by his not very scholarly father and the drawing-school of George

1. Consisting of Lord Liverpool, Lord Farnborough, Lord Goderich, Messrs Peel, Herries, and Arbuthnot.

Maddox. The screen may have been suggested by Holland's Ionic screen to Carlton House, being demolished about the same time.

The 'Pimlico' arch is strictly Roman, on the Arch of Titus model, but with the order brought out *fortissimo* at the expense of pedestal and attic, so that the whole thing has a vertical emphasis, in satisfactory contrast to the more conservative Constantine horizontality of the Marble Arch which, be it remembered, originally formed an incident in the same scenic sequence to which the Hyde Park Corner group was the introduction. Burton's arch was never finished – you can still see the rough panels of masonry prepared for sculptural trophies. In 1840 it suffered the fate of being made the pedestal for a bad equestrian statue of Wellington. Protests and ridicule had no effect and although Burton hopefully inserted in his will a sum for the substitution of the intended quadriga, he changed his mind, seeing the unlikelihood of anything being done. At last, when the arch was moved, the statue was banished, but still no quadriga was forthcoming. In 1912, however, a vast Beaux-Arts equipage settled on top of the arch, curiously distorting its character and generalizing its neat Georgian classicism into Edwardian Baroque.

Burton's other work for the Woods and Forests included an unfortunate building called the Parliamentary Stables in Storey's Gate. To this he was made to give a lavish architectural disguise in deference to the sensibilities of the Dean and Chapter of Westminster – a concession which he had to explain before a somewhat critical Select Committee. These outrageously expensive stables have long since disappeared.

To this review of architecture within the Palace orbit must be added one more building – George Rennie's bridge of five segmental arches over the Serpentine, a sterling piece of masonry construction which owes its existence directly to the master of the scene – King George IV.

While Nash was wrestling with his Palace problems, the disappointed Soane had turned his attention to opportunities at Westminster. Between 1820 and 1824 he rebuilt the seven Courts of Law which clustered round the great fabric of Westminster Hall. And during the same period he built the Scala Regia and the Royal Vestibule to the House of Lords. All this work has disappeared – the Scala Regia after the great fire of 1834 and the Law Courts after the removal of the Judicature to the Strand in the 1880s – and for that reason these fine, mature works of one of our greatest architects have dropped out of the traditional picture of English architecture.

One of these seven courts – the Court of Chancery (Plate 28b) – represented Soane's furthest departure from the academic and his mysterious creation of a 'disembodied' architecture from which not only the orders themselves but nearly all conventional expressions of support are eliminated. The ceiling of this strange apartment was raised on an arcade with no columns – apparently floating over the Court; the circular gallery seemed to derive support from five-centred arches so flattened as to mock the least pretence of usefulness. This highly-strung architecture is hardly Soane's most pleasing work, but it leaves one astonished at the reach of his imagination. The Scala Regia and Royal Vestibule were very different. Developed on sober, classical lines, their arches, vaults, and domes were enriched to the last degree with Soanean ornament of the busiest and most wilful kind.

The Offices of the Board of Trade provided Soane with another opportunity in Westminster, but somehow or other he failed to do it justice and brought an avalanche of criticism on his head. The whole building was brilliantly reconstructed, as the present Treasury, by Charles Barry in 1844–5, using Soane's columns.

Both Soane and Nash were made to suffer much from public and parliamentary criticism during their last years. In Nash's case there was evident ground for complaint, if only because no estimate he gave for a Royal building ever had the slightest relation to what the Treasury would be expected to pay. But Soane's case was different. His advanced and original works were no easier to understand than some of the music Beethoven was writing. And his highest flights are always accompanied by childish odds and ends which it is quite impossible to take seriously. He could never leave out his 'knobs' – more properly *antefixae* and *acroteria* – circles or semicircles filled with Greek honeysuckle and tied up in coils of grooved or beaded moulding. These catch the attention and detain it from appreciation of the larger originalities in the control of space and light. It was easy to mock these mantelpiece mannerisms and the greatness of Soane was felt by few. Today almost all the buildings in which that greatness was expressed have been destroyed, either on purpose, by accident, or blitz.

Next in importance to these major public works by Nash and Soane come the two buildings which house the chief national collections of antiquities and paintings – the British Museum and the National Gallery. Their architects were, in the first case, Robert Smirke, in the second, William Wilkins. Neither Smirke nor Wilkins had genius, but both were able. Their works were much abused by some of the critics of their own time and became targets for Victorian abuse. The truth is that both of them had foibles, and for that there is a reason. The English tradition of architectural training was such as to encourage foibles. It lacked the 'vertical' stiffening of the State academies on the Continent and relied on the 'horizontal' communication of experience from individual master to individual pupil. Individualism – and foibles – were the inevitable results.

Smirke, born 1780, was the son of a Royal Academician painter, received a few months' training from Soane but did not take kindly to it, and was later in a surveyor's office. Wilkins, born 1778, was the son of a Norwich architect, went to Cambridge, graduated Sixth Wrangler, and became a Fellow of Caius. Both travelled and studied much in Greece and Italy and were redoubtable scholars of Greek architecture.

The differences between these two close contemporaries are interesting. Smirke always aimed at breadth and simplicity, at the risk of being dull. Wilkins tried hard for variety and risked becoming trivial. The worst one can say of the colonnaded façade of the British Museum is that it is dull; and it is not wholly unjust to call the ultra-subdivided, pettily domed National Gallery trivial. But both are redeemed, though in different degrees, by the sympathy and taste of the general handling.

Smirke was the more solid and mature designer. He had been in offices and studying at the Academy Schools while Wilkins was reading for his degree; and his travels were less archaeological in intention than those of Wilkins. Moreover, his interest in the technical side of building was remarkable and he was the best constructor of his day. No building of his can share the reproach of 'shoddiness', so justly levelled at some others of the period. All Smirke's abilities, in planning, detail, and technique, are seen at their best in the British Museum, begun in 1823 and completed nearly thirty years later.

The origin of this great building was in George IV's presentation of the Royal Library to the Nation – an act of generosity for which the nation paid him a not inconsiderable sum. The 'gift' had to be suitably housed. Lord Goderich obtained a grant and Smirke began the King's Library in 1823. Old Montague House, which had contained the British Museum since 1759, still stood and the new building was added to it, though conceived from the outset as the eastern side of the quadrangle of an entirely new structure. Gradually, Montague House disappeared as Smirke's Galleries were built; the tremendous southern colonnade was completed in 1847.

The interior of the King's Library is perhaps the best part of the Museum. It has Smirke's admirable feeling for serene breadth. In the centre it breaks into a square space, with Corinthian columns *in antis*, but the main lines echo through from end to end; the ornaments, derived from the decorative tradition of Adam and Dance,[1] are well designed and expertly controlled. The vestibule and main staircase of the Museum are also a grand, unhurried design, worked out in strictly Greek elements, with shallow coffered ceilings and sentinel Doric columns carrying the great beam of the staircase opening. As a whole, the building has, of course, suffered from the constant addition of galleries so that the articulation of Smirke's plan is partly lost; and when the iron-domed reading-room was formed in the

1. From various remarks in the Farington Diary it seems that Dance was Smirke's friend and guide in matters of design in his early days.

centre quadrangle, the stateliness of the lay-out was much diminished. But all the galleries have a cool, impersonal dignity which is admirable. As for the south front, with its unbroken parade of forty-four Ionic columns (Plate 35), coolness and impersonality are carried perhaps a little too far. It was surely a pity to screen the whole bulk of the structure from end to end in this way however magnificent the columnar screen; and the pediment over the eight central columns does not by itself effect a marriage between the mass behind and its open frontispiece. The Greek order is, however, superb in every detail and its scale impressive. But there is too much of it, and it was always Smirke's most pronounced foible to carry a good thing just too far.

The National Gallery (Plate 36b) is a complete contrast. It was begun rather later than the Museum, in 1832, but finished much earlier – in 1838. Sir Julius Angerstein's collection of paintings had been bought (at the King's instance) as the nucleus of a National Collection and the site of the old Royal Mews selected for a building in which to house them. Both Nash and Cockerell submitted designs, but Wilkins, who had had something to do with the selection of the site, put in some drawings at the last moment and, by luck and influence, secured the commission.

Of Wilkins's plan, which provided for the housing of the Royal Academy as well as the Angerstein collection, nothing need be said, for it was a mere succession of top-lit galleries, with other rooms towards Trafalgar Square, to left and right of an entrance hall. Wilkins's whole interest was in architectural effect and here, along the north side of the new Square, he had the finest site in London at his disposal – a fine site and a very long one, and it was its length which made it difficult to handle. Somehow, it had to be subdivided and made interesting. In the centre Wilkins placed a portico and steps. The wings he divided up with intermediate and terminal pavilions and, not content with these, extended the theme of the portico for two bays to left and right in pilaster form : he also left enough room beyond his terminal pavilions for recessed appendages at the extreme ends of the front. Thus the façade is divided into no fewer than thirteen sections, six on either side of the central portico. Unfortunately, all the subsidiary sections have approximately equal value and the two sorts of pavilions are so similar in 'weight' that one is inclined to evaluate them as alternative suggestions rather than complementary parts of a single design. To make his design still more 'interesting', Wilkins set a dome over the portico and turrets over the terminal pavilions, like the clock and vases on a mantelpiece, only less useful.

To compare the composition of the National Gallery with, say, Soane's much cheaper and simpler façade of the Art Gallery at Dulwich (1811–14) is to understand at once that classical composition is a very much deeper thing than mere technical artifice. In the Soane work, each section is clearly evaluated and has its due weight in the whole panorama. In Wilkins's building each addition to the bare mass of the structure increases the ambiguity of the whole.

The National Gallery is redeemed by the taste and scholarship with which every part is handled. The combination of portico and steps is excellent – as good as the sister portico at University College which we shall meet in another chapter. The dome and turrets, too, are in themselves gracious and accomplished. Seen in sharp perspective, the Gallery cannot fail to please; but considered critically as a façade commanding a great square, its weakness is apparent.

We shall meet the works of Wilkins again in another chapter. He and Smirke are an entertaining study. We know little of the lives of these temperamental opposites, but there is not, perhaps, much to know. Smirke seems to have been serious, methodical – a man of understatement. As a young officer in the Militia, he wrote a handbook to battalion-drill[1] and his career was built on discipline and ambition. Wilkins, on the other hand, was a rather gay character, quite extraordinarily vain, a well-informed connoisseur of painting, and a great amateur of the theatre. On

---

1. *Review of a Battalion of Infantry*, 1799. Attributed to Smirke's father in the British Museum catalogue, and admitted by Sir Edward Smirke to be at least a joint production.

the whole, the evidence tends to show that the personalities of Robert Smirke and William Wilkins are pretty well reflected in their architecture.

Two more public buildings (neither now existing) remain to be mentioned and the more important of them is the General Post Office at St Martin's-le-Grand. The Post Office moved to this site from a set of converted mansions in Lombard Street which had grown inadequate to its expanding needs. Commissioners, appointed under an Act of 1815, invited architects to send in designs for the new building and nearly a hundred did so. This was evidently too many for the Commissioners who promptly, and for no recorded reason, sent them back and called in Smirke who, on principle, never went in for competitions. The competitors grumbled and one of them, Joseph Kay, the Post Office's own excellent surveyor, never quite got over his annoyance. But Smirke, safely enthroned, proceeded to build in 1823 and completed the work in 1829. And, of course, the building he provided was in the highest degree competent. The chief room – the letter-carriers' room – was a long hall lit by two tiers of large windows, below and above an iron balcony reached by an iron spiral stair in the centre of the hall. The façade to St Martin's-le-Grand was, inevitably, Greek Ionic, with three handsome porticos. The building was demolished in 1913.

Smirke was such a safe, reliable man, that he was often called in when some other architect had got himself and his clients into difficulties. Croker called him 'the Dr Baillie of architects' after the celebrated author of *Morbid Anatomy*. The case of the Customs House, where the patient was subsiding into the Thames mud, will be cited later. Another Thames-side casualty, rescued by Smirke, was the Millbank Penitentiary. This gloomy building, begun in 1813, on the site now occupied by the Tate Gallery, was a humanitarian experiment in jail design for convicts who might be expected to benefit more from 'classification, employment, and reform' than from being sent to the hulks. Jeremy Bentham was the prime mover and the plan, with its central hexagon and six radiating pentagons, was the perfect embodiment of his *panopticon* principle. An architect called Harvey was the first executive and presumably designed the pentagons with their conical towers, which made the whole group look like a medieval French château of vast extent. Harvey proved incompetent, however, and Hardwick was called in. Hardwick found the job difficult and unremunerative and promptly backed out; and Smirke's help was finally sought to get the Government, the managing committee, and the building out of an appalling mess. This long-forgotten humanitarian Bastille, finished in 1816, cost the country nearly £500,000.

That George IV's public buildings were, on the whole, a credit to their authors and to the nation can, I think, be fairly and frankly admitted. They were all victimized and slandered at the time by chatterbox critics and it was not long before they were convicted wholesale under the devastating edicts of Gothic Revivalism. Today, with public opinion gone mad after anything Georgian, they tend to be over-praised. So let us admit (as the wiser heads of the time admitted) that few of them are quite as good as they might have been. Let us admit that Nash was sometimes culpably negligent, that Soane's 'knobs' need not be admired, that Smirke was prone to prolixity, and that Wilkins had a strong dash of the amateur. When that is admitted, there is much – very much – to admire and enjoy. There is the tact and delicacy in the handling of classical detail; the effortless ability to harmonize the fruits of archaeology with the plain, traditional elements of building; there is the good craftsmanship in Portland stone and stock brick; and there is the exquisitely fine joinery and ironwork in staircases, doors, windows, and fittings. By any reasonable standards these buildings are worthy of admiration.

CHAPTER 16

The Church and the State

In Chapter 6, we reviewed a great phase of church building. In this chapter we come to another. The two phases are not unlike in their origins. In both, the expansion of London offered the main reason for new church building; in both a great and direct part was played by the State, and the Act for Fifty New Churches of 1711 is echoed by the Church Building Act of 1818. On a closer view the two movements look less alike. Queen Anne's Act was a political gesture of some warmth; the churches were intended to be, and, indeed, were in fact, costly and dignified symbols of the State religion as conceived by Tories. The Act of 1818 took the business more coolly. No number of churches was specified but a sum of money – one million pounds – was put down wherewith an indefinite number of churches was to be built. The initiative in the whole affair came from a group of laymen headed by Joshua Watson, a retired City wine-merchant.[1] The Bill was introduced by the Primate and passed into law without difficulty. Any member of either House could see the need for it. The peril of 'democracy' among the lower orders had been obvious since 1789; the enormous spread of nonconformity was an allied threat. Now, dissenters could build their preaching boxes wherever they could get the land, the money, and the congregation. The Establishment could do nothing except by Act of Parliament. John Wesley had raised a great porticoed hall in the City Road in 1777–8; Whitefield another, as conspicuous, in Tottenham Court Road in 1756; and Rowland Hill his octagonal auditorium in the Blackfriars Road in 1783.[2] People flocked to these places and others like them.

1. See M. H. Post, *Six Hundred New Churches*, 1961, for an admirable account both of the legislation and the buildings resulting from it.

2. Of these three, only Wesley's chapel survives. Whitefield's was demolished in 1898. Rowland Hill's, after serving as a boxing-ring, was bombed and demolished in 1940.

The Church of England on the other hand had nothing new to show but a few proprietary chapels and chapels-of-ease, served from the mother churches and regarded without loyalty or affection by perfunctory suburban congregations.

The period between George III's accession and Waterloo – fifty-five years – is so bare of churches that the few which were built strike one as architectural oddities. A few suburbs, like Battersea and Clapham, provide a straggling tail to the rebuilding movement which produced churches like Hampstead and Islington around 1750. These two are carpenters' or surveyors' jobs. Battersea (1775-7) was by Joseph Dixon, Clapham (1774-6) by Kenton Couse, an officer of the Works. Both have immense carpentry roofs and, by availing themselves to the full of Baltic scantlings, eliminate the problem of the internal columns altogether. Neither church, however, shows a very high degree of artistry. For this we must look at Dance's rebuilding of All Hallows, London Wall (1765) where the very beautiful neo-classical handling of an Ionic order under a barrel vault has already been described. We shall also find originality at St Mary's, Paddington (1788-91), another medieval derelict rebuilt this time by John Plaw, an architect known chiefly as the author of books of cottage designs. Plaw's church is a neat cube with a variety of excrescences rather quaintly related to it. The internal arrangement is odd, comprising an octagonally planned gallery and a shallow dome. The thing is thoughtfully worked out and quite undeserving of the scorn which later church-builders heaped upon it.

A rebuilding of exactly the same date as Paddington is James Carr's church of St James, Clerkenwell. Carr, evidently at a loss for a recent precedent, imitated late Wren and produced a competent result. His spire, conspicuous from around Farringdon Street, looks like a lost and unhappy cousin of the Wren family.

All but last among these sporadic rebuildings came St John's, Hackney, 1792-7. Hackney is by James Spiller, a friend of Soane's and a clever man, with a difficult temperament which perhaps was against his emerging into the front rank of architects. His church resembles Paddington in that it is basically symmetrical on both axes, though the plan is not square but cruciform. Like Paddington, too, the main porch (added 1812–13) is bowed, and so are the other four smaller porches. But unlike Paddington and unlike almost every other building of the day, the scale of Hackney Church is huge – a dark brick monster with umbrageous eaves as weighty as Hawksmoor, though with only a fraction of Hawksmoor's pathos and beauty. Almost the whole building is in dark brick, but the steeple, added in 1812–13, and riding over the west end, is entirely of Portland stone. The effect of this contrast is dramatically and (one imagines) unintentionally odd. The steeple, with its flamboyant curves, has less relation to the structure below than that of any other London church. Beautifully weathered and gleaming white, it seems to float in sublime independence of the sturdy brown temple which really supports it.

Spiller's steeple at Hackney, with its Grecian character and Regency idiosyncrasies, is a real departure from the Wren–Gibbs tradition. But it was not quite the first. The astonishing tower of St Anne's, Soho, preceded it. This, built in 1802–6 to take the place of an older tower, is by Samuel Pepys Cockerell. The design shows some French influence and elucidates the problem of combining a bell stage and a conspicuous clock with uncommon rationality. The usual devices for making an effective silhouette – balustrades, urns, colonettes, and pineapples – are discarded; we are given simply a massive louvred bell-stage, surmounted by a cylinder and a shape which can crudely be compared with two interpenetrating beer-barrels. This contains the four-faced clock. Above is a weather-vane. The whole thing is original, if a trifle freakish, and well worth preserving, even though the seventeenth century body of the church has gone, having been destroyed by a direct hit early in the aerial attacks of 1940.

Apart from these rebuildings, church construction in the late eighteenth century is represented only by a few proprietary chapels built by popular clergymen or by the landlords of the expanding estates and chapels-of-ease in outposts of the enormous parishes. Of the former, Fitzroy Chapel in Maple Street, south of Fitzroy Square, was a fairly typical example; a pedimented brick box with some trifling frontal adornments and a

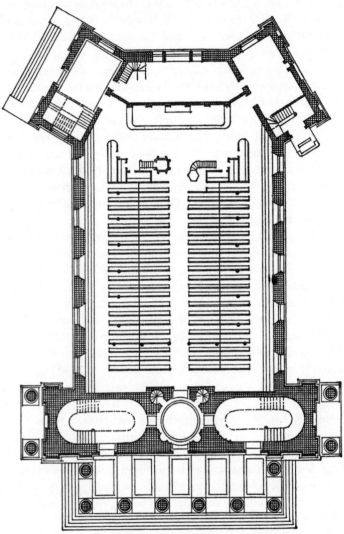

Fig. 28. Plan of St Marylebone Church

bell turret. Of the latter, there is the neat chapel in West Street and there used to be two quite interesting churches by Thomas Hardwick – St James's, Hampstead Road, 1791–2 (destroyed

215

about 1960), and the much later (1814) chapel which is now the parish church of St John's Wood. Hardwick was a pupil and staunch follower of Chambers and his churches barely deviate from Chambers's Roman standards. St John's Wood Church, with its Ionic portico and bell turret, is the best of the three. To Hardwick's later church-work we shall return in a moment.

The 'Million' Church Building Act, as we have seen, became law in 1818. By that time a church-building movement, born with the return of peace, had already begun. Marylebone and St Pancras, enormous parishes, swelling with the wealth and pride of merchants and 'nabobs', were already thinking of re-placing their tiny hamlet-chapels with something more in pro-portion to their numbers and their means; and Stepney, less wealthy but even more extensive, was doing the same.

Marylebone had secured a design from Sir William Chambers during his lifetime, but now relied on the assistance of his suc-cessor, Mr Hardwick. In 1770, a committee had obtained an Act for building a church. Further Acts were obtained in 1772 and 1773 but nothing was done until 1813 when, with the help of yet another Act, a chapel was proposed. The site, already acquired, was on the south side of Marylebone Road, a fact which caught the attention of John Nash and induced him, characteristically, to form York Gate on the axis of the new church. Hardwick's design was modest enough, comprising a four-column Ionic portico and a small bell-turret, exactly like St John's Wood. When the church was half built, however, the committee, headed by the Duke of Portland, suddenly deter-mined that the new chapel should become the new parish church. A sixth Act was obtained, and Hardwick was told to alter the plan and heighten the architectural character accordingly, which he did by adding two columns to the rising portico, sub-stituting a Corinthian for the Ionic superstructure and elaborat-ing the bell-turret into a conspicuous steeple adorned with miniature caryatides. The result, completed in 1818, is coldly imposing and acquires its greatest merit from the excellent en-semble it presents in conjunction with Nash's façades when viewed from the Park.

Meanwhile, a St Pancras committee was working on a still

more ambitious scheme, for a plot of land they had acquired on the east side of Euston Square. The Act for St Pancras New Church dates from 1816. Three architects, William Inwood, Francis Bedford, and Thomas Rickman, were premiated in the limited competition for designs. Inwood's was chosen, perhaps for its originality and for the attractiveness of the drawings but perhaps equally because Inwood had long been associated with the district and must have been known to members of the committee. In any case, the selection resulted in the brilliant building which stands today very much as it was left by Inwood. Though dismissed, even by so perceptive a critic as Lethaby, as a mere copy of the Erechtheum, it is better worth study than most classical churches since the time of Gibbs.

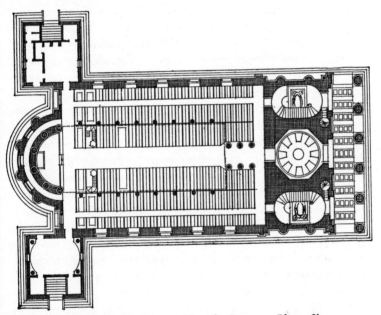

Fig. 29. Plan of St Pancras Church. Compare Plate 38b.

Old Inwood was surveyor to the Kenwood and other estates in St Pancras parish and there is nothing to show that he was very much of a designer. But he had a son, Henry William, who travelled for a short time in Greece, returning in time to help (at the age of twenty-four or twenty-five) with the design of the new church (Plate 38b). One must presume that it is to the genius of this young man that we owe this skilful and mature work. In general plan and form it owes less to the Erechtheum than it does to St Martin-in-the-Fields, the only obvious theft from the Greek building being the placing of the caryatid tribunes so that they extend slightly beyond the east wall of the church — a curious freak of the original structure which no scholar has been able to explain. Apart from that, the church is simply a great hall, with an apse at one end and a vestibule, tower, and portico at the other. This west end is clearly modelled on St Martin's: it tackles the same problems of combining a portico and tower and solves it in the same way. No amount of skill can ever make a happy marriage between a portico and a tower, when the latter is set on top of the former, though it is very remarkable how determined English architects have been to try. The tower does not, of course, really ride on the pitched roof and this important fact must, somehow or other, be expressed. Gibbs settled the business by recessing pairs of columns in the first bay of each side elevation, emphasizing the correspondence between these bays and the tower. Inwood did the same. But the resemblance to St Martin's stops outside the church. Inside, Inwood did what most other architects of the time would have done, introduced a flat ceiling and used columns only to support the galleries. The availability of big timbers from the Baltic probably accounts for the abandonment of nave arcades, and doubtless architects were glad to be relieved of the dreadful complexities of an internal order supporting nave and aisle vaults. But the result is a bareness, an 'institutional' character which has done more than anything to make early ninetenth-century church architecture disliked.

Nobody can accuse St Pancras of bareness, either inside or out. On the outside, the rich ornaments of the Erechtheum are imitated with much ingenuity in terra-cotta, elaborately fixed up with metal supports and cramps. Some are copied from casts of the originals, brought home by the architect. The caryatides are from a paraphrase by Rossi, built up in terra-cotta chunks round cast-iron columns. The tower goes to another

Athenian building for its make-up – the Tower of the Winds – but the adaptation is free and astonishingly successful, for whenever Inwood leaves his avowed prototypes he shows himself possessed of a power of invention which is always fresh and appropriate.

You enter the church through an octagonal vestibule corresponding with the tower above and rather subtly ceiled over a ring of dwarf Doric columns standing in a freize. Beyond this is the great airy space, the body of the church, terminating in an apse with six *verd-antique scagliola* columns. It is rather gloomy now, but was originally well lit, the windows being filled with ground-glass with coloured borders. All the details are well worth looking at – the coffered ceiling, the fanciful gallery columns, the oak pews, the organ case, the superb mahogany pulpit; and some of the earlier mural tablets share the Grecian refinement of their surroundings. Besides all these there is the clerk's vestry occupying the north tribune, a room of much beauty with Ionic columns supporting an oval ceiling.

It is hardly necessary to state that St Pancras was an expensive church. Over £70,000 was spent on it, a few thousand more than Marylebone and about four times as much as the most grandiose products of the Church Commissioners. St Pancras is the queen of early nineteenth-century churches; its architecture earns it the title, as much as its size and cost. Inwood's flair for recapturing that nervous intensity of Greek architecture of the fifth century is very remarkable, and he seems to have had no difficulty in applying it to the commonplace objects of English practice.

The Inwoods were responsible for three other churches and two National schools in St Pancras parish. Two of the churches have, in a less degree, the virtues of the greater building. All Saints, Camden Town, built under the same Act in 1822-4, has a delightful semicircular portico and a cylindrical tower surrounded by columns, but much too thin to be successful. The Ionic order is based on fragments found by Inwood in Greece and now in the British Museum, and very lovely it is, with the shallow metallic delicacy of marble transferred to Portland stone with surprising success (Plate 40a). The other two churches were paid for by the Commissioners. St Peter's, Regent Square, 1824–6 (Plate 39) was half destroyed by bombs and finished off in 1967. It was Greek, again the special Inwood Ionic, but showed a falling off from its predecessors. Again, the circular tower was grotesquely emaciated. St Mary, Somers Town, (1824–7), is one of the most pitiful performances in Gothic revivalism ever perpetrated. It must have been very cheap: one can only suppose that the architect, reluctant to dilute his precious Hellenism under financial stringency, resolved that Gothic might bear the stigma of poverty with less discredit to himself.

By the time St Pancras was completed, the first wave of church building under the Act of 1818 was in full swing. The years 1822–5 saw the commencement or completion of nearly thirty large churches in London, most of them costing between £15,000 and £20,000 and designed to hold about 2,000 people. The Commissioners were advised on architectural matters by the Board of Works, whose three architects, Nash, Soane, and Smirke, had been asked for specimen designs and estimates as soon as the Act was passed. None of these three had a natural predisposition to church building. Soane, although he produced a most original paper design, was not really very interested. Nash was chiefly concerned with the effect of churches as part of the metropolitan scene. Smirke, of course, would slog away at any problem that came his way and produce results never quite lacking in taste but always supremely dull. Besides working on paper and in an advisory capacity, each of these three carried out a few churches for the Commissioners.

Nash, with great wit and ingenuity, contrived to adapt a site at the top of Regent Street so as to provide his new street with an important terminal feature. All Souls, Langham Place, lies approximately at an angle of forty-five degrees to Upper Regent Street, but its circular vestibule, tangential to the church and placed on the axis of the street, closes the vista beautifully, and there is not the least suggesetion of laboured compromise. It is really a case of the application of Nash's circus principle – the introduction of a circus when an abrupt change of direction is necessary – in town planning, extended to the plan of a building. The vestibule, with its effective Roman order and an upper stage comprising a spire rising out of a second colonnade, is amusing and unconventional, and the M.P. who, in 1824, said he 'would give a trifle' to have it pulled down was dull as well as spiteful. The church itself is a hall of some dignity with Corinthian columns rising from the gallery to the flat ceiling. The cost was rather over £18,000 and Bath stone was used to bring the church into harmony with the painted stucco of its surroundings.

There were two other churches in Regent Street, both partly paid for by the Commissioners, and designed under Nash, one by Nash's assistant, George Repton, and the other by the son of an old colleague, C. R. Cockerell. The former, St Philip's, had a Roman Doric portico with a Greek turret above and an interior with two tiers of galleries and a shallow dome. Cockerell's church, St George's or Hanover Chapel, was something quite out of the ordinary, brilliantly planned on the principle

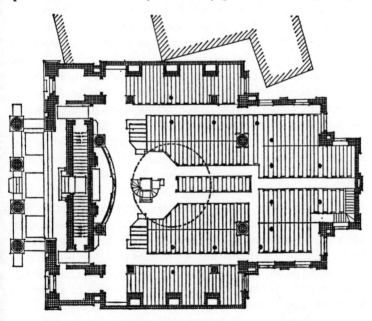

Fig. 30. Plan of Hanover Chapel. Compare Plate 38c.

of a classical atrium and with real and unique appreciation of the achievements of Hawksmoor and Wren, a fine Greek Ionic portico coming over the pavement with towers to either side of it (Plate 38c). Both these churches have been demolished.

Nash's only other personal contribution to the church-building movement was the ridiculous cheap Gothic church of St Mary, Haggerston, with its tall thin western tower surmounted by a trivial lantern. It was a contemptible production, though one could not help being fascinated by its extreme oddity. A bomb hit it in 1941 and left not one stone standing on another.

Sir John Soane contributed three churches and to compare them is to see how difficult it was even for Soane's remarkable mind to grip the problem and resolve it into that harmonious unity of which in other spheres he was capable. His thesis design for the Commissioners is an improvisation on a theme basically Gothic but transposed into Soanean geometry. His executed churches are more conventional. Two, St Peter's, Walworth, and Holy Trinity, Marylebone, are much alike in general outline, but to study the variations is to see some of the workings of Soane's mind. The anomaly of a tower riding on a roof Soane put out of court at once so that in neither case is there a pediment. At Walworth (1823-4, the first to be built) the columns are recessed in the façade, an unbroken cornice proceeds serenely across them, and above is a very slim tower. One is conscious of Soane's delicate sense of surface and contrast, but also of a weakness in the opposition of vertical and horizontal, which he evidently recognized himself. At Marylebone (Plate 40b) he corrected it by bringing forward the columns and elaborating the tower, aiming at a more complicated equilibrium between 'up' and 'across'; but at Marylebone the Soane sensibility is lost, and neither church is wholly successful. The interiors of both are interesting, with their round-arched arcades reminiscent of the thesis design. The ceilings are flat, but prominence is given to the chancel by the introduction of segmental cross arches. At Walworth, the original altar-piece survives.

Soane's third church, at Bethnal Green, is totally different. Here is neither portico nor tower, but a west end with a recessed centre under a segmental arch and a tiny bell cote above, very conspicuously in the Soane manner, but not very beautiful. The body of the church has been practically rebuilt. It is curious what an ill effect the Commissioners' requirements seem to have had on this remarkable man, especially when one remembers that he designed things as beautiful as the chapel at Wardour. Admittedly, he considered the money provided inadequate, but the whole spirit of the Act, which insisted on the least expense for the largest number, seems to have discouraged him. Perhaps, even more, it was the spirit of the times, and the deflated condition of early nineteenth-century churchmanship, which saw to it that no metropolitan church can be counted among the masterpieces of Soane.

It took more than an Act of Parliament and more than an unfavourable psychological atmosphere to put the third member of the Board of Works trio off his stroke. But Robert Smirke was even-tempered to a fault and so long as he was allowed to put up a good big Greek Ionic order he was content to let the rest of the building take shape in easy subservience. His interiors are quite without emotion and have only enough thought in them to ensure the neatness and respectable finish which, to be fair, Smirke always gives us. External effect did interest him and at St Mary's, Wyndham Place (1821–3), on a site at the end of a newly created vista on the Portman estate, his portico does look very handsome (Plate 40c). The tower which rises above it, however, is as witless as Nash's at All Souls is witty; it has nothing to say and goes to enormous lengths to say it. Smirke evidently felt that if Greek Ionic must keep company with a tower, the tower should exhibit no trace of the un-Grecian tradition of Wren and Gibbs. A very proper point of view; but Smirke's mere evasion is put to shame by Inwood's clever results at St Pancras and Camden Town.

The Wyndham Place church was preceded by the very similar church of St Anne, Wandsworth (1820–2), where the tower is raised on a vestibule, preceded by an Ionic portico, and succeeded by another, duller church, St John, West Hackney (1821–3)[1], where, probably for cheapness' sake, the architect had to substitute Greek Doric for his beloved Ionic.

1. Destroyed 1940–1.

So much for the churches designed by the three leaders of the profession. It now remains to say something of the churches handed out by the Commissioners and the parish committees to other, less famous men. Four of these churches demand to be considered as a group. They are the four which were built in the enormous parish of Lambeth, which stretched from the Thames right down to Brixton, and which, some time after their erection, were christened the 'Waterloo' churches. Who named them thus, when and why, we do not know. The idea of constituting some of the churches thank-offerings for Victory was canvassed in the Parliamentary debates of 1818 but never officially adopted.

The four churches are St Matthew, Brixton, St Mark, Kennington, St Luke, West Norwood, and St John, Waterloo Road (Plate 40d). All were built between 1822 and 1824. All cost between £15,000 and £18,000. All have Greek porticos. All have towers. The architects got their commissions by combining success in competition with local interest (the Act recommended that architects who were parishioners should receive special consideration). St Matthew's, Brixton, is by C. F. Porden, nephew of the designer of that remarkable Gothic adventure, Eaton Hall, and of the Prince Regent's Indian stables at Brighton. Porden had supervised the building of St Pancras for the Inwoods, and some of his details – the doors and altar rail – have the Inwood touch. Very boldly, he put his tower at the east end, leaving his Greek Doric portico to speak its classical language without interruption. The east window, flanked by Doric columns, gets indirect light through the tower. St Mark's, Kennington, is nominally by D. R. Roper, a well-known surveyor in the parish; but here the real architect was A. B. Clayton, a rather mannered designer whose work is apt to appear under other people's names. Here again the portico is Greek Doric. The tower which broods over it is ingeniously composed of Greek elements.

The other two churches are both by one architect, Francis Bedford, of whom we know little, except that he travelled in Greece, corresponded with Cockerell on the subject of Greek architecture, and that he was one of the runners-up in the com-

petition for St Pancras. St John's, Waterloo Road, is a church
with a Greek portico and a tower – a tower which does its best
to be the *kind* of tower Ictinus *might* have put on the Parthenon
if the Athenians had had the advantage of belonging to the
Church of England. I mean that it avoids the traditional silhouette tricks and has the ears of a Greek stele. Bedford's other
'Waterloo' church, at Norwood, magnificently sited on rising
ground, has a Corinthian portico embodying the details of the
Epidauros tholos. The tower is merely a modification of that
at St John's.

The Waterloo churches certainly made a fine show and there
are a dozen or so other churches in London designed on the
same scale and about the same time. Bedford designed two
other churches – one in Trinity Square, Southwark; the other
a duplicate of St John's, in Camberwell. Basevi, Soane's brilliant
and favourite pupil, did St Mary's, Greenwich (demolished
1935); Gandy-Deering achieved a high level of success at St
Mark's, North Audley Street, where columns *in antis* and a bell
turret are combined in the most accomplished way; Francis
Edwards, the public house and brewery man, did St John's,
Hoxton, perhaps the least honourable of the classical churches;
Hardwick the younger did the soulless Christ Church, Marylebone, while his father combined an Ionic portico with a Gothic
spike quite charmingly at King Square, off Old Street; Hollis
attempted a Grecian purification of St Martin-in-the-Fields in
the expensive church of All Saints, Poplar (not a Commissioners' Church); Hakewill, at St Peter's, Eaton Square, tried the
Hawksmoor device of giving solid epaulettes to his west front
to suggest a basis for the tower; Lapidge, a good bridge-builder,
built the clumsy church in St Peter's Square, Hammersmith;
William Chadwell Mylne was responsible for the square-cut
Gothic church of St Mark, Myddleton Square, on the New River
Company's Estate. That is nearly all, but I have left two
really able architects to the end – James Savage and Charles
Barry.

Savage designed two churches in London, the first being the
new parish church for Chelsea – St Luke's – begun in 1820 and
only partly paid for by the Commissioners (Fig. 31; Plate 38a). It

is a Gothic church and Savage took his Gothic seriously, even adventuring as far as a complete stone vault from end to end of the building, propped by flying buttresses spanning the aisle roofs. Magdalen Tower, King's Chapel, and Bath Abbey have evidently been carefully studied (no doubt in Britton's engravings) and there is an air of competence and consequence about the design which makes one respect its architect very much. The interior has real dignity and the fittings are carefully detailed. The criticisms of the building are, of course, obvious. Eastlake remarked that it had a 'machine-made' look, meaning, of course, that there is no real *experience* of Gothic building behind it, only a professional acquaintance with Gothic pattern. And the fact that this acquaintance is rather more than superficial makes it all

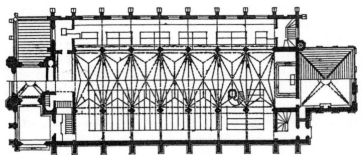

Fig. 31. Plan of St Luke's Chelsea. Compare Plate 38a.

the more difficult to judge the building objectively, as one can judge a Gothic building of the time of Adam and Wyatt objectively. The really trivial 'machine-made' Gothic of the eighteenth century is pretty enough; but Savage means us to take his scholarship seriously and it is rather embarrassing.

Savage was, of course, an architect in the current academic tradition and his later church, St James's, Bermondsey, leaves no doubt about his merits. Built in 1827–9, a few years later than most of the churches mentioned in this chapter, it carefully avoids the stupidities and assembles the merits of most of them. The boldly silhouetted tower stands over a four-column portico, but a podium intervenes heavy enough to destroy the roof-riding impression which was the bane of church architects of those days. The detail is Greek but never pedantic; and the interior is, for once, a really fine thing, with an Ionic order rising from the galleries. St James's is not so original as anything of Cockerell's, or so intriguing as Soane, but it has solid merits.

And now Barry. In 1820, this gifted young man – he was only twenty-five – returned from his travels. He had seen Italy, Greece, Asia Minor, Palestine, Syria, and Egypt. He came back to London and started with industry, humility, and hope to build a career. The very first job he got was the remodelling of the little old church at Stoke Newington. Then came two Commissioners' churches in the Manchester area, the first begun in 1822. Next year he won the competition for St Peter's, Brighton; and in 1825 or 1826 he was commissioned by the Rector of Islington to build three churches in that parish – one at Holloway, one at Ball's Pond, and one in Cloudesley Square. It is not clear why Barry, with his accumulated knowledge of Greek, Roman, and Italian work, should have elected to dive at once into the one thing he had not studied at all – Gothic. Presumably his employers had decided leanings that way, or we might have had some London churches as delightful as the Italian Brunswick Chapel at Brighton. Anyway, Barry's London churches are all Gothic. Sir Gilbert Scott in his *Recollections* calls them 'really respectable and well-intentioned', and that, from a Gothic Revivalist's point of view, is as much as can be said; while from a broader angle there is certainly nothing to add. They show as little genuine experience of Gothic as St Luke's, Chelsea, and if they have slightly greater copybook accuracy than Inwood's dreadful church at Somers Town or Nash's silly steeple at Haggerston, it makes them less, not more, interesting than these. Barry did not think much of them either, referred to them in later life with half-humorous contempt, made a point of destroying the drawings, and, says his biographer, 'would have still more gladly destroyed the originals'. Each church cost round about £11,000, much less than the Waterloo churches, but expensive compared with many of the skinflint products of the succeeding decades. They are in brown brick with stone dressings and there is nothing about them which suggests that they are, in fact, the products of an architect of exceptional powers.

These, then, are the churches of the early nineteenth-century movement in its earlier and least parsimonious phase. Most of them have high architectural pretensions, and some few – but only a few – have architectural qualities of a high order. There is an element of indecision, of weakness, in all of them. This was felt at the time. John Britton, not a perceptive critic certainly, but one who voiced the views of educated feeling, said this of the churches: 'By some singular circumstances and coincidences of the times which we cannot easily account for ... there have been scarcely any pre-eminent specimens of art in the edifices erected. There are few we can fully approve and admire, but many that provoke censure.'[1] Almost any responsible writer would have said the same. Here was a great opportunity which had missed fire. People had expected something better, though what they had expected they probably hardly knew themselves. Some certainly felt that Gothic should have been more used; others that cast-iron with its capacity for precision and its indestructibility by fire should have been exploited. All agreed with Soane's view[2] that the church-building period of Wren and Hawksmoor had produced very much nobler results. But the general disappointment and dissatisfaction did not find voice until Pugin, with furious hyperbole, announced that 'a more meagre, miserable display of architectural skill never was made, nor more impropriety and absurdities committed than in the mass of paltry churches erected under the auspices of the Commissioners – a disgrace to the age – both on the score of their composition, and the miserable sums that have been allotted to their construction'.[3]

This is going rather far, but certainly there was something wrong. What was it? The answer is supplied by the social scene and the church's relation to English life at the time. The church was the preserve of a secure class – that alloy of new wealth and faded aristocracy which, whether under Whig or Tory guise, complacently weighed the scales of Government in its own favour. Security is the enemy of vital religion and

1. *Public Buildings of London*, Introduction to vol. 2.
2. *Lectures*, ed. A. T. Bolton, P. 166.
3. *Contrasts*, 1836, p. 50.

the church, which a century before had been a harvest field of political ideals, became a conservatory of social conventions; such a situation could hardly produce great churches. Where nobody is much interested in the function of a building it is hard for its architect to be so; and even if churches like Marylebone and St Pancras required and stimulated a certain style and glamour, the same could not be said of churches handed out by the State to sparse, anonymous suburbia. Here there was not even the stimulus of a rich, educated, and critical congregation. Parliament asked simply for 'fit and proper accommodation for the largest number of persons at the least expense', and the requirement was fulfilled.

These churches were designed at a time when the mysteries of ritual were contemned and rhetoric, at least in the Church of England, had declined to platitude. It was not the age of the preacher any more than it was the age of the priest. It was the age merely of the congregation. It follows from this that the architect was inhibited at the outset from being anything but wholly non-committal. On the other hand he was fully conscious that in an age which talked as much about 'improvements' as we do about planning, external display was expected from him; and it was natural perhaps that he should turn to the Greek Temple as a type of building whose exterior was imposing and whose interior, so far as the knowledge of contemporary scholarship went, was a complete blank. That is the distressing thing about these churches; their interiors are nothing, and the building which is designed to contain a *nothing* is not likely to be a good building however much care is given to its exterior.

Nevertheless, the London churches of 1820–30 have a certain interest; and as subjects for the exercise of criticism they afford endless entertainment and delight, with their faults and follies and their occasional brilliant successes; while to the architects of the greatest talent and who struggled hardest – to Soane and Cockerell, Inwood and Savage – we owe a genuine debt of gratitude and admiration.

A mere postscript to this chapter must suffice for the architecture which proceeded from religious bodies other than the established church. In its earlier phases it might well be called the architecture of repression, since a Roman Catholic chapel, a Synagogue, and a Methodist preaching house of the eighteenth century presented to the street a façade indistinguishable (except in the matter of a bell-cote) from the very plainest proprietary chapels of the national church.

The Roman church suffered the severest repression and, until the second Relief Act of 1791, only the Embassy Chapels, the Church in Moorfields, and a few missions were allowed to the Catholics of London, and almost all of these had suffered disaster at the hands of the Gordon rioters in 1780. Catholic church architecture in London really begins with the rebuilding of the 'Bavarian Chapel', Warwick Street, in 1788: its well-proportioned brick front still remains. Then, after the Act of 1791, came St Patrick's, Soho (rebuilt 1892), St Aloysius, Somers Town (about 1800; now, alas! to be demolished), St Mary's, Cadogan Street (1812; demolished 1879), and St Mary's, Hampstead (1816; the present front dates mostly from 1850). These are, or were, buildings of the simplest kind, inviting no protestant animosity by outward display and providing the worshipper with the merest shreds of sculptural symbolism and imagery. In 1817, however, came the handsome church of St Mary, Moorfields, where, for the first time in nineteenth-century London, the setting of the mass was lavishly and splendidly dramatized. The architect was John Newman, one of Smirke's assistants, and he provided an elliptical apse with an internal colonnade executed in Como marble by G. B. Comolli, a pupil of Canova, who seems to have visited London solely to execute this commission. Behind the colonnade concealed lighting, contrived in the French manner, irradiated a panorama of Calvary, painted by Allio Aglio (Plate 41a). The exterior of the church had a pretentious Corinthian façade for which Newman disclaimed responsibility; its composition suggests it, fantastically enough, as the prototype of many Congregational churches of the forties and fifties. St Mary's, Moorfields, was demolished in 1899 but Comolli's carved marble columns were skilfully re-used by George Sherrin in his new St Mary's, Eldon Street, where they may still be admired.

The Jews were represented in Georgian London by a very small number of synagogues, the most ancient being that of the Spanish and Portuguese Jews, Dukes Place, rebuilt with great splendour after the Great Fire and still happily in existence. To this was added, in 1788–90, the very fine German Synagogue, built by James Spiller, the architect of Hackney Church, with tall Ionic colonnades and a flat panelled ceiling. This interesting work, the only substantial contribution of the Jewish faith to the architecture of Georgian London, was lost in the blitz of 1940–41.

The places of noncomformist worship have a much more expansive and complicated history – a history, however, of shelter rather than of architecture. An early noncomformist chapel invariably represents the initiative of a preacher, supported by his congregation. A dividing line scarcely exists between a 'proprietary chapel' of the establishment, built by a landlord or a clergyman, and a nonconformist preaching-house, built by a preacher and congregation. Wesley's Chapel in the City Road, Whitefield's in Tottenham Court Road, and Rowland Hill's in Blackfriars Road, all three individual adventures by ordained clergymen, were mentioned at the beginning of this chapter. There were many others, from the 1780s onwards, and by the time of Waterloo chapel-building by the Methodists was being conducted with enormous vigour. So much so that in 1815 the Methodist chapel-building committee was obliged to issue a warning 'to remember especially Mr Wesley's advice, "Beware of building *expensive* Chapels",' and 'not to engage without moral certainty that income from seat-rents, with subscriptions would avoid embarrassment.'

Methodist Chapels were scattered throughout suburban London and a few survive, though often converted to other uses. They are of the plainest description, with pedimented brick fronts and galleried interiors. A chapel of special interest, long since demolished, was Lambeth Chapel in Lambeth Bridge Road (Plate 41b), which was perhaps the prototype of nearly identical chapels in Hull, Stockton, and elsewhere in the north.

Two Scottish Presbyterian clergymen with markedly individual conceptions of the conduct of worship, contributed buildings of some character to the latest phase of Georgian London.
The Rev. Alexander Fletcher filled the domed Albion Chapel
in Moorgate[1] from 1816 till his suspension (as the result of a
breach-of-promise case) in 1824, when he quitted the Scots
Secession Church and employed William Brooks (whom we
shall meet again) to build the Finsbury Chapel, a clever design,
with portals flanking a raised Ionic portico. Neither of Fletcher's
chapels now stand.

The other Presbyterian adventure was until lately represented
by the arrogant 'York Minster' frontispiece of the Rev. Edward
Irving's church in Sidmouth Street, Regent Square, designed by
young William Tite, and executed in Bath stone, about 1827,
with a common stock-brick preaching-box behind.

The Unitarians, with their strong intellectual following,
might have been expected to produce architecture of distinction;
but nothing is recorded of greater mark than the Greek Doric
Chapel in Stamford Street and a grossly detailed Ionic chapel
situated, like so many temples of the unorthodox faiths, in Finsbury.

The Baptists, for all their long history, have left little architecture in London. A late-seventeenth-century chapel survives
at Deptford. Of the important Keppel Street Chapel, said to
have been designed by Heathcote Tatham, no records are dis-
coverable.

The Friends were active builders after Waterloo and their
meeting-houses at Wandsworth (1778) and Peckham (1826)
survive – buildings of endearing simplicity, whose architecture
reproaches the childish pretentiousness of Fletcher and Irving
and their like, who brought nonconformist architecture to the
brink of that awful abyss in which, throughout the succeeding
era, it remained.

1. Elmes, in *Metropolitan Improvements*, records that it was 'designed
by a young architect of the name of Jay'. William Jay (*c.*1794–1837) went
to America in 1817 and practised in Georgia.

CHAPTER 17

Private Wealth and Public Architecture

THE State, urged and rallied by the Sovereign, was the first and principal provider of monumental architecture. But the picture of late Georgian London shows us good buildings and large buildings paid for by corporate bodies of many kinds, from ancient religious foundations to joint-stock companies. To analyse and group them all would render this chapter a mere table, and it will be wiser to select representative buildings which not only indicate the sources of wealth which became available for building but have some artistic value in their own right.

At the foot of Highgate Hill stands Whittington College, a Gothic building ranged round three sides of a quadrangle, with a gabled chapel in the centre. George Smith was the architect, in his capacity of Surveyor to the Mercers' Company and his Gothic is meant to mark the antiquity of the foundation which his building was to serve. The Whittington charity had its medieval home on College Hill but moved to the sentimentally appropriate site near the 'Whittington Stone' in 1822; the Mercers, who administered the charity under the founder's will, finding at their disposal an accumulation of wealth sufficient to pay for a statue of Whittington as well as a great many crockets.

Medieval wealth paid for other buildings of the same kind. St Katherine's Hospital, in Regent's Park is a similar case. The old buildings of this twelfth-century foundation stood near the Tower of London, but in 1829 yielded place to St Katherine's Dock, and the Royal Hospital of St Katherine-by-the-Tower was royally rehoused in Gothic buildings by one of Nash's pupils – Ambrose Poynter. There is a graceful 'King's College' chapel showing a Bath stone front to the park and brick to Albany Street. Opposite, in the Park proper, was a comfortable Gothic residence for the master.

A third case of a charity rebuilt is that of Aske's Hospital or the Haberdashers' Almhouses[1] at Hoxton. Here the rebuilding took place in 1825 on the site of the previous building, which was by Wren's colleague, Robert Hooke. As there was no medieval tradition to be signalled by crockets the new building was allowed to be Greek and has a Doric portico of four columns, the architect being D. R. Roper.

Plenty more examples still exist of ancient charities rehoused. Many have been destroyed. The really excellent Tudor buildings which John Shaw, senior, designed for Christ's Hospital disappeared at the beginning of this century, when the school moved to Horsham. George Smith's classical front to St Paul's School came down in 1885, coincident with the move to Hammersmith.

The lawyers, the physicians, and the surgeons all rehoused themselves, wholly or partly. The Inner Temple chose Smirke for their architect; the Middle Temple employed Hakewill. In both cases, the architect bowed to the venerable ghosts of the site and worked in Gothic – Smirke in his Inner Temple library, Hakewill (followed by Savage) in his Plowden Buildings. Smirke's best work in the Temple, Harcourt Buildings, was, however, classical. This and the library were gutted in 1941, revealing an extensive structural use of iron 'fire-proof' sheeting in the library, and J. W. Hiort's patent flues. To the new College of Surgeons, in Lincoln's Inn Fields, Dance had already given a noble Ionic portico in 1806–13; to the new College of Physicians, on the west side of Trafalgar Square, Smirke gave a not less admirable Ionic portico in 1824–5. Neither portico has any particular purpose except to signalize the academic status of the corporation lodged behind it.

More interesting, in many ways, than these rebuildings is the architecture which came out of certain new tendencies in education and religious thought. Quite a number of buildings can be grouped together as representing the vein of radical enlightenment in early nineteenth-century life. They are without exception classical and the most interesting of them is the one

1. Now the Shoreditch Technical Institute.

designed to house the greatest educational adventure of the time – the London University (Plate 36a).

Thomas Campbell brought the idea of a metropolitan, non-sectarian university back with him from Bonn in 1820.[1] He and Brougham and Jeremy Bentham worked on it so fast and with such good indications of success that by 1825 a site in Gower Street had been bought and Bentham had advertised for architectural drawings in the Press. William Wilkins's design was accepted, against those of C. R. Cockerell[2] and others, chiefly, one imagines, because he had built Downing College, Cambridge, and other buildings in that University, and partly, perhaps, because of the immediately striking character of his design.

This 'adopted design' was published in 1826 and the plan is shown to contain all the elements – decidedly continental – of the new university idea. There is, of course, no chapel – this pointed omission allowing a great assembly hall to be made the central feature of the building. The wings adjoining the hall comprise suites of museums and libraries; returning towards Gower Street they accommodate various minor offices, while at four points big semicircular lecture theatres project to the rear and sides. Architecturally, the great feature is the central decastyle portico, raised on a podium and prefacing the assembly hall, behind which is an octagonal vestibule surmounted by a dome.

In the execution of this design (1826–7) a very unfortunate thing happened. The assembly hall was omitted. But its decastyle portico and the great array of steps leading up to it were retained. The result is that the steps and portico now lead to nothing except a disappointing octagonal lobby with a light-well in the centre; so that the portico is now, in fact, nothing more than a 'set piece', an architectural charade which reminds one forcibly that Wilkins was very much a man of the theatre.

The portico, by itself, is one of the most delicate in London;

1. H. Hale Bellot, *University College, London, 1826–1926* (1929).
2. Whose design, preserved in the Victoria and Albert Museum, is extremely fine.

but the whole design of University College has just those qualities and just those weaknesses which we saw in his Trafalgar
Square building. The wings have a too abrupt relation to the
centre, being married to the portico neither in rhythm nor
alignment; the dome, moreover, though charming in detail,
is as petty as the one over the National Gallery – a mere model
of a dome. The two lesser domes which Wilkins proposed for
the centre pavilions of the forward wings would merely have
mocked the initial mockery; but the wings were not begun
till 1868, when Professor Hayter Lewis wisely thought out something quite different. The portico is a treasure; but it must be
owned that an ability to plan would have been a rather valuable
asset in an architect so closely associated with the aspirations of
Utilitarianism.

The foundation of the University of London had a remote but
curious architectural repercussion which must be mentioned
in passing. To counterbalance the free-thinking radicalism of
Brougham and Bentham, a group of Tory churchmen, headed
by the Rev. George d'Oyley, set about founding an opposition
or complementary establishment with an Anglican bias – King's
College. With King and Government on their side, they were
able to secure the gift of a site – the land adjoining Somerset
House on the east.[1] But one of the conditions imposed was that
the new College should be responsible for completing the river
front of Somerset House according to Sir William Chambers's
very costly and elaborate design. It was a hard condition but it was
fulfilled. Just within the time-limit (1835) and with the college on
the verge of bankruptcy, Sir Robert Smirke finished the job.

The provision of educational facilities for the middle classes
was undertaken with enthusiasm all over England. 'Athen-
aeums', 'Lyceums', 'Porticos', and 'Literary and Philosophical'
institutions were founded everywhere by groups of people who
could collect sufficient subscribers to build an appropriate home
and furnish it with a library. Most of them belong to the
provinces. London's pioneer establishment was the Royal Institution, founded in 1799. The London Institution (Plate 37a)

1. F. J. C. Hearnshaw, *The Centenary History of King's College*, 1929.

followed in 1806 and built its home in Finsbury Circus in 1815–19. The building no longer stands; it was acquired for the School of Oriental Studies in 1912 and demolished in 1936.

But the London Institution should not be forgotten. Its architect, William Brooks, designed for it one of the best small libraries in London (Plate 37b) – a long first-floor room, with projecting book-stacks forming six bays on each of the long sides, these stacks supporting a gallery to give access to the higher shelves. In addition, there was a splendid horse-shoe lecture-theatre, neatly linked to the main building by an octagon vestibule. And the façade of the building, which commanded Finsbury Circus, was a well-balanced composition, with details tinged by an admiration for Soane.

There were plenty of other institutions, some educational, some charitable, some newly born, some perhaps half a century old, which housed themselves with some grandeur. Almost all were Greek, with good, simple fenestration, and a portico – Doric or Ionic – to mark the status of the institution. Some of these buildings still stand. For instance, there is the London Orphan Asylum at Hackney (W. S. Inman, c. 1823), now used by the Salvation Army. Here is an immense Greek Doric chapel with colonnade wings, the detail throughout being executed in Hamelin's patent mastic. There is the pleasant, spacious court-yard and porticoed chapel of the Licensed Victuallers' Asylum at Peckham, built about 1831. Others were damaged in the war and have disappeared since. There was Highbury College, a training college for the Independent ministry, built from designs by J. Davies in 1825–6; the order was Greek Ionic and the design owed something to Smirke. Homerton College (Samuel Robinson, 1823), another seminary for dissenting ministers, architecturally less ambitious, stood in Homerton High Street.

Others again can be recalled in T. H. Shepherd's careful drawings. None are first-rate architecture but almost all evince that curious ambition to possess an Athenian portico, even at the expense of all other architectural amenity. The New Caledonian Asylum (George Tappen, 1827–8), whose purpose was the wholly practical one of keeping the orphans of Scottish soldiers out of the gutter, was prefaced by Parthenon columns carried up the full height of the façade. And the Asylum for Female Orphans in Lambeth (L. W. Lloyd, 1826) admitted its poor little inmates through a portal guarded by Greek Ionic sentinels.

Robert Smirke's insistence on the exhibition of Athenian beauties against a non-committal background haunts all these buildings, but few architects could emulate Smirke's subtle spacing and conscientious finish. Nevertheless, the porticos sanctioned the worthiness of the institutions in the eyes of governors and subscribers and stamped their efforts with a conspicuous and respectable seal, even if the users of the building were not thereby greatly edified.

Vauxhall Bridge, Waterloo Bridge, and Southwark Bridge were built between 1813 and 1819 and it is an astonishing fact that all three of these great 'public works' were projected by private individuals and carried through as financial speculations by companies incorporated under private Acts of Parliament. It is also remarkable that they were projected during one of the gloomiest phases of the Peninsular War. And, having regard to this speculative origin in bad times, it is impressive to note that all three, when completed, were first-rate examples of the art and science of the engineer.[1]

The original Hammersmith Bridge came a few years later and was projected by the Hammersmith Waterworks Company. Only the rebuilt London Bridge of 1824–31 was built by a public body – the City Corporation – and assisted out of Treasury Funds.

The explanation of the very striking initiative displayed in the first three cases is probably the simple one that a great many people were making a great deal of money during the war and were glad to adventure some of their profits in so solid and unquestionably useful a thing as a Thames bridge. Whatever the

1. For descriptions and engravings of the bridges see Britton and Pugin, *Public Buildings of London*, 1825–8, and, for further particulars, *Wheatley and Cunningham, London Past and Present*, 1891. Also *Select Committee . . . to inquire into the State and Condition of the Bridges over the Thames*, 1854, and L.C.C. *Bridges*, 1914.

outcome of the war, nobody could doubt that toll-receipts from these privately owned bridges in central London would maintain a high and more or less calculable level. They might even prove to be a safer as well as a more profitable investment than Government stock.

In June 1809, within a few weeks of each other, the Acts for Vauxhall and Waterloo Bridges received the Royal Assent. Vauxhall was begun as Regent's Bridge in May 1811, Waterloo at Strand Bridge in October of the same year. Both companies retained John Rennie as their engineer; Rennie being then fifty and the famous designer of docks, harbours, and canals, as well as the wonderful bridge over the Tweed at Kelso. But at Vauxhall Bridge, Rennie's work proceeded only a little way before the company ran short of funds. Rennie revised the design from a seven-span structure of blue Dundee limestone to an eleven-span structure with iron arches, but it was still too costly; and when the work was resumed Rennie was superseded by James Walker. Walker's bridge had nine iron arches; it was completed in 1816 and replaced by the present bridge in 1906.

For Waterloo Bridge (Plate 44a) funds were more easily forthcoming, perhaps partly because of the energetic personality of Ralph Dodd, the projector-in-chief. The Act of 1809 provided for the raising of £500,000 and an additional Act of 1813 allowed for another £200,000. A third Act of 1816 bestowed further powers on the company and gave the bridge its patriotic name. The ultimate cost, including the approaches, was £1,050,000. It turned out a bad speculation because people could so easily avoid the toll by using the free bridges of Blackfriars or Westminster.

The magnificence of Waterloo Bridge was amply acknowledged during the long and unsuccessful struggle for its preservation from 1923 onwards, and there is no need for further emphasis on its excellence. But the reasons are worth inquiry. In the first place its scale was enormously impressive. The scale of London architecture, and indeed of English architecture as a whole, is small; it easily descends to meanness. Hawksmoor and Vanbrugh aimed at bigness of scale, but the middle and late Georgians – Chambers, Adam, Soane, and Nash – designed small and even diminutive; they were always prone to subdivide and

elaborate so as to give an interesting and eloquent play of
shadows.

Rennie's first interest was not in shadows, but in structure.
The noble *larghetto* of his nine semi-elliptical arches provided
in itself enough architectural excitement, especially with the
hard geometric pattern of the radiating granite voussoirs. Nevertheless, following Mylne at Blackfriars and his own precedent at
Kelso, Rennie gave the bridge an order. To Rennie as to Telford
and Fowler, the Greek Doric had a simplicity and structural
nobility more consonant with engineering works than any of
the Vitruvian orders. So he raised pairs of Doric columns on
each pier, making them support a continuous entablature of
the simplest character, breaking outwards over each pier. He
added a grey Aberdeen granite balustrade of the traditional
Roman pattern, and there he left the design, all the better for
the lack of 'modelling' which a Smirke or a Wilkins might
have given it – and which would have reduced its scale. The
scale of Waterloo Bridge was dictated by the structure, not by
the designer's handling of detail. Hence its sheer magnificence.

Waterloo Bridge was bought by the Metropolitan Board of
Works for £475,000 and opened free of toll in 1878. In 1923 a
serious movement was observed in one of the piers and in 1926
the L.C.C. decided to remove the bridge and build a new one.
This they achieved in the face of lively public and parliamentary
opposition. The new three-arch structure is very fine, but it is
instructive to note how the architectural embellishments, few
and discreet as they are, have managed to rob the bridge
of that impersonal grandeur of scale which the old structure
possessed.

Rennie's next work was for the Southwark Bridge Company,
who had obtained an Act in 1811 (Plate 44b). This company
found itself up against City opposition, on the score that the
bridge at first proposed would form an obstacle to river traffic.
The only way to satisfy the Corporation and obtain the Act had
been to undertake to cross the river in three spans. This had
never been attempted, although Telford had put forward his
famous one-span iron proposals as early as 1801. Rennie, like
Telford, resorted to iron.

The centre arch spanned 240 feet, which was 4 feet more than the bridge over the Wear at Sunderland, finished in 1796 and considered one of the engineering marvels of Britain. The voussoirs constituting the eight segmental ribs in each arch were of solid cast iron bolted together so that each rib was a more or less self-supporting structure and the thrust of the exceedingly flat arches was minimized. The piers, of Bramley Fall and Whitley stone, were bonded vertically as well as horizontally in their lower parts, ensuring maximum stability. The spandrels between the ribs and the roadway were filled with triangulated iron strutting. The bridge was, from an engineer's point of view, more ambitious and more masterly than Waterloo Bridge. Architecturally it was less striking, for the obvious reason that three very flat segmental arches have a less exciting rhythm than a succession of nine semi-elliptical arches. But Rennie's faculty for giving engineering an architectural twist was as manifest at Southwark as at Waterloo. The iron ribs were gracefully framed by the stone piers, cornice, and balustrade; and the criss-cross strutting in the spandrels was in perfect geometrical harmony with its bounding lines. Once again, the scale of the structure must have been inspiring; Dupin, a French engineer, said[1] of it 'c'est le pont des géants'.

Southwark Bridge cost the company about £800,000 and was opened in 1819. Like Waterloo, it was a bad speculation[2] and the directors 'never had a halfpenny for forty years, nor even a cup of coffee'. It was bought by the City Corporation, in 1866, for £218,868 and rebuilt unadventurously with five arches in 1919.

Rennie's third great undertaking was the rebuilding of London Bridge, but he only lived to make the preliminary designs, and the credit for the realization belongs to his son. The rebuilding had been under consideration since 1801, when a great volume of advice was obtained from architects, engineers, professors, generals, and others and it was then that Telford's famous one-span proposal was put forward – and shelved with the rest. The resumption of the war stopped everything and it was not till 1823, two years after the elder Rennie's death, that

1. *Notice Nécrologique sur John Rennie, Esq.*, 1821.
2. *Select Committee*, etc., *ut supra*.

an Act was obtained. The main cost was borne by the City, but the Treasury contributed substantially (out of the Coal Tax) on condition that a greater width of roadway was adopted and certain improvements effected at the approaches. These improvements were placed in the hands of Smirke. Rennie, who had hoped that his brother-in-law, C. R. Cockerell, would be employed, observed[1] that 'a more unworthy set of buildings was never designed', and the little Smirke façade, which still lurks in the shadow of Adelaide House, endorses the judgement.

London Bridge still stands, though slightly altered in the widening of 1903–4. Its five semi-elliptical arches broaden the precedent of Waterloo Bridge, but the ellipses are flatter and consequently the rhythm is less arresting; and there is no classical order. It is a worthy building and it is no fault of the Rennies that it lacks the engineering excitement of Southwark and the architectural grandeur of Waterloo. It was opened by King William IV in 1831.

The fifth Thames bridge of the period was William Tierney Clark's suspension bridge at Hammersmith built by the Hammersmith Water Works Company, under an Act of 1824. Clark adopted the technique which Captain Samuel Brown had used in his chain pier at Brighton and his Union Bridge (1820) over the Tweed near Berwick. The bridge was finished in 1827 and lasted till the present one replaced it in 1887. It was very much cheaper than any of the other bridges and when the company was bought out in 1900 the public had to pay more than twice the cost of the original construction, whereas in other cases they had paid little more than half.

The great clubs of the early nineteenth century were to a great extent a product of the war. Thus, the Travellers'[2], the first to appear, was founded by Castlereagh to encourage the exchange of ideas between Englishmen and foreigners at a time when the Continent had been closed to civilians for twenty years. Founded in 1814, the Travellers' did not build till 1829. The architectural pioneer was, therefore, the United Service, founded by Lord

1. *Autobiography*, 1875.
2. Sir A. Fitzroy, *History of the Travellers' Club*, 1927.

Lynedoch in 1815 for Army and Militia Officers.[1] This Club almost immediately proceeded to look for a site and found one in Lower Regent Street. Smirke (of the Militia) was employed as architect and his design, executed in 1816–17, struck the key-note for the new club architecture of London (Plate 45a). The older clubs, which were really proprietary coffee-houses – White's, Brooks's, and Boodle's – had been designed very much like private houses, though with a little extra ostentation. Smirke designed an unmistakable public building, with no ostentation at all. For once, he omitted to introduce an order, except for the Greek Doric porch in Charles Street. He grouped his windows in an effective, rather Parisian, way and introduced panels with sculpture in relief. This *astylar* treatment became the rule for club-houses and was followed for more than thirty years. The building soon proved too small for the club, which moved to the corner of Pall Mall in 1827, occupying a new building by Nash, to be described later. Smirke's building was given over to the Junior United Service Club, rebuilt in 1855–7 and demolished in 1951.

The United Service inaugurated the grand era of club building. The University Club, the Union Club, the Oriental, and the Athenaeum followed in quick succession, and by 1830 club life had quite superseded the traditional coffee-house life of the pre-war period. And club architecture had staked out an important claim, later substantiated by Charles Barry in his Travellers' building of 1829–30, in the Reform of 1837–8, and in the much later and more grandiose buildings of the younger Smirke, Basevi, and Parnell & Smith.

The University Club was founded by a group of M.P.s in 1822 and opened in 1826, on a Crown site at the corner of Pall Mall East and Suffolk Place. William Wilkins was the perhaps almost inevitable choice for a University venture of this kind and he designed a building of some distinction, with the Erechtheum order deployed in *anta* form to decorate the principal storey. The plan (Fig. 32) was very much that of a large country villa, adapted to a partially enclosed London site. The coffee room, with the saloon over it, ran from front to back of the

1. Sir L. C. Jackson, *History of the United Service Club*, 1937.

building at the Pall Mall end. Wilkins followed Smirke in providing a Greek Doric porch, but he departed from Smirke's modest reticence by introducing a portico at first floor level on the Pall Mall front. The club was rebuilt in 1906.

The Union Club was founded in the same year as the University for a more general membership (hence the name) and took a Crown site in Trafalgar Square. Smirke was the architect (1824–7) both for the club and for the College of Physicians adjoining it on the north and he united the two in a single monumental block to form an effective west side to the square. The plan of the club was similar, in essentials, to that of the University Club. The principal feature was the morning room running across the south end of the site with a pleasant bay-window in the centre. The Union Club moved to new premises

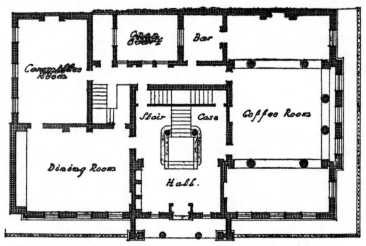

Fig. 32. Ground-floor Plan of the University Club.

in 1925 and Smirke's building was altered to become Canada House. The exterior design was reproduced in stone and some of his exteriors preserved; but the bay window disappeared with the formation of a new entrance.

Crockford's[1] and the Oriental[2] followed in 1826–7 and it is

1. H. T. Waddy, *The Devonshire Club and 'Crockford's'*, 1919.
2. A. F. Baillie, *The Oriental Club and Hanover Square*, 1901.

convenient to describe them together, though no two clubs could be less alike in social character. Crockford's (rebuilt as the Devonshire Club in 1875) was a gambling hell of the most lavish and patrician character. The Oriental (still in existence) was principally designed as a resort of men who had served in the East India Company or whose duty or business had taken them abroad to the eastern hemisphere. Somebody described it as a *nabobery*. It had the early reputation of being a dull club, which nobody could say of Crockford's.

But Crockford's and the Oriental both had the same architect, Benjamin Dean Wyatt. The eldest son of the last architect Surveyor-General, Wyatt might well have qualified for membership of either of his own clubs. After an education at Westminster and Christ Church, Oxford, he accompanied Wellesley to India as his secretary and there will, no doubt, have met the Oriental Club's eventual founder, Sir John Malcolm. Wyatt threw up his diplomatic career in a fit of home-sickness; little else is recorded of his life, but it is known that he passed some part of it in the King's Bench prison, which looks as if he had inherited his father's extraordinary ability to dissipate money. Crockford's would surely have opened its doors to him; perhaps it did.

Architecturally, Wyatt's clubs were very like each other. Both were ponderous in scale (like his earlier Drury Lane theatre) with great slabs of Corinthian pilaster surmounted by an entablature of coarse Greek profile. Crockford's was in St James's Street, and the pilasters were grouped in the centre of the street façade. The Oriental (demolished 1962) had a poor site, facing north, in Tenterden Street, with one end overlooking Hanover Square; here, Wyatt pilastered the ends and slightly recessed the centre (again like Drury Lane).

To the same years as Wyatt's two clubs belong Decimus Burton's Athenaeum and John Nash's new home for the United Service, facing each other in Waterloo Place on the site of old Carlton House. The Athenaeum took the site on the west, the United Service that on the east and in the first instance the idea of the Commissioners of Woods and Forests, and indeed of Nash himself, was that the two buildings should have identical exteriors. There followed two years of extraordinary muddle in the course of which Nash flouted the Commissioners' instructions, misled the Athenaeum committee (although himself a member of the Club), and finally announced that he was 'persuaded of the bad effect ... of an attempt of perfect uniformity'.[1] Nash's building, with its northward-facing double portico, seems almost studiously to avoid looking at Burton's Athenaeum. The latter, perhaps the more interesting of the two, has a generous Doric porch opposite the flank of the United Service.

The virtual founder of the Athenaeum was James Wilson Croker who confessed that he 'thought of it because the University Club, the Travellers', the United Service and other such clubs had superseded and destroyed the old coffee-houses, and I considered that literary men and artists required a place of rendez-vous also'.[2] Decimus Burton was appointed architect in 1824 but his efforts to produce a design must have been bedevilled for some years by the alleged necessity of copying the United Service. When at length the Athenaeum was declared free to live its own architectural life, Burton was able to add what is today its most noticed feature – the full-size copy of the Panathenaic frieze under the cornice. This, executed by John Henning and his sons, is not only effective in itself but has the satisfactory effect of giving the building something of the massive effect of an Italian *palazzo*. This effect Burton was eventually able to echo in the United Service Club where he was brought in, twenty-three years after Nash's death, to give the exterior a handsomer character than its original architect had provided.

Both clubs have interesting interiors, with noble staircase halls of rather similar type – Nash's less ornate but with a finer sense of space – and at least one 100-foot room divided by pairs of classical columns. The Athenaeum, appropriately perhaps, is more ornate and more Grecian. Here, Apollo Belvedere, plaster and gilt, presides over the staircase. Across the road, it is the noble Duke of York, in marble, who has the place of honour.

The story of the post-Waterloo clubs is closed by a smaller but,

1. *Survey of London*, vol. 29: St James, Westminster, Pt i (1960), p. 390.
2. Humphrey Ward, *History of the Athenaeum*, 1926.

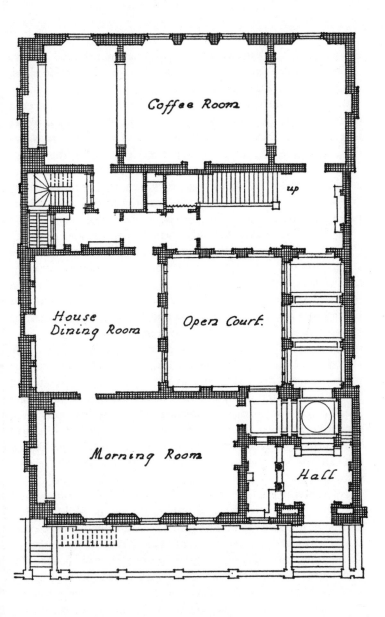

Fig. 33. Ground-floor plan of the Travellers' Club. Compare
Plate 45b.

in another sense, perhaps greater building than the Athenaeum – Charles Barry's new home for the pioneer of all these clubs, the Travellers' (Plate 45b).

Barry was thirty-four when he was commissioned, after a limited competition, to design the Travellers'. His work before that date (1829) had been of three kinds : Gothic *à la mode*, as in his Islington Churches, Greek *à la mode*, as in the Manchester Art Gallery, and, thirdly, an experimental line in the Italian, but emphatically not Palladian, taste. It was mere chance that Barry and not one of his contemporaries introduced this more adventurous Italian manner. All the young men who went abroad after Waterloo seem to have been struck with the idea of giving Vicenza a rest and looking for a change, towards the churches and palaces of Rome, Venice, and Florence. Barry was extraordinarily quick and shrewd in his perceptions and won by a head in the race to exploit the new discoveries. He built a little church at Brighton in Italian as early as 1824 and Mr Attree's villa near the same town was built about the time of the Travellers'.

But it was the Travellers' which made Barry and his style famous. Not content to follow the Smirke-Nash-Burton plan, he placed his principal apartments at front and back of the site and lit the centre from an open court, in the manner of an Italian *palazzo*. He folded up the staircase into a modest space and, generally speaking, economized where his predecessors had been perhaps ostentatiously lavish. The result is that the Travellers' strikes less awe and is more domestic than the earlier clubs.

But it was the handling of the elevations which surprised and delighted both profession and public. Instead of hiding a slate roof behind a balustrade, he constructed an elaborate *cornicione* at the eaves and covered the roof with a passable imitation of Roman tiles. Instead of supplying the garden front with a wrought-iron balcony of the ordinary 'Georgian' kind, he projected a solid-looking balustrade, pierced with an intersecting pattern, on a row of decorative console-brackets; instead of smoothing his rustications into a reluctant enhancement of surface, he enriched them with chamfers, sinking, and vermiculation. To the garden windows he gave shell tympana, Florentine pilasters, and archivolts. The whole effect was vigorous and picturesque, in contrast to the extreme restraint imposed by the Athenian school. The building was the answer to the *malaise* discernible in all the work of the later Greek Revival, the feeling that the capture of Periclean refinement was not an absolute goal after all: that there was still beauty in roughness and vigorous relief.

The Travellers' closes the Georgian chapter in the history of club-houses. Barry's next club, the Reform, the first avowedly political club since the coffee-house days, was begun in the first year of Victoria's reign. There he pursued the Italian theme still more vigorously and from that moment Italian became the Victorian style for every building which could not or would not be Gothic.

At the beginning of George IV's reign most of London's private palaces were elderly buildings in the Palladian taste. Northumberland House was considerably older. But Spencer House, Devonshire House, Burlington House, and Chesterfield House were all Palladian; and some of these could only be called palaces by courtesy.

All were eclipsed when, in 1820, George IV's brother, the Duke of York, was granted a site in St James's on a 999 years' lease. He borrowed money to build the house we now know as Lancaster House and employed Smirke as architect. But George IV so much disliked Smirke's design that the work was stopped, to be recommenced in 1825 on the basis of new plans by Benjamin Dean Wyatt. The Duke died in 1827, £2,000,000 in debt. The Crown became possessed of the unfinished house and sold it to the Marquess of Stafford who roofed it before his death in 1833. His successor, the second Duke of Sutherland, had the task of finishing and decoration and in this he continued to employ Wyatt as designer but placed the execution in the hands of – of all people – Smirke; while at some stage he also introduced Charles Barry.[1]

1. H. Colvin, 'The Architects of Stafford House' in *Architectural History*, vol. i, 1958.

From this unhappy history ensued a house of very indifferent exterior effect but great internal splendour. The difficulty is to know to whom this splendour should be attributed. The tremendous staircase hall was doubtless planned by Wyatt but may have received its finishing touches from Barry. There is evidence, too, that Wyatt initiated the scheme of decoration, harking back to the France of Louis XV, which is the glory of the principal rooms. This was probably the first occasion of a revival, in London, of French interior decoration of the previous century. We find the same kind of thing in Apsley House which the same Wyatt enlarged and remodelled for the Duke of Wellington in 1828. Apsley House, like Lancaster House, has a rather tame and very English exterior but the Waterloo Gallery is gloriously French. Did Wyatt really turn his hand to the mastery of a forgotten (and exceedingly difficult) technique of decoration; or was, perhaps, some French designer found to bring his skill across the Channel and remain the nameless author? Whatever the case, the interiors at Lancaster House and Apsley House established Louis XV as the decorative rule in London high society for seventy years and more – from Buckingham Palace to the Ritz.

Wyatt's two palaces were the only private palaces built in George IV's London; and although the Duke of Clarence made a determined effort to squeeze into St James's alongside his elder brother, the result (for which Nash was reluctantly responsible) was a long way from palatial. Clarence House still exists, but the interior has been entirely re-cast.

There was, however, one other house, which may just be admitted to the category on account of its considerable size and architectural elaboration. This was the double residence, Nos. 14–16 Regent Street, designed by Nash for himself and his relative and friend, John Edwards. It stood on the east side of the street and was built in 1818–24. The two houses interlocked, the office of Nash's house being beneath the principal living rooms of the Edwards establishment. Nash and his wife lived on the first floor of the south wing in a magnificent 'flat' with a long gallery linking the drawing-room and staircase to the dining room; the bedroom suite running alongside the gallery. The

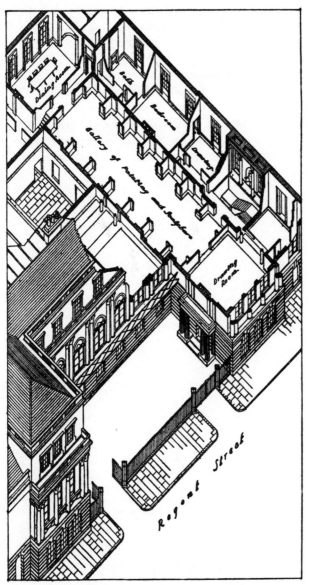

Fig. 34. Axonometric view of Nos. 14 and 16 Regent Street, the houses of John Nash and John Edwards.

house was destroyed in 1923, but the gallery was dismantled during Nash's lifetime and transported to East Cowes Castle, where, among the ruins, scraps of it may still exist.

The category of 'public buildings', in the liberal sense of buildings privately owned but either useful or conspicuous to the public, could be almost indefinitely expanded. The main omissions from our present review are theatres and commercial buildings. The first are always, the second sometimes, of 'public' significance and in any case are of sufficient importance in the general picture of Georgian London to claim our separate attention in subsequent chapters.

CHAPTER 18

A Note on Theatres

THE theatres of Georgian London defy all attempts at chrono-logical grouping and their distribution throughout the chapters of this book would be too confusing to contemplate. The same theatre would have to make several appearances, each time with a different architect, and perhaps for no more significant reason than that its predecessor had just been burnt down. Moreover, theatre-design is a rather special branch of architecture, and the main points about the subject can best be made in a comparative review. As no Georgian theatre interiors survive in London the interest of the subject is somewhat limited, so I shall confine myself to notes on a few really important buildings.

At the beginning of the eighteenth century, Wren's Drury Lane stood much as he had left it. Its ample apron stage pro-jected into an auditorium decorated on either side with giant Corinthian pilasters. At the back were three curved tiers of seats, supported on small Doric columns, in this respect slightly resembling the famous late-eighteenth-century Theatre Royal at Bristol.

Vanbrugh, in 1704–5, built his ambitious opera house in the Haymarket, which, according to Soane[1] was 'no contemptible proof of his genius and abilities'. But we know very little about it except that it had a dome supported on a Corinthian order and was acoustically deplorable.[2] It was much altered, then finally burnt in 1789, when it was rebuilt by a Polish architect, Novosielsky, whose auditorium introduced the horse-shoe shape.

Novosielsky's theatre was probably the first in England to take advantage of the originality displayed in the Grand Théâtre at Bordeaux, a classic of theatre design completed in 1780. London theatres before that date – for instance, Adam's exquisite recast-ing of Drury Lane (Plate 46a) for Garrick in 1775–6 – were

1. *Lectures*, ed. A. T. Bolton.
2. L. Whistler, *Sir John Vanbrugh* (1937), p. 108.

mostly *rectangular*. Bristol (1764-6) is supposed to have been the first English theatre to copy the normal French *semicircular* end. The Haymarket opera house went a step further in borrowing the *horse-shoe* from Bordeaux. The horse-shoe remained the standard shape for large London theatres; it lent itself to the introduction of a circular or domical ceiling, with two spandrels at the proscenium end, and could be considerably elongated without losing the obvious advantages of the shape.

The horse-shoe was used again when Henry Holland rebuilt Drury Lane (Plate 46b) for Sheridan in 1791-4. He gave it a fantastic and rather beautiful interior with a ceiling supported on near-Gothic vaults; it survived only fifteen years.

Adam's Drury Lane and, after 1794, Holland's Drury Lane are theatres of what I have called the Golden Age of Georgian London, illustrating its early and late phases respectively. The appearance of both is accurately preserved in engravings; they are lighter and more fragile in design than their Continental contemporaries and were among the decorative but unhappily transient masterpieces of their age.

In 1808-9 both Covent Garden and Drury Lane were burnt to the ground. The rebuildings which followed produced the two pre-eminent theatres of late Georgian London – Robert Smirke's Covent Garden and Benjamin Wyatt's Drury Lane. Smirke was twenty-seven when he started, with break-neck speed, the designs for Covent Garden. Wyatt was twenty-six when Samuel Whitbread put the commission for Drury Lane into his hands. To each architect the theatre was his first great opportunity – an opportunity as unexpected in war-time as it was tremendous at any time.

Covent Garden was burnt on 20 September 1808; Smirke's new building opened its doors on 18 September 1809. In the circumstances one might expect the design to show symptoms of hasty decision; and in fact the exterior did have the academic defect that the Bow Street façade, with its Greek Doric portico, was unsatisfactorily related to the side and rear elevations. Soane very unkindly made a feature of this defect, with specially drawn diagrams, in his R.A. lectures. He and Smirke had never been particularly good friends.

Covent Garden (Plate 47a) seems to have been a successful theatre. The plan was cleverly put together (on a site totally inadequate to the accommodation demanded) and included a grand staircase directly imitating Chalgrin's very recent work for the Paris Directorate at the Palais du Luxembourg – an example, incidentally, which Soane was to follow many years later in his Scala Regia. This staircase Smirke packed in *alongside* the auditorium and to one side of the central vestibule.

The auditorium was horse-shoe shaped, though less pinched at the proscenium end than Novosielsky's; the decorations appear to have been simple, relying for effect on the unbroken sweep of the five tiers of seating. The theatre was burnt to the ground in 1857 and rebuilt in its present form by E. M. Barry.

At Drury Lane Benjamin Wyatt was more fortunate in his site, which permitted a generous preamble in the way of vestibule and staircase between the entrance and the auditorium. He introduced a domed Corinthian rotunda, approached by grand staircases from left and right. All these features survive and are, in fact, the only interior parts of a Georgian theatre remaining in London (Plate 47b).

In his auditorium, Wyatt followed the Bordeaux plan fairly closely, and his decorations were on much the same scale of enrichment as Smirke's at Covent Garden. But the theatre was very far from successful. In spite of elaborate theoretical studies made and published[1] while the design was in progress, Wyatt failed to grasp the practical issues. His circulation at the stage end was tortuous and constricted and in 1822–3 parts of the building, including the proscenium, were remodelled by another architect, Samuel Beazley.

The exterior of Wyatt's Drury Lane still exists, almost intact (Plate 47b). The façade to the Lane has the inert heaviness of the architect's clubs and palaces, and the square-piered portico, added by Spiller in 1820, provides no light relief. The Ionic colonnade (cast iron), on the north side, was added by Beazley in 1831–2. The Wyatt-Beazley auditorium survived, with sundry alterations, till 1922, when the present one was built.

1. B. Wyatt, *Observations on the principles of a design for a theatre* (1811). Another version appeared in 1813.

It was Samuel Beazley, Wyatt's successor at Drury Lane, who built the old Lyceum in 1816. His auditorium here was part of an ellipse and the decorations, in salmon pink with oiled and burnished gold ornaments and crimson upholstery, were a foretaste of what we think of as the Early Victorian style. Beazley, in fact, was to become the pre-eminent theatre designer of that age. He rebuilt the Lyceum once again in 1831–4 giving it the present portico. And in 1836–7 he built the St James's Theatre which, in spite of much alteration, retained its essential character till its demolition, amid loud public protest, in 1957.

After the Lyceum came two important rebuildings by Nash in the Haymarket, both engaging with 'metropolitan improvements' in that area. The Theatre Royal, Haymarket, was rebuilt in 1820–1 a few yards south of the site which it had occupied for a hundred years, so that the new portico formed, as it still forms, the closing feature of Charles II Street. This theatre, much smaller than the others I have mentioned, was a delightful and wholly successful building. The auditorium was rather old-fashioned, with straight sides and a segmental end and was covered by a flat dome on pendentives. Palm-tree columns, recalling the Brighton Pavilion, supported the ceiling and proscenium and the decoration consisted principally of a network pattern, raised and gilded, on the reddish-purple ground of the box fronts; the interiors of the boxes were finished in maroon. The whole effect must have been gay and charming in the extreme and of all the Georgian theatres it is the Haymarket which one would most willingly recreate. The interior was completely rebuilt in 1879 and again in 1904, but the exterior is intact. Not only the porticoed front to the Haymarket, but the amusing rear elevation in Suffolk Street are worth study.

The other rebuilding in the Haymarket consisted in the reconstruction, by Nash and Repton, of the whole island block in which the King's Opera House was situated. Novosielsky's old auditorium of 1790–1 and the adjoining concert-hall were retained and provided with a grand front in the Haymarket. At the base of this front was an arcade which continued round the sides of the block in Pall Mall and King Charles Street, and again round the western boundary of the site in the form of a long vaulted passage with shops on one side. This passage, the Royal Opera Arcade, still exists, the nostalgic relic of a bold and effective marriage of town-planning and architecture. The remainder of the block was demolished for the construction of Her Majesty's Theatre and the Carlton Hotel in 1892. Now, the Carlton has give place to the sky-scraping New Zealand House; but Royal Opera Arcade has been suffered to remain.

Today, the theatre architecture of Georgian London is irrecoverable except through prints and drawings. We have, it is true, Wyatt's aristocratic staircases and rotunda at Drury Lane and his stucco façade with its four votive altars at the entrance. We have Nash's really fine exterior of the Haymarket. That is all. Something of the Georgian style is certainly recoverable at Covent Garden, where Barry adhered closely to tradition. But the enchantment of the older theatres is completely lost. And what is, perhaps, worse is that no theatre architect of the present has given us an auditorium which rises above mediocrity.

CHAPTER 19

The Trail of Commerce

BUILDINGS manifestly designed for the functions of trade hardly existed before the later part of the period. In the early years, the port of London was a mere succession of timber wharfs, ranged in antique disorder along both banks of the Thames. Warehousing was largely an affair of cellars and out-buildings. The offices of merchants were formed in the ground-floors of their houses. Shops were merely front rooms with en-larged window-openings; markets were streets or squares where booths or shambles were erected. The only buildings associated with the flow of commerce which were architectural in intention were exchanges and customs houses. These, it is true, had an ancestry of great architectural respectability.

But about half-way through the eighteenth century the tide of commerce – the life-stream of the capital – began to leave, so to speak, an architectural deposit in its course, and this is the architecture which now concerns us. As a suggestive pre-liminary, let us glance for a moment at the graph of Britain's eighteenth-century trade.

In 1700 imports and exports together were valued at £13,000,000. The line plods slowly upwards till, at the close of Walpole's ministry, £19,000,000 is reached. Then it sags and recovers only just in time to register £20,000,000 at the begin-ning of the Seven Years' War. That war secured to Britain the trade of both the Indies, of Canada and America, and at its close the curve is already stronger; it sinks again during the American war but rises to £34,000,000 by 1790. Finally, in one mighty leap, the graph touches nearly double that figure in 1800. Now, London was Britain's chief port. The Thames was the resort of an ever-increasing fleet of merchant vessels: east-indiamen with the bulk and silhouette of men-o'-war, west-indiamen from America, ships bringing wine from Spain and fruit from Africa, bulky colliers from Newcastle, whalers from

Greenland, coasting vessels, packets, brigs, lighters, barges, dinghies, and ferry-boats.

All this highly picturesque traffic – excluding only the greater merchantmen – crowded into the Pool. There was only one port authority, the City of London. There was a system of 'legal quays' which was, in effect, a monopoly of dockage exercised by the City to its own enormous profit and, as time went on, to the acute disadvantage and distress of commercial life. At one period, such was the delay in unloading, that scarcity prevailed while plenty lay idle on the water.

It was in the year of the outbreak of war, 1793, that anxiety at the appalling situation resolved itself into action. Tracts opened the subject; meetings, a petition to Parliament, the setting up of a Parliamentary Committee, and the presentation of a Report followed in due order.[1] Vested interests made a mighty show of indignation but crumpled up before the invincible case for reform. Ultimately, an Act enabling the City and a joint stock company to buy land and build a dock and a canal in the Isle of Dogs, received the Royal Assent in July 1799.

That event marks the opening of seven years of vigorous dock construction and the beginning of dockland as we know it today. Previous wet docks on the Thames there had been, but they were private ventures outside the favoured ring of 'legal quays', and necessarily too far down stream to meet the real needs of earlier London trade. There had been the Howland Dock at Bermondsey, built around 1700, with the Dutch-doll symmetry of the age of William III, with double lines of poplars to reinforce the banks and a brick homestead for the Howland family framed in the vista. There had also been Perry's less impressive Brunswick Dock of 1789, with its soaring mast-house. But both these were outside ventures. The dock construction which began in 1799 was radical. It was to clear the river of shipping and to form the mainspring of a whole new district of London.

The cargo-handling docks of the early nineteenth century came in this order. First, the West India Dock, in the Isle of

1. For the history of the Docks see Sir J. G. Broodbank, *History of the Port of London*, 2 vols., 1921.

Dogs, begun 1800. Second, the London Dock at Wapping, begun 1802. Third, the Surrey Docks, begun 1804. Fourth, the East India Dock at Blackwall, begun 1805. Then, after an interval of more than twenty years, the St Katherine's Dock, adjoining the Tower, was added to the number. All were promoted by private companies; all were planned broadly and well; and all availed themselves of the best ability in engineering and produced architectural results whose magnificence can, in a few cases, still be seen and appreciated.

The West India Dock was the first and, till 1940, remained the finest. The engineer in charge was Ralph Walker, with John Rennie, just then engaged on his great bridge at Kelso, as consultant. Two rectangles – the Import dock and the Export dock – lay side by side with the main range of warehouses, designed by George Gwilt and his son, along the north side of the former. The extraordinary engineering grace of the scheme as a whole has, of course, been diminished by alterations and today there is scarcely anything left. One must refer to Daniell's dramatic pictures and the steel-engraved plans of the period to appreciate the clean lines of the approach as it was first cut in the sodden earth of the Isle of Dogs, finished with masonry and cast-iron work of superlative quality.

The London Dock (Plate 48b) at Wapping is less ambitious and less shapely than the West India, but the warehouses are remarkable. They are the work of Daniel Asher Alexander, the constructor of Dartmoor and Maidstone gaols, a genius whose practical ability was inflected by admiration for the megalomaniac visions of Piranesi, a predilection which Alexander shared with many other architects, artists, and poets of the time. While Coleridge turned the plates of the *Opere Varie* and young de Quincey drugged himself into Piranesian frenzy, Alexander built his reminiscences of the Carceri into jails and warehouses. At Wapping, some of his sheer brick walls, set off by imposts and rustics, still remain.

The complex Surrey Dock system, projected by Ralph Dodd, the engineer-speculator who, later on, was the promoter of Waterloo Bridge, never offered much of architectural interest and was elaborated out of all recognition in Victorian times.

The canal which was to have linked up the dock with all the market gardens between Rotherhithe and Epsom got no further than Camberwell where its stump end can be seen to this day.

Neither was architecture conspicuous when the East India Company, following with dignity the example set by less exalted interests, projected a new dock at Blackwall; for the Company already had great warehouses in the city, including some off Bishopsgate, built in 1782, which still stand. At the entrance to the docks, Rennie, the Company's engineer, built a granite portal, which survives (in reconstructed form), witnessing that the quality, if not the quantity, of the great Company's patronage of architecture was respectable.

The last of the early nineteenth-century docks was St Katherine's, a venture which squeezed in higher up the river than any of its predecessors, displacing a medieval college and a Georgian slum in the very shadow of the Tower of London. The engineer was Telford. He raised his brown brick warehouses on Greek Doric columns of cast iron, and Philip Hardwick was brought in to design the Greek Doric office building. The dock has proved incapable of expansion and, apart from bomb damage, remains very much as Telford left it, a grand piece of construction with that tough refinement which the early engineers invariably achieved. The office building, however, has gone.

Directly associated with the docks is the Custom House, whose rebuilding was undertaken immediately following the peace of 1814. The story involves catastrophe both to a fine design and a distinguished career and is worth telling for the light it throws on professional affairs of the period.

It was the custom of public departments, corporations, estates, charities, and the like to employ a surveyor – a man with some architectural qualifications, remunerated by means of a small retaining fee and a fixed percentage on work executed. Where extensive and heavy responsibilities were involved, an architect of the first rank – a Soane, a Holland, or a Cockerell – would be retained. Where the work extended only to survey and dilapidation routine, the qualifications required were more modest. In the latter event, a delicate situation would sometimes be brought about by the decision of a committee to undertake the one big building adventure to which they were liable – the rebuilding of their own premises. If the surveyor inspired confidence he might be employed without hesitation; otherwise, he might be passed over in favour of a man of greater eminence[1]; or, thirdly, he might be invited to produce a design for consideration side by side with designs produced from other quarters. This is what happened in the case of the Custom House. David Laing, son of a city tradesman and a pupil of Soane's, secured the surveyorship of H.M. Customs about 1810. His building experience was limited, but he was a good designer and, when it was decided to erect a new Custom House, in place of the old Queen Anne building, his project stood the test of challenge from other quarters. The new building was finished in 1817. The triple-domed hall with its battery of windows was something of a new departure in English architecture; it recalled Durand and the Napoleonic innovators who flourished in Paris a decade earlier. It was much praised; Laing told a journalist that everything had been done 'to insure the stability and duration of the edifice' and, feeling himself securely lodged among the great men of the profession, he published a book of his work, including some pleasant villas and farms and forty-one splendid plates of the Custom House.

But in 1825 an unfortunate thing happened. One of the piers of the vaults under the great hall subsided. It seems that beech piling, used without sufficient knowledge of the timber, had decayed. Perhaps, too, Laing had not sufficiently considered the distribution of loads involved in his daring design. We do not know; but anyway, he was held to blame; and as by that time the care of all public buildings in London had been put into the hands of the architects at the Board of Works, one of them, Robert Smirke, was instructed to take over at the Custom House. Smirke demolished the whole of Laing's centre and rebuilt it with Ionic columns as we see it today.

Leaving the docks and warehouses, the trail of commerce leads us to the markets and shops. The distinction between

1. For instance, Jupp, the East India Company's surveyor, was replaced by Holland in the case of East India House, Leadenhall Street, rebuilt 1799–1800.

wholesale and retail distribution was not marked, geographic-
ally and architecturally, as it became marked in the nineteenth
century. It was still an age of bargaining and the market was
often a centre where wholesale and retail commerce proceeded
side by side. Architecturally, the first step from the street market
where the traders provided themselves with what primitive
gear they could, was the provision of a building in the centre
of an open space, probably with an open ground floor on the
lines of the sixteenth-, seventeenth-, and eighteenth-century
buildings still familiar in country towns. Such a building was
the Oxford Market, which Gibbs erected on the Harley Estate
(it stood just behind Peter Robinson's). From that time, as we
have seen, estate plans almost always made provision for markets,
sometimes merely open spaces, more rarely with market buildings. In the City, the elder Dance covered in the Fleet river in
1737 and built a long arcaded market which survived till 1829.
Nothing as substantial as this seems to have been attempted
again in London for nearly a century and the later markets were
mostly blocks of shops planned in isolation from the neighbouring thoroughfares. A good example, only recently destroyed, was
the Mortimer Market on the small Mortimer estate just off
Tottenham Court Road. And there are others.

The most important markets come right at the end of the
period. The fruit and vegetable market at Covent Garden had
grown up during the eighteenth century in the square opposite
Inigo Jones's church. In 1828–30, coincident with the demolition of the Fleet Market, the agriculturally-minded Duke of
Bedford provided it with a building, employing Charles Fowler as his architect. The building still stands (Plate 48a), but has
been so much extended and elaborated that it is difficult to make
out the logical and pleasing lines of the original plan. There is
a central arcade, lined with shops; on either side are long
narrow courts, now covered in, while beyond these are the
outer ranges of shops, set behind a Greek Doric colonnade;
this colonnade continues all round the market, except where it
is interrupted by the square corner pavilions and (on the long
sides) the central pedimented halls designed for the 'casual'
fruit and potato markets.

Fowler was an architect with an original sense of structure and planning which places him alongside engineers like Rennie and Telford. Covent Garden was the first London market of its kind (the prototype of such markets was built in Liverpool in 1819); it was followed in 1831–3 by Hungerford Market, a larger and more magnificent structure, also by Fowler, which was demolished for the building of Charing Cross Station in 1860. Fowler built a third great market in his native Devonshire – the Lower Market at Exeter, destroyed in the raids of 1942.

Shops and shop-fronts emerged slowly from the mere contrivance of extra large sash windows to full architectural consciousness. It is doubtful whether any existing shop-front in London is earlier than the middle of the eighteenth century. By that date, bowed fronts were beginning to be preferred to straight-up-and-down framing; and the 'pent-house' projections prescribed in the Rebuilding Act, having been rendered unnecessary by the compulsory introduction of rain-water pipes, were giving place to elaborate classical cornices. In Artillery Lane, off Bishopsgate, in a quarter associated with the silk-weaving industry, is a wonderful example of a Roman Doric shop-front of about 1756. It was made for a silk-merchant's shop, forming the lower storey of his house, which was entered separately at the side. Dozens of the late eighteenth- and early nineteenth-century shop-fronts still exist in London, often scarcely recognizable after the excision of their window bars. A row of such shops is usually a pleasant parade of individualities in detail, rendered harmonious by a reasonable uniformity of height and character.

A famous shop-front of the later eighteenth century is the double-bowed specimen at Fribourg and Treyer's, 34 Haymarket, remarkable, however, rather as a survival in modern surroundings than for any special merits of its own. More artistic is the front originally made for Birch, the confectioner, in Cornhill, and removed to the Victoria and Albert Museum in 1926. It is an unusual and beautiful piece, done by a craftsman who well understood the spirit of Adam innovation.

Up to the Napoleonic period a shop-front was never con-

sidered either as part of the façade of which it formed the base
or as part of a consistent architectural panorama at street level.
The designed shopping street belongs to the Regency and after,
and even then such streets were modest affairs, often mere
passages, situated at the edge of big residental districts. They
were minor speculations, depending for their success on the
prosperity of the neighbourhood. The best example in London –
Woburn Walk (formerly Woburn Buildings), just south of St
Pancras Church – has already been mentioned (p. 193 and Fig. 35).

Fig. 35. Houses and shops, Woburn Walk.

A special case of the shopping street was the covered alley
known by the not very appropriate euphemism of 'arcade'. The
earliest of these intimate and enticing bazaars, and the only one
whose popularity has never waned, is the Burlington Arcade.
It was part of Lord George Cavendish's remodelling of Burlington House in 1815–19 and was designed by his lordship's architect, Samuel Ware, the author of an essay on vaulting. The
original façade to Piccadilly, which tactfully affected the Palladianism of its proto-Palladian neighbour, suffered a curious
fate. The late learned Professor Beresford Pite was employed
many years ago to add an additional storey, which he did with
sympathetic skill; shortly before the war he was again called in,

this time, unfortunately, to remove the original lower part. Perhaps in revenge on the taste of the times, he replaced it by the cynically outrageous Baroque frontispiece of the present day.

A few years after its completion, the Burlington Arcade was imitated, as we have seen, by Nash and George Repton, when they constructed the Opera House in the Haymarket. Later still came the rather similar Exeter and Lowther arcades, both forming part of the Strand improvements, planned by Nash, and executed by others. Both declined in public favour and were eventually built over.

All these arcades reduced the shop-front into a disciplined pattern, sparkling and delightful in general effect, to which top-lighting, introduced through holes in a stuccoed vault, contributed satisfactorily, until the sooty air and high buildings of Victorian London got the better of it.

Separate from the docks, markets, and shops but inseparably part of the trail of commerce were London's Exchanges. Here tradition provided ample precedent for architectural assertiveness.

The Royal Exchange, the centre of international business, and, from 1777, the headquarters of 'Lloyd's Coffee House', already had an architectural history of great distinction. Gresham employed a Flemish architect and gave London one of its first really civilized public buildings. It was burnt in the fire and rebuilt by Jerman, an able contemporary of Wren's and one of the City Surveyors.

This building of Jerman's, built on Elizabethan foundations, survived till 1838, when it was burnt; but on two occasions during the eighteenth century it was considerably tidied up. Parliament spent £10,000 on it in 1767, during the period of general improvement and grooming in the City, the western side being wholly rebuilt by Dance. Later, from 1820 onwards, a further £33,000 was spent, and George Smith, the architect to the Mercers' Company, replaced Jerman's wooden tower, on the south side, by a stone tower, of less interesting outline. A tower, surmounted by the Gresham grasshopper, was always felt to be a necessary attribute of London's *bourse*, and when Sir William

Tite rebuilt the Exchange in 1842, he placed a revised, but hardly improved, version of Smith's tower in the centre of the façade towards Throgmorton Avenue.

The original universal competence of the Royal Exchange as a mart for merchandise was supplemented when a separate Corn Exchange was built by George Dance the elder in 1749-50. To this rather fine building, with its open Doric colonnade, a new and larger Corn Exchange, designed by George Smith in collaboration with A. B. Clayton, was added in 1827. The new building also had a Doric colonnade, but of the Greek variety and standing between two pavilions rather heavily designed in the Soane idiom. This was demolished between the wars.

Another Exchange arrived in the City in 1802, when the stock-brokers, who hitherto had conducted their business in a coffee-house, built a Stock Exchange in Capel Court. Stock-broking was then a very limited business, the stocks comprising only those issued by the Government, the Bank, and the East India and South Sea Companies. It was not until the age of limited joint-stock companies and the arrival of international exchange that the London Stock Exchange attained its prodigious, world-shaking importance. The stockbrokers' architect was James Peacock, Dance's assistant and the designer of the excellent houses in Finsbury Square. The plain basilican room, with continuous clerestory lighting, which he designed was demolished some twenty years after its erection.

The subject of commercial architecture could be considerably elaborated towards the end of the Georgian period, when the beginnings of the general commercial patronage of architects became clearly visible. Private banks and insurance companies, brewers and manufacturers and shopkeepers were beginning to employ architects of repute. The County Fire Office took the first site in the new Regent Street and supplied the terminal feature to the vista from Carlton House. Another insurance company employed C. R. Cockerell to build its head office in the Strand. Brewers were handsome patrons of architecture. Francis Edwards, a Soane pupil, acquired a large brewery con-nexion and built, among others, the Lion Brewery (1836) whose façade was conspicuous on the south bank of the Thames till 1950. He also built the works and offices for the Imperial Gas Company (1823 onwards) near the Regent's Canal at Hoxton, where some of his buildings are yet in use. D. R. Roper was the architect of the famous shot-tower on the South Bank near Waterloo Bridge which has only recently been demolished. And J. B. Papworth was responsible for some excellent warehouses in Milton Street, City, whose brick and iron construction defied the blitz, though severe damage necessitated their demolition soon afterwards.

All these examples are indications of the commercial patronage then in its infancy but which was bestowed on an increasing number of architects after 1830 and eventually resulted in the rebuilding of London streets as a Babel of all the styles in nearly every possible combination. The patronage of art by commerce is an excellent thing, but incalculable in its results.

CHAPTER 20

Greater Georgian London

IT is only towards the end of the story that London's circumferential spread calls for a chapter to itself. The rough edges of George II's London and the estate developments flung out under his successor were still an integral part of the metropolitan body and the surrounding country was still only slightly differentiated from other tracts in the counties of Middlesex, Essex, Kent, and Surrey. The land around London was good farm-land – most of it pasture but a proportion arable – and it bore the typical marks of its manorial ancestry. The villages were much like any other south-country villages, with their modest and dilapidated Gothic churches, their manor houses and their demesnes richly expanded by Enclosure Acts; their brick or half-timber farmsteads, with great tent-like barns such as still survive in the extreme outer edges of the modern sprawl.

But spread over the whole area was the influence of the capital, with its demands for fruit and vegetables, for rural pleasures and occasional rural residence, and for a certain number of industrial products – china, calico, Windsor chairs, soap, bricks, to name a few. In the loop of the Thames round Fulham was London's 'kitchen garden', and there were market-gardens, orchards, and nurseries in other districts. The orchard areas were also holiday areas, with tea-gardens and lodgings to let. Islington was the special holiday village of the City people. A City family, mewed up in a brick court all the week, would trek out on a summer Saturday to a tea-garden or else to their own private pleasure-garden with its neat cottage. In one way and another the semi-rural pleasures of eighteenth-century Londoners made considerable demands on the countryside and the desire to have one foot in *rus* and one in *urbs* was common in every class which could in any degree choose its mode of life.

The essence of suburban life is the townsman's deliberate pursuit of health and relaxation : this in contrast to the draggled, straggling suburbia which is the poverty fringe of the town. As the town expands, the two intermingle, elements in the poverty-fringe sticking, here and there, to the outward wave of amenity-seeking. But the suburbia which we are now considering is essentially the suburbia of prosperity, of the townsman's search for a country foothold.

For the sake of analysis, London's suburban growth can be described in terms of four types of development, all becoming interwoven in a countryside already embroidered with the old manorial pattern. The types are :

(a) *Village development:* the overgrowth of villages, chiefly by the building of large houses in and around their centres.

(b) *Country villa building:* the erection of small but often luxurious houses, in ample grounds.

(c) *Roadside development:* a miscellaneous increase of building along the traffic routes leading out of London.

(d) *Estate development:* in the form of regular groups of streets accessible from a main road.

(a) *Village development.* This is the first architectural effect of the influence of London on the surrounding country. It was already forecast in the seventeenth century, developed strongly in Queen Anne's reign, and consists essentially in the building of houses by or for merchants and professional men. They are sometimes in terrace form, sometimes standing in their own grounds and they often survive as admirable architectural groups. The terraces were speculative ventures; the individual houses usually turn out to have been built by a Turkey merchant, Riga merchant, Spanish merchant, an unusually successful tradesman, a lawyer, a doctor, or perhaps a famous actor or painter. They are rarely architect-designed, but good substantial bricklayers' or carpenters' jobs with a hooded door, panelled rooms, and a stair with twisted balusters. There are four rooms on each floor, all squarish and rather small : on the ground floor one room may be the entrance hall.

Hampstead was one of the richest and remains one of the most interesting of these village developments. Church Row is typical of the terrace arrangement and its partial regularity (especially Nos. 18–28) suggests a speculative origin. Elm Row, off Heath Street, has houses of a similar kind, one of them repeating the fleur-de-lis device cut in the brickwork which appears on some houses in the Row. Of individual Hampstead houses, the most remarkable is Fenton House in the Grove, built on a square plan in 1693. The builder is unknown. The modillion eaves-cornice of Fenton House is typical of several in Hampstead, most dating from the early eighteenth century: Burgh House, Well Walk, said to date from 1703, is a good example – a three-storey brick house, five windows wide, with an excellent wrought-iron gate to the garden. In Frognal, north-west of the parish church, there was a close group of big houses, many now demolished. 'The Old Mansion' is a survivor with a long two-storey front of narrow Queen Anne windows. Frognal House, across the road, westwards, is another survivor, while at the top of Frognal, approached by way of a lime avenue, is Frognal Grove, which incorporates something of the house built for himself by Henry Flitcroft, the architect.

Round the church and on either side of the High Street, Hampstead developed its overload of rows and mansions. And they sprang up, too, in the remoter parts of the parish – at North End, West End, and in Pond Street – the latter a curiously isolated group, mostly inhabited by doctors and still retaining some excellent carved woodwork and wrought iron.

Most of Hampstead's characteristics can be paralleled in the other village centres round London. Highgate, always less accessible and less popular than Hampstead, has its early eighteenth-century mansions in the Grove. There are three fine specimens in Stoke Newington High Street (Nos. 187–91) and both houses and terraces are to be found at Edmonton, Clapton, Hackney, Bow, and Bromley-by-Bow; Greenwich, Rotherhithe, Peckham, Camberwell, Dulwich, Streatham, Battersea, and Wandsworth; and indeed any village within a radius of ten miles of London Stone. There are counterparts of Hampstead's Church Row at Wandsworth (Nos. 1–6 Wandsworth Plain), at Clapham (North Side), at Twickenham (Montpelier Terrace), and at Richmond (Maids of Honour Row).

To complete the social picture of village-centre development here are some quotations from Harrison.[1] At Peckham there are 'many handsome houses ... most of which are the country seats of wealthy citizens of London, or the fixed habitation of those who have retired from business'. At Kentish Town, 'the air being exceedingly wholesome, many of the citizens of London have built houses; and such whose circumstances will not admit of that expense, take ready furnished lodgings for the summer, particularly those who are afflicted with consumptions, and other disorders'. Here and at Hammersmith Harrison notes the prevalence of boarding schools. At Tooting there are 'merchants' seats', at Fulham 'many good buildings belonging to the gentry and citizens of London'. And so for village after village. And after two hundred years the impress of the middle-class suburbanite on the village of his choice is still perceptible.

(b) *Country villa-building.* The word 'villa' and the conception it denotes came in with the Palladians, and the villa of villas in the London area is Lord Burlington's lovely house at Chiswick, built on the general plan of Palladio's Villa Rotonda, in 1729. Although very magnificent, this villa was not large and modesty of extent is an essential attribute of the true villa. Marble Hill, Twickenham, by the Earl of Pembroke with Robert Morris, and the White Lodge in Richmond Park are two other Palladian examples. Small country houses near London began to multiply in the second half of the century and many had the true 'villa' character, which is to say that besides being smallish they were strikingly symmetrical and decidedly classic. Their planning was very different from that of the earlier villas, or indeed of the early eighteenth-century village mansions we mentioned in the first section of this chapter. The main innovations were the elimination of the basement and the intercommunication of the principal rooms. The basement was an Italian feature which had the effect of raising the principal floor to a height which required the introduction of a formidable array of steps on the entrance and garden sides of the house. This made for a certain aloof nobility which pleased the earlier Georgians, but it was later felt to be more agreeable to walk straight out of the French windows of the drawing-room on to the lawn. There-

1. *History of London*, 1775.

fore the basement was suppressed into being a mere cellar and the service quarters were designed as an appendix to the house, not participating in its symmetry and usually half-screened by trees.

The second innovation was a break-away from the stodgy room-by-room planning of the earlier period when a house was conceived as an assemblage of square or oblong boxes, some devoted to the use of the male, others to that of the female occupants of the house. The more polished manners which came to prevail in the 1770s and the freer mixing of ladies and gentlemen in everyday life led to the planning (largely under the Adams' leadership) of rooms *en suite*, with wide folding doors. Much ingenuity was needed to combine this more open planning with a perfectly trim exterior, but here the architects achieved wonders. These later villas are, of course, almost always architects' work; and in the Academy catalogues one finds over and over again entries reflecting the demand for these small and convenient houses.

Inevitably, a great many of these suburban villas perished in the flood of Victorian house-building, that torrent of 'villadom' which mocked its victims by borrowing and degrading their name. Many of the lost villas are recorded in contemporary prints; John Hassell's *Picturesque Rides* and *Views of Seats* give a good selection. Here, for instance, will be found the domed 'Casina' at Dulwich, designed by Nash for a solicitor and landscaped by Humphry Repton. Of the survivors of these houses, two good examples have become public property. The house in Clissold Park, Stoke Newington, designed in the first decade of the century by Joseph Woods, has an open Greek Doric colonnade along its west front. In Brockwell Park is another example, built for a glass-manufacturer by D. R. Roper with stucco and joinery detail of great delicacy. Both houses are built on eminences, natural in origin but improved by art. Both have considerable parks with artificial water.

A later comer than the villa, but in the same category so far as the creation of suburbia is concerned, was the 'ornamental cottage' or *ferme ornée*. This was a miniature residence, usually in a more or less Gothic style and very often thatched. A rich amateur of the Picturesque might spend a small fortune on one of these cottages, and if the lordly prototype of the villa was Burlington's house at Chiswick, the ornamental cottage owed something indirectly to Horace Walpole's work at Twickenham. There were dozens of these bizarre little toys in the London countryside, but hardly any have survived. Some achieved a special reputation – for instance, Craven Cottage and Ivy Cottage, both at Fulham and both long since destroyed. Craven Cottage was a fantasy of its owner, Walsh Porter, the interior decorator who worked at Carlton House for the Regent; it contained an 'Egyptian Hall' in miniature and there was ancient glass in the windows. Sir Robert Barclay's 'Ivy Cottage', at Parsons Green, was Gothic, with a marvellous Gothic-painted dining-room with medieval glass from Rennes. It was perhaps the reputation of these two little houses which sent the names 'Ivy Cottage' and 'Craven Cottage' flying through all the later Georgian suburbias of England. Another cottage, rather less expensively got-up, was 'Woodlands', built by a Mr Lynn among the cornfields near Clapham. It had Tudor windows and crow-stepped gables; the service wing was out of sight among trees. The description of it given in one of Hassell's books[1] is quoted because it characterizes the genus to which many of these cottages belonged.

For this purpose [retirement] and to relax from the fatigues of a professional employment, the proprietor erected this homely, yet elegant little cottage: a humble thatch covers its roof and a plain, unostentatious, but convenient fitting up, are its internal advantages. A small, well-chosen collection of paintings, chiefly by modern artists decorate its walls. The simplicity of the external appearance of the cottage, which is modern Gothic, has a corresponding accompaniment with its inside; in the dining-parlour, the same style is pursued; the tables, chairs, wainscoting and sideboard, resemble in miniature, the ancient appearance of the best of our old castles, to which the stained-glass windows give a sombre finish.

It will not have escaped the reader that a measure of silliness was one of the ingredients of the typical 'ornamental cottage'.

1. *Picturesque Rides and Walks . . . thirty miles round the Metropolis*, vol. 1, 1820.

Fig. 36. Fountain Cottage, Camberwell Grove.

Few of these architectural baubles survive, least of all near London. At Hampstead, however, there is the triple-towered, pointed-roofed 'Hunter's Lodge' in Belsize Lane, a very pretty example which must date from the end of the eighteeenth century. In the Grove at Camberwell was, until 1944, the thatched 'Fountain Cottage' with a veranda supported on rustic columns. This was on the estate of Dr Lettsom, the quaker physician and philanthropist.

(c) *Roadside development.* This is what is now commonly called 'ribbon-development' because the long strips of roadside house-building fly out from the centre of a map like loose ribbons. It represents the most obvious and natural form of expansion for a town and goes back in principle to the Middle Ages when the 'fore-streets' began to straggle outwards from the principal gates.

But the use of the borderlands of main roads was for long inhibited by two factors: first, the desire for safety in grouping and a reluctance to settle in sparse spacing in open country; second, the bad condition of the roads themselves. The roads improved slightly with the multiplication of turnpike trusts in the second half of the century and more rapidly under the influence of Macadam after Waterloo. Traffic was greater, safety greater and from 1815 onwards the stretches of road between London and the nearest villages attracted all sorts of building. It was utterly miscellaneous. There were the moderately large private house, the speculative terrace, the cottage or group of cottages, the nursery garden with the nurseryman's house, the brickyard, the soap-factory, the brewery – a panorama of uses which unfolded unattractively enough along most of the roads leading out of London.

Among the earliest and most conspicuous 'ribbons' was the road from London to Islington. Islington had been a magnet for City people since the seventeenth century. It was, as we have seen, their holiday village, and in the direction of Islington the social traffic of the City had an irresistible tendency. By 1735 High Street and Upper Street were 'well lined' with houses, so that a long thin finger of built-up area pointed north-wards on the map.[1] The northward trend continued with High-bury Place, built in 1774–9 and Highbury Terrace, 1789. Cole-brook Row was built alongside the New River in 1768; Duncan Terrace arrived opposite in 1799, and before 1800 the terraces in Liverpool Road had been begun. Compton Terrace belongs to the first years of the new century. All this work was specu-lative housing of a moderately good class. Some of the terraces carry the names of their builders – as Rosoman's Row (Roso-man being the owner of Sadlers Wells Theatre) and Annett's Crescent; all are of brown brick with sparse ornament of a grace-ful kind.

The only line of roadside building comparable to the Isling-ton strip was the southward stretch of housing lining the road which led south from London Bridge. Here, in the parish of Southwark, was ribbon-development of very ancient origin. Here were the innumerable inns of medieval and later date, of which only the famous George now survives. This 'ribbon', a crowded, stunted approach to the metropolis narrowing to the bottle-neck of London Bridge, retained its medieval character till half-way through the eighteenth century. While London had but one bridge the south bank of the Thames remained a

1. J. Nelson, *History of St Mary, Islington* (1811) and S. Lewis, *History of St Mary, Islington*, 1842.

marshy desert, partly drained by stinking ditches and sparsely strewn with cottages where fisher-folk and glass-workers eked out a poor living.

Westminster Bridge was opened in 1750 and, in the following year, an Act ordered a straight road from the bridge, across the fields, to Borough High Street. This attracted no building. Blackfriars Bridge was begun in 1760 and it was only then that extensive development on the south side could be foreseen as inevitable and important. The City, which had been responsible for the bridge, took the initiative in forming the roads which were intended to be and still remain the 'bony structure' of South London. Robert Mylne, the able young architect of the bridge, made the plan and an Act was obtained in 1769, the year the bridge was opened. In his plan, Mylne produced the line of Blackfriars Bridge as a dead straight road entering a circus at the point where it met the east-west road joining Westminster Bridge to the Borough. From this circus, two roads forked south-west and south-east, the one leading to Lambeth, the other to Walworth. No buildings were projected in the first instance, the only architectural feature of the scheme being an obelisk placed in the centre of the circus. This circus is known today as St George's Circus; the obelisk has been relegated, since 1905, to a site 200 yards away in Lambeth Road.[1]

None of the roads was begun to be built up for about ten years. In the 1780s and 1790s, however, the buildings arrived – long rows of brown brick terraces at frequent intervals along both the new and the old roads, rapidly drawing the map of London out to Kennington and Camberwell and Peckham.

In every direction, but especially northward, southward, and eastward, the same thing happened. Starting at Islington and going clockwise round London, there are strings of roadside terraces in Liverpool Road, Kingsland Road, Hackney Road, Mile End Road, and Commercial Road; and, crossing the river, in the Old Kent Road, Walworth Road, Kennington Road, Kennington Lane, and Lambeth Bridge Road. Almost all were built after Waterloo, though here and there one finds a group of houses unmistakably stamped with the careful elegance of the war

1. *Survey of London*, vol. 25: St George's Fields (1955), Chapter v.

period. The western sector provides a less obvious and monotonous pattern, probably because there was more competition over a longer period and land was more expensive. The road between Kensington and Hammersmith naturally attracted attention early and in 1787–9, G. Wightman, a carpenter, built the beautiful Phillimore Place,[1] destroyed about 1935. Later came Earl's Terrace, built by M. Changier, a Frenchman, during the war period; Changier is alleged to have spent over £100,000, failed, and taken an early opportunity of crossing the Channel.[2] Then there are later terraces in the King's Road, Fulham Road, and Kensington Gore. Northwards they straggle out from Camden Town and Kentish Town.

It would be wrong to pretend that many of these terraces are very good architecture. They are least good when they affect emphatic symmetry, which is absurd in a composition which is only seen in perspective and where there is no possible pretext for central emphasis. Adam, it is true, did this sort of thing in Portland Place; but Portland Place was a close, not a thoroughfare, and at least some of the central houses were mansions of exceptional size. The suburban builder rigged his pediments and end pavilions for no particular reason except the obvious one of striking a West-End note. The joinery and stucco details, on the other hand, are often very charming. There are pretty door-cases and fanlights and plaques bearing in large Roman letters the name of the terrace and perhaps the date.

Roadside development was by no means entirely a matter of terraces. In the west, as I have said, it was more varied – here and there a terrace, here and there a big house in its own grounds; in the intervals an occasional pair of tall semi-detached houses, or a small stucco-Gothic box with a tiny garden in front and some characteristic name – Milan Cottage or

1. Faulkner's *History of Kensington* mentions a Mr Porter as the architect. This should be *Porden*. Porden exhibited a view of the terrace in the R.A.

2. Changier's speculation is probably at the bottom of Leigh Hunt's story (*The Old Court Suburb*, Chapter xi) of a Frenchman who built Edwardes Square with a view to housing the officers of Napoleon's invading army. Actually, Edwardes Square is a post-war development of about 1819.

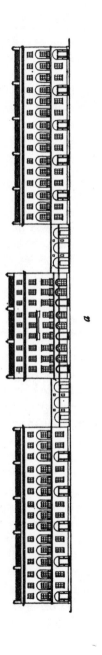

Fig. 37. Three types of suburban housing development. *a*. Linked terraces. *b*. Semi-detached houses. *c*. Quasi-semi-detached houses.

Gothic House – lettered on its front. You can still discover these oddly-strung beads in any direction you like to go; often their cornices or gables peep over the shops built in late Victorian times on their front gardens.

As the ribbons tailed off into the country they often straggled and draggled into miserable squalor – squalor of a kind still only too familiar and accurately painted by Dickens in describing the location of Harriet Carker's house, somewhere up the Finchley Road:

The neighbourhood ... has as little of the country to recommend it as it has of the town. It is neither of the town nor country. The former, like the giant in his travelling boots, has made a stride and passed it, and has set his brick-and-mortar heel a long way in advance; but the intermediate space between the giant's feet, as yet, is only blighted country, and not town, and here, among a few tall chimneys belching smoke all day and night, and among the brickfields and lanes where turf is cut, and where the fences tumble down, and where the dusty nettles grow, and where a scrap or two of hedge may yet be seen, and where the bird-catcher still comes occasionally, though he swears every time to come no more – this home is to be found.

There was a good deal of squalor in London's country and there were the beginnings of the bleak anonymity which makes present-day suburbia a no-man's land, inhabited by people whose sense of location recognizes only a shopping centre, a tube station, and a bus-route. In among all the one-man projects and get-rich-quick speculations along the roads, however, were some of wider ambition. These belong in our next category.

(d) *Estate development.* As ribbon building proceeded, leap-frogging along the highways, great unbuilt-up wedges of agricultural land were left. All sorts of things could happen in these gulfs. They provided cheap sites for factories, breweries, brick-kilns, and, of course, nursery gardens, all with attendant cottages. But here and there they were built up solid with streets and squares, set out in a tidy design. This was estate-development, akin to what had been happening in west London since Hanover Square, the only differences being that these estates did not grow out of the pattern of London proper but were planted between the main roads at points dictated by the watchful opportunism of landowners and builders.

These estates often styled themselves 'new town' or else affixed the word 'town' to the family name or title of the free-holder. Many of the names have dropped out of use, with the loss of the estate's topographical identity; others have stuck. Thus, Somers Town and Camden Town are still recognizable localities, while Agar Town, now mostly railway yards, has almost passed out of use. Nor does anybody now speak of Kensington New Town, a charming little group of streets off Kensington Gore, or of Walworth New Town, or Bromley New Town. Pentonville, on the other hand, a romanticization of the same idea, has stayed, if only because of the celebrity of its gaol.

Many of these 'new towns' are worth attention, either historically, or, more rarely, because their planning and architecture are distinguished. 'Hans Town', which consisted in the first instance of Sloane Street and Cadogan Place with Hans Place on the west, is one of the earliest distinct examples. It owes its existence to the initiative of Henry Holland, the architect, who took a lease of eighty-nine acres from Lord Cadogan in 1771. Hans Place imitates, on a modest scale, the shape of the Place Vendôme in Paris. On its long axis and to the south, Holland built himself a house which he called Sloane Place but which in later years came to be called the 'Pavilion', perhaps in reference to Holland's association with George IV's famous building at Brighton.[1]

Holland christened his Hans Town after Sir Hans Sloane, whose daughter-heiress married an Earl of Cadogan; and the name was retained till the 'town' lost its identity after the building-up of Belgravia. The original houses were plain brick buildings of three or four storeys, not aiming very high in the social scale. A few still survive.

Somers Town, lying north of the 'New Road', is the next prominent example. It was begun on the land of the first Lord Somers of Evesham (second creation, 1784) in 1786. The principal

1. D. Stroud, *Henry Holland* (1950), pp. 14–18.

speculator was a builder called Leroux.[1] At first it consisted
of a few streets, a crescent on the east and the Polygon on
the west, standing more or less in open fields. This Polygon
was a kind of inverted circus, composed of detached blocks of
houses facing outwards and having courts or gardens running
to the centre. It was demolished early in the present century.
The district was developing at the time of the Revolution and
refugees in search of cheap housing came there in numbers. One
of them, the Abbé Carron, building the Catholic chapel of St
Aloysius in 1808; the little building is still there with its Pro-
testant-looking altar-piece and its classical west front added in
1830, preserving like no other Catholic church in London the
atmosphere of the age before emancipation. The square round
the site of the Polygon still has a few substantial early nineteenth-century houses.

Camden Town came in 1791. It was set out eastwards of the
road to Hampstead on the property of Lord Chancellor Camden
who seems to have retained Joseph Kay as surveyor. Terraces
were built along the Hampstead Road, with a grid of streets
behind. The architecture is of no account except in the case of
College Place and the corner of Crowndale Road, where sites
were taken by Thomas Cubitt round about 1825. College Place
is a model of what good proportion and good building can
make of an elementary subject. Camden Town remained isolated
until the contiguous Agar estate on the east was built up in
Victorian times, Camden Town and Agar Town eventually
filling in the wedge between Hampstead Road and Maiden Lane
(now York Way).

Further east and lying off the roads leading north through
Islington is a group of important estates with some good plan-
ning and architecture. On the Canonbury estate, behind Henry
Leroux's Union Terrace, Canonbury Square was begun soon
after 1800. Two other estates lay on either side of Liverpool
Road, which became a 'ribbon' from 1796 onwards; on the west
the property of the Stonefield family, on the east that of Mr John
Milner Gibson. On the Stonefield Estate, Cloudesley Square

1. *St Pancras Book of Dates*, 1908, where it is stated that a lease was
granted by Lord Somers and the Hon. J. Somers Cocks in 1783.

was laid out, with streets leading into the centre of each side, shortly before 1824. Land in the centre of the square was conveyed to the Church Commissioners and the church, by Barry, erected 1826-7. The houses are mere routine stuff, the work of five speculating builders. The Gibson estate across the road, was developed some years later, with the quite ordinary Gibson Square and the perfectly extraordinary Milner Square (about 1841), the latter the work of Gough and Roumieu whose architecture is of the most sinister description. They (I think R. L. Roumieu was the man) attempted here to redeem the Georgian house-front from its negativeness by resolving it into a pattern of vertical *anta*-like ribs with windows and wall-panels in the intervals. The principle is reasonable enough but the mannerisms in the modelling give the design an unreal and tortured quality, only slightly modified by the destruction, shortly before the war, of the curious porches. It is possible to visit Milner Square many times and still not be absolutely certain that you have seen it anywhere but in an unhappy dream.

These Islington layouts have not the same morphological character as Somers and Camden Towns. They are incidents in the considerable stream of residential building flowing north from the City and never had quite the 'new town' identity of the others. A good many smaller estates merged in the same flow, including the pleasant Barnsbury Square, a square of detached and semi-detached houses of various sorts with circular 'closes' at the north-west and south-west corners.

In the East End, in the vast parish of Stepney, the Wentworth property was developed untidily and sporadically, and fragmentary nuclei – hardly 'new towns' – occur frequently – like the Tredegar group off Mile End Road, John Beaumont's layout round Beaumont Square, southward of the same road, and the group of houses on Bow Common known as Bromley New Town. Again, in the south, all the wedges were loosely filled with small developments of the same sort, mostly rather poor architecturally, though an interesting exception was the Paragon on the Rolls Estate in the New Kent Road designed by Michael Searles and destroyed (except for two houses and the gate-piers) before the war. The plain Union Crescent, opposite the Paragon, survives, together with some other streets and the estate office in the Old Kent Road. North of the Thames again, the wedges between the river and King's Road, between King's Road and Fulham Road, Fulham Road and Kensington all show the same kind of thing. Kensington New Town was a late-comer and survives in the neat well-designed houses of Victoria Grove and Launceston Place – its identity as a new departure now completely lost.

This cursory outline of Georgian suburbia is all that the scope of a chapter permits. The analysis of the whole subject, while the buildings yet stand, is an urgent task for topographical students. But it is a very big task, for research into land-ownership, involving the inspection of leases and estate records is slow, laborious, and not lacking in obstacles. For the purpose of this book, all I am concerned to do is to illustrate the principles of development. This I have done by distinguishing four components – the expanding village, the building of villas, the development of highway 'ribbons' and, finally, of estates between the 'ribbons'. Of course, the division is to a great extent arbitrary. Thus, the expansion of a village may include villa-building, the formation of 'ribbons', and the laying out of estates; a 'ribbon' itself may comprise quite a number of private villas; or, again, the development of a large estate in a 'wedge' may contribute houses and terraces to one or two of the limiting 'ribbons'. But we are dealing with a fairly complex morphology which cannot be neatly categorized.

As a postcript to this chapter it is perhaps worth saying something about the nomenclature of late Georgian suburbia. Every terrace, however humble, had at one time its particular name, occasionally still preserved on a plaque though ignored by the present-day numbering. The builders were very local in their point of view and did not scruple to repeat a name already occurring many times in adjacent districts. Generally speaking the names of streets and other groups of houses fall into eight categories, as follows:

(1) *Names and Titles of the Royal Family.* 'George' and 'Hanover' were general throughout the period. 'Brunswick'

came in with the Prince of Wales's marriage to Caroline of Brunswick in 1795; 'Caroline' is usually ascribable to the same person. 'Charlotte' usually indicates a date shortly after 1796, when the Prince's daughter was born and is rarely referable to George III's queen. 'Regent' and the less common 'Regency' obviously belong to 1811–20. 'Coronation' is rare, belonging exclusively to 1821 or 1831. George IV's brothers provided the extremely popular series, 'York', 'Albany', 'Clarence', 'Kent', 'Cumberland', 'Sussex', and 'Cambridge'; to which was added 'Gloucester', after the Duke who married Princess Mary in 1816. 'Coburg' occurs after the Duke of Kent's marriage in the same year.

(2) *Landlord's Names, Titles, and Residences*. This nomenclature was already familiar in the seventeeth century when the names and titles of George Villiers, Duke of Buckingham, were attached to streets off the Strand, built on land which he sold in 1675. The Cavendish-Harley estate used not only names and titles but from 1719, country estates such as Wimpole and Welbeck, and this was followed on the Grosvenor (Eaton), Bedford (Woburn), and Portman (Orchard Portman gives Orchard Street) lay-outs.

(3) *Builders' Names*. These occur fairly low in the social scale, at a level where the practice would not give offence to potential occupiers. 'Webb's County Terrace' in the New Kent Road, with the name written very large on the centre of the building, was a good example. Many Christian names, male and female, are ascribable to the desire of builders to compliment themselves or their wives or daughters.

(4) *Amenity*. This class advertises the siting or healthiness of the buildings, as in 'Prospect', 'Belmont', 'Monte Video', 'Bellevue', or 'Montpelier' or the rural character of the place as in 'Grove', 'Ivy', 'Rose', 'Rosemary', 'Almond', 'Willow', 'Oak', or 'Woodbine'. Or simply abstract charm as in 'Eden', 'Paradise', 'Elysium', or 'Pleasant'. Naturally, the sites for which such names were selected were precisely those where the existence of the amenities advertised was most precarious.

(5) *Public Men*. In this group, 'Wellington' is by far the most common, with 'Nelson' a very poor second. 'Chatham', 'Pitt',

and 'Rodney' had distinct phases of popularity. 'Addington' occurs twice, and belongs only to the years of his premiership, 1801–4. 'Sidmouth', his later title, sometimes occurs. Liverpool, a later premier, is honoured at least twice.

(6) *Victories*. 'Waterloo' is easily first, with 'Trafalgar' second and 'Copenhagen' third. Victories being, like Coronations, occasional affairs the opportunities for attaching their names to newly-built properties were limited. Some latitude seems to have been allowed, however, in the resounding instance of Waterloo. A 'Trafalgar' usually belongs to 1805–6, except, of course, for the more famous of the two Squares which had that name which is retrospective by more than a quarter of a century.[1]

(7) *Patriotic Sentiment*. 'Albion' and 'Britannia' are common everywhere after Trafalgar and 'Patriot' occurs in the East End.

(8) *Architectural Shape*. Squares, Crescents, and Circuses are usually qualified by a name from one of the above-mentioned categories. But 'the Paragon' stands by itself. I know of three Paragons in the London neighbourhood. Much the earliest is at Richmond; it is simply a short terrace of identical houses built about the first quarter of the eighteenth century and overlooking the river. I have found no other London Paragons between that and the two built by Michael Searles, one in the New Kent Road and the other at Blackheath. The fourth is Paragon Road, Hackney, which has a clear affinity with the Blackheath Paragon. It is a curious word to apply to a group of buildings, though not more curious perhaps than the later 'model' villages and 'model' dwellings. The point of the word was underlined in the two cases by Searles by strict architectural regularity on a rather unusual and decorative plan. Other virtues, such as sound construction, were perhaps implied.

A 'Polygon' I have already mentioned as having existed in Somers Town. There is another, dated 1792, at Clapham. The name is as self-explanatory as 'square' or 'circus', and both these examples were built on a many-sided figure.

The only other name in this category is 'Oval'. London has two 'Ovals' and I doubt if it ever had any more. One is the very

1. Trafalgar Square, Chelsea, has been re-named Chelsea Square.

large Oval on the Duchy of Cornwall estate at Kennington, which was perhaps started as a formal project but was built up irregularly during the early nineteenth century. The other Oval, later and much smaller, runs north-east of the Hackney Road; it is really two facing crescents of detached houses, one of which was demolished before the war and the other rendered derelict by bombing.

CHAPTER 21

The Ends of the Threads

In this, the last chapter, I shall pick up the ends of some of the threads laid bare in earlier chapters and tie them into a Victorian bow. It would be a pity to guillotine them at 1830, which would seem the only alternative.

First, then, *Metropolitan Improvements*. What became of this energetic movement, heralded by Gwynn in 1766 and so magnificently prosecuted by Nash? It did not die with Nash; he had a loyal successor in James Pennethorne, whom he had brought up and trained in his office and who was his chief assistant from 1826 onwards. After Nash's retirement, Pennethorne was commissioned independently, in 1832, to prepare plans for the further improvement of London and he produced a remarkable scheme. It was curtailed and mutilated in a horrible way and only some bits and pieces of it were carried out.

It was Pennethorne who cut New Oxford Street through the slums of St Giles's, under the Improvement Act of 1839. A few of the façades are his, but most of them are the florid and decadent attempts of unremembered architects to be more handsome and picturesque than Regent Street. Cranbourn Street (1843) and Endell Street (1846) are other fragments of Pennethorne's great plan; while Garrick Street and Southwark Street (both 1864) and some others which were carried out by the Metropolitan Board of Works after 1855 owe their origin to him. These fragments, excerpted from a complete and organic design and unworthily executed under third-rate architects, show how utterly the sense of urban responsibility, so strong under George IV, his ministers and architects, had broken down.

It broke down for a number of reasons. The Reform Bill of 1832 gave the first shock to the old oligarchic traditions and responsibilities and opinion in Parliament hardened against anything in the nature of State initiative. The Coal Duties, which constituted the only source of revenue considered applicable to public improvements, were utterly inadequate. And up to 1855 there was the paramount administrative difficulty that there was no one body responsible for London's welfare as a whole. The Office of Woods and Forests had sponsored Nash's plans (quite reasonably, since two Royal Parks were involved) and this anomalous precedent constituted them the (all too ineffective) sponsors of Pennethorne's schemes. They had no powers of compulsory acquisition except under *ad hoc* Acts of Parliament and their authority cut awkwardly across the parochial government system. In Parliament it was felt that if improvements were really necessary (which was always arguable) they should receive as little help as possible. The acquisition of land for non-profitable purposes such as parks was conceived to be the business of philanthropists; when exceptions were made, the Treasury managed to find some pathetically inadequate windfall to meet the situation. Victoria Park was bought with money received from the Sutherlands for the lease of York House. Disraeli strongly opposed the acquisition of Battersea Park. In both cases, Pennethorne's design for the lay-out and approaches were massacred with sadistic parsimony.

After Pennethorne, 'improvement' became the responsibility of the Metropolitan Board of Works, created in 1855 and the direct precursor of the L.C.C. The M.B.W. possessed substantial powers and achieved much, notably the Thames Embankments (1862–74), but its architectural control was negligible and the nadir of 'improvement' came when Shaftesbury Avenue and Charing Cross Road were opened in 1886 and 1887, and speculative architecture romped unbridled from Oxford Street to Piccadilly. The lines selected were not bad, but the handling was beneath contempt – a morass of irresponsibility, ignorance, and peculation. There the history of the old tradition of improvement ends. Kingsway (1906), with all its inadequacies, represents the first faint glimmer of a new epoch of civic responsibility.

The development of *Great Estates* in what is now inner London continued vigorously until the seventies, on lines somewhat resembling those on which Cubitt had developed Belgravia. Indeed, Cubitt's formation of Pimlico, with its massive terraces and ample squares, remains one of the most obvious continuations of the Georgian tradition. Another was the building up of Bayswater and Notting Hill, chiefly by very substantial builder-speculators who acquired the freehold of the soil and laid out immense residential strongholds covered from top to toe with Italian ornament. John Crake's Hyde Park Gardens (1836) and George Wyatt's Leinster Square and Princes Square (1856) are among the most imposing, exceeded in richness only by Lancaster Gate (1857) where the speculator called in Sancton Wood and the elaborate magic of the French Renaissance.

The decline in taste and competence was more marked in the remoter regions of Paddington, Chelsea, and Islington, where a less prosperous class of tenant was anticipated. But one of the chief single factors in the descent was the loss of status on the part of the architect in his capacity as 'surveyor'. The later Georgian landlords had retained the services of men at the top of the profession. Architects like S. P. Cockerell, John Shaw, Thomas Cundy, and D. R. Roper had had the superintendence of one or two or more estates at a time, for which they provided plans and typical elevations and often prepared the leases. It was, of course, to a large extent 'bread-and-butter' work and that, no doubt, is why it was scorned by the idealistic Gothic-church men of the fifties and sixties, when the profession became tragically split between art and piety on the one hand and 'bread-and-butter' on the other. In any case, the fact remains that the surveyors of the Victorian epoch were men of very little account indeed, and their control of the builders was an affair of estate management rather than architecture. After 1850 it is rare to find an architect of any reputation meddling with estate development. Exceptions are curious rather than edifying; like the case of George Godwin, who developed the Chelsea Park Estate in the seventies, leaving Elm Park Gardens as his (singularly forbidding) memorial.

Precisely the same applies in the further developments of the town where the vacant spaces in what I have called *Greater Georgian London* were filled up in successive waves of building enthusiasm. One can watch the process at work in detail. Thus, the admirable John Shaw conducted the building on the Eton

College estate at Chalk Farm in the good old-fashioned way and a fair standard was maintained till a nonentical surveyor, George Pownall, succeeded him and all quality vanished. At Tufnell Park, the same Shaw made an excellent start, but the thing went to pieces under George Truefit. At Roupell Park, the attempts of Banks and Barry were equally destined to failure, as were those of Henry Kendall at St John's Wood Park. The truth is that the builders began to know too much (thinking themselves Cubitts) and the surveyors too little. The old methods ran down completely. When Bedford Park was begun in 1876, with Norman Shaw as chief designer, the aim and relationships of promoters and architect were something entirely new. Letchworth and Hampstead and Welwyn were adumbrated and the Georgian chapter in estate development was left to reach its miserable and long-protracted end in our own day.

The grand corollary to the Victorian expansion of London was the rebuilding of the City – the *Commercial Stronghold*; and the link between the two processes was the arrival of the railways. The first terminal station in London opened at Euston Square in 1838. By 1844 there were six terminals, none of them however, very near the centre. King's Cross was opened in 1852, Paddington in 1853, the East Kent Station at Blackfriars in 1858, Charing Cross and Cannon Street in 1863–5, St Pancras in 1871, Liverpool Street in 1875, and Holborn Viaduct in 1877. Thus, between 1852 and 1877 the railway systems placed before Londoners the basic facilities for railway travel with which we are familiar today. And, of course, these facilities included suburban as well as long-distance journeying. The first stretch of the Metropolitan, linking Farringdon Street to Paddington, was opened in 1863.

It was exactly this period which saw the first general rebuilding of the City since the Fire. Already in 1858 the Georgian streets were described as being in a state of 'general demolition'. Merchants were moving into the new squares and terraces of Bayswater and Pimlico, their ancient houses yielding place to warehouses and office buildings unattached to residences. After 1861 the process was accelerated by the drift to the outer suburbs accompanied by daily travel on the railways; and this process continued as more and more facilities became available. Thus the inchoate and remote 'dormitory suburbs' were born.

Rebuilding in the City started well, with the banks and insurance offices of men like C. R. Cockerell and John Gibson and the warehouses of George Somers Clarke and Sancton Wood. The greater banks and joint-stock companies upheld a reasonable standard, but the operations of smaller firms and of property companies building rentable offices were conducted on a lower level. Nevertheless the rebuilt City as it stood at the end of the Victorian period contained much remarkable architecture, most of it absurdly ornate for its function and situation, but a proportion of it honourable both in structure and design.

The metamorphosis of the City was, in effect, the broadening of what I have called the *Trail of Commerce* to affect a whole area of London, transforming it into one great depository and whole-time counting-house. This transformation, the outward thrusts of suburbia, and the improvements to ease the communications between city and suburbs were all three interdependent, so that the first of my Victorian knots is duly tied.

The second knot must involve some of the less tangible aspects of the growth of towns. *Taste*, which was the subject of one of my earliest chapters, entered into a phase of revolutions at the close of the Georgian era; and the first and greatest revolution was the revolution against taste itself. Too often, this phenomenon is represented merely as a pietistic intensification of the antiquarian revival of Gothic. It was far more than that. Its intuition was deep and formidable, perhaps more clearly conscious of what it wanted to destroy than what it wanted to build. To disrupt the rule of taste was the first objective, performed with incredible ease. The three-centuries-old fabric collapsed within ten years of the publication of Pugin's *Contrasts* in 1836; the common stuff of early Victorian architecture was made up out of its ruins. What to create in its place was the problem which baffled and puzzled three generations of architects. Ruskin, poet and geologist, revealed an extensive landscape of possibilities, all of which became impossibilities when refracted in the still half-Georgian minds of English architects. Butterfield, the builder, married his imagination to the adolescence of Gothic, worshipping its hardness of limb, and produced a few buildings of immense and far-reaching importance. After him, Morris and Webb began to lay the foundations on which the future of architecture still rests.

The revolution against taste expressed itself first and chiefly in *Church Building*, but not in the kind of church building with which either of my chapters on that subject was concerned. The State built no more churches, nor was it called upon to do so. It was felt that church building by the State had no heart : and for the Commissioners' churches, as we have seen, no degree of contempt could be too high. Sacrifice was necessary and the greatest churches of Butterfield, Carpenter, and Street were built from the purses of pious and wealthy benefactors. Yet some of the habits of Georgian church building continued. The work of the Commissioners, indeed, penetrated into Victoria's reign and the parallel activity of the Incorporated Church Building Society, dating from the same year as the Church Building Act, saw to it that in whatever direction London expanded, Gothic steeples soon rose above the clustering house-tops. All the great estates developed in Victorian times have their Gothic churches, sometimes designed by the surveyor to the estate. Cundy, for instance, built the Gothic churches of Pimlico. But in such buildings there was little of the new fervour and vitality. That is chiefly to be found in the churches which pious benefactors and their pious architects planted in the distressed and mournful suburbs – in Kilburn and Plaistow, Kennington and Southwark. The overthrow of agreed and inherited canons of taste produced countless eddies of architectural fashion and these gradually dyed the fabric of Georgian London, one after the other, till it became a motley purplish mosaic instead of a brick and stucco criss-cross. *The London House* proved wonderfully constant in essentials of plan and arrangement, but its externals changed every ten years. The semi-detached villa, born, as we have seen, on the Eyre Estate, made an absolute conquest of suburbia, its frail morality proving susceptible at one and the same time to influences (at third hand) from modern France and ancient Venice. In central London, Georgian leases fell in rapidly before and after the 99th anniversary of the wonderful year 1774. But few houses were rebuilt and, instead, they were buttoned up in Italianate cement to face another fifty years or so of London life. Portland Place was rusticated, the Adelphi capped by an eagle in a pediment, Charlotte Street and Great Russell Street were swathed in compo detail; while Russell Square underwent a Doulton face-lifting, ingenious and inglorious. Where houses, in mass, were rebuilt they were sometimes Gothic, but not often; and after 1870 the discovery of a marvellous Anglo-Flemish hybrid called 'Queen Anne' carried the day. But my second knot is tied in the taste of the sixties. 'Queen Anne' marked the beginning of the Georgian Revival.

The picture of Victorian London is, in reality, nothing but the picture of Georgian London 'made over'. The alterations were superficially rigorous, not radical. If we were to watch the movement of the nineteenth century as we watched that of the two previous centuries at the beginning of this book, from a station in the clouds, the spectacle would be turgid, intricate, plethoric. We should see London spreading furiously in great blotches of no definable outline; we should see the railways coalescing into a sort of cat's-cradle round central London; we should see the occasional incision of streets, viaducts, and embankments and the ubiquitous upshot of churches, schools and public-houses, gasworks, waterworks, sewage-works, factories, and industrial dwellings.

The change from Georgian to Victorian London was quantitative and qualitative. But although the change in quantity – the outward spread – was the more conspicuous, the *significant* change was in quality. The quantitative change derived its momentum from the eighteenth century though constantly stimulated by the increasing population and industrialization of the country. But the qualitative change reflects kinds of taste, initiative, and endeavour which belong exclusively to the Victorian age. The gradual assumption of responsibility for public welfare, first by philanthropic individuals and groups and then gradually by the State, is seen in the detailed modulation of the capital rather than in its general forms and outline.

The story of all these changes, the gradual emergence of urban life of a new social character, the conflicts of new requirements

with old assumptions and with the old structural framework –
all this is the subject for another book, with a rather different
approach and laid out in a very different way. The purpose of
this present chapter is only to show to what extent the Georgian
character of London penetrated into the succeeding age – and
where it finally stopped. We have seen the continuation and
decline of 'metropolitan improvements', the out-thrust of estate
development towards an incontinent suburbia created by the
railways, the metamorphosis of the City, and, lastly, the overthrow of Georgian standards of taste under the assault of a new,
combative attitude of mind, better able to destroy than to create.
There, in a profuse tangle of florid ends and stern beginnings,
of complacence and criticism, cynicism and faith, our story
finishes.

APPENDIX I

Existing Georgian Buildings in the City and County of London

THE following lists comprise the churches and public buildings and some of the more significant streets and houses surviving from the Georgian period. It is based on the list in previous editions of this book but has been checked, amplified, and re-arranged. Most of the Borough lists have been sub-divided into areas for convenience of study, while streets are listed so far as possible with respect to contiguity on the map. Churches erected entirely or largely from grants by the Church Building Commission (1818) are designated by the letters C.B.C. All areas were revisited by the author in May–September 1962. Professor Pevsner's perambulations in the two London volumes of his *Buildings of England* series (Penguin Books, 1952 and 1957) have been consulted throughout with incalculable advantage.

CITY OF LONDON

1. *Churches rebuilt in the Georgian period, in chronological order:*

    St Mary Woolnoth (Hawksmoor, 1716–24); St Michael, Cornhill: tower only (probably Hawksmoor, 1721); St Botolph, Bishopgate (J. Gold, 1725–9); St Botolph, Aldgate (G. Dance I, 1741–4); All Hallows, London Wall (G. Dance II, 1765–7; interior rebuilt to original design, 1962); St Botolph, Aldersgate Street (N. Wright, 1789–91); St Dunstan-in-the-West (J. Shaw, 1829–33).

    Synagogue: Spanish and Portuguese Synagogue, Bevis Marks (1700–1).

2. *Public buildings:*

    Bank of England. Sir R. Taylor's Court Room, Sir J. Soane's outer wall, and certain Soane interiors were retained (though with severe modification) in the rebuildings, 1925 onwards.

    Custom House (D. Laing, 1813–17; centre rebuilt by Smirke, 1825).

    Mansion House (G. Dance I, 1739–53).

297

St Bartholomew's Hospital (Hall and Ward Blocks by Gibbs, 1730 onwards; later work, including Church of St Bartholomew the Less, by T. Hardwick from 1808, and by P. Hardwick, 1851).

Trinity House, Tower Hill. See STEPNEY (*Tower Hill Area*).

3. *City Companies' Halls built mainly in the Georgian period:*
Apothecaries' Hall (remodelled in late-18th-c); Fishmongers' Hall (H. Roberts, 1831–3); Goldsmiths' Hall (P. Hardwick, 1829–35); Skinners' Hall (façade *c.*1790; mid 18th c. staircase); Stationers' Hall (east front by R. Mylne, 1800); Watermen's Hall (late-18th-c. façade).

4. *Domestic buildings:*
Crescent, Circus, and American Square (off the Minories). Layout by G. Dance II, *c.*1760–70. A few original houses survive in the Crescent.

Crutched Friars, No. 42 (early 18th c.).

Devonshire Square, Nos. 7, 12, and 13 (mid and late 18th c.)

Fredericks Place (speculation by the Adam Brothers 1776).

Idol Lane, No. 9 (early-18th-c.; fine staircases).

Laurence Pountney Hill, Nos. 1 and 2 (1703 with finely carved doorcases).

New Street (off Bishopsgate). Former East India Company Warehouses (from 1782 onwards). Nos. 5–7 (1775).

Salisbury Square, No. 1 (early 18th c., with angle pilasters).

CITY OF WESTMINSTER

1. *Abbey area:*
Westminster Abbey. West towers by Hawksmoor and James, 1734-40.

Westminster School. Dormitory (Lord Burlington, 1722–30).

St John, Smith Square (Archer, 1713–28). *Outer walls only survive.*

Smith Square. Built about 1726. Original houses survive on the north side.

Lord North Street. Nearly complete street of *c.*1720.

Barton Street. A complete street, built 1722.

Cowley Street. As Barton Street.

Great College Street, Nos. 16–18 (*c.*1720).

Old Palace Yard, Nos. 6 and 7 (John Vardy, *c*.1750-60).

Queen Anne's Gate, Nos. 15-25 and 26-46 (*c*.1704 with finely carved doorcases); Nos. 5-13 and 14-24 (late 18th c.).

2. *Whitehall area:*

Whitehall. Admiralty (Ripley 1723-6; screen to court-yard by Adam, 1760); Admiralty House (S. P. Cockerell, 1786); Dover House (Paine, 1755, with extension to Whitehall by Holland, 1787); Gwydyr House (J. Marquand, 1722); Horse Guards (Vardy after Kent, 1750-8); Paymaster General's Office (John Lane, 1732-3); Treasury (elevation to St James's Park by Kent, 1734-6; Whitehall elevation by Barry, 1844-5, re-using Soane's columns of 1824-7).

Richmond Terrace (T. Chawner, 1822-5).

Downing Street, No. 10 (front part probably by Kenton Couse, 1766-74; at the rear is a 17th-c. house, entirely remodelled, probably by Flitcroft, *c*.1735; dining-room and breakfast room by Soane, 1825); No. 11 (contains a dining-room by Soane).

Parliament Street. No. 43 (*c*.1753; stairs with 'Chinese' balustrade).

3. *Strand area:*

St Paul, Covent Garden (Inigo Jones, 1631-2; largely rebuilt by Hardwick, 1795-8).

St Clement Danes: tower (Gibbs, 1719-20).

St Mary-le-Strand (Gibbs, 1714-17).

Somerset House (Chambers, 1776-86; east wing, Smirke, 8128-34; west wing, Pennethorne, 1852-6).

Fleet Street, No. 37, Hoare's Bank (Charles Parker, 1829).

Gough Square (off Fleet Street). Dr Johnson's house (*c*.1700 with later alterations).

Strand, Nos. 430-449, with buildings in Adelaide Street and William IV Street ('West Strand Improvements', *c*.1830).

Charing Cross Hospital (D. Burton, 1831-4).

Buckingham Street, 17th-c. houses with many 18th-c. alterations.

Covent Garden Market (C. Fowler, 1828-30; many later additions).

King Street, Covent Garden, No. 43 (Archer, *c*.1704; Baroque façade).

Adam Street, Adelphi, No. 7 (The only surviving house in the Adelphi illustrating the original decorative treatment).

APPENDIX I

John Adam Street, Adelphi. Royal Society of Arts (R. Adam
1772–4).
Drury Lane Theatre (exterior, rotunda, and staircases by B. D.
Wyatt, 1810; portico and colonnade by S. Beazley, 1831).

4. *St Martin's area:*
St Martin-in-the-Fields (Gibb 1722–6).
Trafalgar Square (laid out by J. Nash). National Gallery (Wil-
kins, 1834–8; many additions). Royal College of Physicians
and Canada House (former Union Club), forming west side
of square (Smirke, 1824–7).
Haymarket, No. 34 (Fribourg and Treyer; late-18th-c. shop-
front).
Haymarket Theatre (Nash, 1820, with modern interior).
Royal Opera Arcade. Surviving portion of Royal Opera House,
Haymarket, as reconstructed by J. Nash 1816–18.
Suffolk Street and Suffolk Place (laid out and generally designed
by J. Nash, 1820–3). Royal Society of British Artists Gallery,
Suffolk Street (Nash, 1823).
St Martin's Place, Nos. 1–4 (St Martin's National Schools, 1830);
No. 5 (former Vestry Hall); Nos. 6–8, houses. All part of the
'West Strand Improvements' of c.1830.
Goodwin's Court (off St Martin's Lane). Late-18th-c. shops.

5. *Soho area:*
St Anne, Soho. Tower (S. P. Cockerell, 1802–6). Church demolished.
Soho Square, No. 26 (late 18th c. with Venetian window); No.
37 (big corner house, mid 18th c., with Greek Doric shopfront
of c.1820).
Greek Street, No. 1 (House of Charity; fine interiors of c.1740);
No. 50 (c.1730).
Frith Street, No. 5 (c.1750); Nos. 58 and 59 (late 18th c.); No.
60 (late 17th c. with late-19th-c. doorcase).
Dean Street, Nos. 67 and 68 (return of Meard's Street, see
below); No. 76 (large house with rusticated windows,
c.1740); No. 78 (Meard's Street type); No. 88 (late-18th-c.
shop-front).
Meard's Street (off Dean Street. Dated 1732.)
Broadwick Street. Nos. 48–58 (c.1730; doorcases as in Meard's
Street).

300

Golden Square, No. 11 (late 18th c. with fine doorcase).

Great Pulteney Street. 18th-c. houses, especially Nos. 37–9.

6. *St James's area:*

St James's Square, No. 4 (Leoni, *c.*1725); No. 5 (Brettingham, 1748–51, refaced); Nos. 9 and 10 (Flitcroft, 1736); No. 15 (James Stuart, 1763); No. 20 (Robert Adam, 1775–89); No. 32 (S. P. Cockerell, for the Bishop of London, *c.*1820).

St James's Street, Nos. 3 and 6 (late-18th-c. shop-fronts); No. 28 (Boodle's Club; J. Crunden, 1775); No. 60 (Brooks's Club; Holland, 1778); Nos. 69–70 (Carlton Club, former Arthur's Club; T. Hopper, 1826–7).

Arlington Street, No. 22 (Kent *c.*1740–55; much altered).

St James's Place. Spencer House (J. Vardy, after General Gray, 1756–65; interior work by J. Stuart and H. Holland).

Pall Mall. Athenaeum Club (D. Burton, 1829–30); Travellers' Club (Barry, 1829–32); United Services Club (Nash, 1827; altered by Burton, 1858).

Carlton House Terraces (J. Nash, 1827–32). Surviving interiors by Nash at Nos. 5, 11, 12, and 13. Interior of No. 1 by J. P. Gandy-Deering, 1820–30.

Carlton Gardens. Lay-out and general design by Nash, *c.*1827.

Duke of York's Column (B. D. Wyatt, 1833).

Lancaster House, St James's Palace (B. D. Wyatt, after Smirke and followed by Barry, 1820–33).

Marlborough House (C. Wren, jr. 1709–10; alterations by Chambers 1771).

7. *Band Street area:*

St George, Hanover Square (J. James, 1720–4).

Hanover Square, No. 24 (remarkable brick front, *c.*1717).

St George Street. Nos. 12–14, 16, and 17 (German-style fronts, *c.*1717); No. 15 typical *c.*1720); Nos. 30 and 32 (German style).

Conduit Street, No. 9 (James Wyatt, 1779; interior much altered).

Clifford Street, Nos. 8 (with painted staircase) and 9 (both *c.*1720); No. 18 (1717).

Burlington Arcade (Samuel Ware, 1815–19, with modern entrances).

Burlington Gardens, No. 7 (former Uxbridge House, now Bank of Scotland; Leoni, 1721, altered 1792).

Old Burlington Street, No. 6 (*c*.1720); No. 31 (important Palladian house, *c*.1730).

Savile Row. Laid out by Burlington, 1733. The east side was a uniform terrace, of which Nos. 3 and 11–17 survive.

Sackville Street. Prevailing date of surviving houses, *c*.1740–50; Nos. 16–21 is a representative group.

Albany, Piccadilly (Sir W. Chambers, *c*.1770, as a private house; blocks of chambers and forecourt added by Holland, 1804).

Albemarle Street. Nos. 5 (stone front, c.1765) and 7 (1732, with fine elliptical staircase, *c*.1810).

Grafton Street, Nos. 3–6 (probably by Taylor, *c*.1750–60).

Dover Street, No. 37 (fine stone façade by Taylor, for the Bishop of Ely, 1772).

8. *Mayfair:*

Grosvenor Chapel, South Audley Street (B. Timbrell, 1730).

St Mark, North Audley Street (J. P. Gandy-Deering, 1825–8; interior reconstructed 1878).

Grosvenor Square. No original houses now survive. The streets around Grosvenor Square are still basically Georgian, the prevailing date being c.1725–30; but no single house has escaped alteration in later Georgian, Victorian, or modern times. The houses listed below are either outstanding in themselves or good representative examples.

Brook Street, Nos. 25 and 27 (survivors from the original street).

Upper Brook Street, No. 33 (Sir R. Taylor, *c*.1765); Nos. 35 and 36 (with rusticated stone doorcases, *c*.1750).

Grosvenor Street. Houses dating from *c*.1725–30 include Nos. 16 (five-window front with quoins), 45, 49–53, 60, 66, 67, and 68.

Upper Grosvenor Street. Original houses (*c*.1725) include Nos. 44, 45, and the well-preserved No. 48.

North Audley Street, Nos. 11 and 12 (stucco front of *c*.1825; the interior of No. 12 includes a fine staircase and gallery of *c*.1740).

South Audley Street, No. 71 (exceptional house by E. Shepherd, 1736–7).

Davies Street, Nos. 51 and 53 (Grosvenor Office, stucco front probably by T. Chundy, *c*.1825. Interior earlier but with many 'period' alterations). Bourdon House (small house with walled garden, 1721–5).

Berkeley Square, No. 44 (Kent, 1744, with staircase and saloon of exceptional splendour); Nos. 45 and 46 (stone-fronted, with rusticated doorcases and fine iron lamp-holders; probably by Isaac Ware, c.1750–60). The streets adjoining Berkeley Square, including Charles Street, Hill Street, and Bruton Street, are still basically Georgian, the prevailing date being c.1750–60. Of this period Nos. 17, 40, and 48 Charles Street and 36 Hill Street are good examples. No. 10 Hill Street has an exceptionally fine Adam-style doorcase (spoilt by later balcony).

Curzon Street with adjoining streets, including Chesterfield Street, Hertford Street, and Half-Moon Street. The area is still largely of the period 1750–60, the most perfect exterior of that date being No. 2 Chesterfield Street. No. 29 Curzon Street appears to be c.1730; No. 30 contains decorations by Adam, 1771–2; Nos. 17–23, 31, and 32 (c. 1750–60). Hertford Street is somewhat later, Nos. 10, 18, 46, and others being late 18th c.

Clarges Street. Laid out 1718; houses at the south end may be of this date (mostly now stuccoed, but Nos. 7, 8, 9, and 45 show early brick-work). Nos. 14, 15, 32, 33, and 34 (c.1780, with Coade ornaments). The street is remarkable for its completeness and variety of types.

Park Lane, Nos. 93–99 (group of bow-fronted houses, originally mid 18th c., now much altered). See also Dunraven Street, No. 100 (Dudley House; W. Atkinson 1824–7; originally stuccoed).

Dunraven Street, Nos. 22 and 25–31 are 18th- and early-19th-c. houses with bowed fronts to Park Lane.

Piccadilly. Apsley House (remodelled by B. D. Wyatt for the Duke of Wellington, 1828, but retains interiors by Adam, 1771–8); No. 94 (Naval and Military Club, formerly Egremont House; mid 18th c.); No. 106 (St James's Club, formerly Coventry House, c.1766, with interiors by R. Adam).

Marble Arch (Nash, 1828; originally built in the forecourt of Buckingham Palace).

Hyde Park. Screen at Hyde Park Corner and Park Lodges (Burton, 1825 etc.). Bridge over Serpentine (G. Rennie, 1826).

9. *Belgravia*:
St Peter, Eaton Square (Hakewill, 1824–7; interior reconstructed 1873–5).
Belgrave Square. Designed by George Basevi, 1825 onwards,

except for separate houses in the N.W., S.W., and S.E. corners, viz: Nos. 12 (by Smirke), 24 (originally by Hakewill, 1827, but altered out of recognition), and 37 (Seaford House, by P. Hardwick, 1842).

Eaton Square and adjacent streets, mostly designed by T. and L. Cubitt, 1825 onwards.

St George's Hospital, Hyde Park Corner (Wilkins, 1827).

10. *Buckingham Palace area:*

Buckingham Palace (J. Nash, 1824–30; incorporating the shell of old Buckingham House. Additions by Pennethorne and Blore; present front to the Mall, 1913).

Buckingham Gate, Nos. 13–18 (18th c., various dates); No. 16 (1706).

Constitution Hill. Arch (Burton, 1828; moved to present position, 1883).

BATTERSEA

St Mary's Church (Joseph Dixon, 1775–7). A typical Georgian village church.

Vicarage Crescent, No. 44 (early 18th c. with good iron gates).

BERMONDSEY

1. *Bermondsey area:*

St James, Spa Road (Savage, 1827–9; one of the finest of the C.B.C. churches).

Long Lane, Nos. 146–8 (early 18th c.), 175, and 135–45 (early 19th c.).

Grange Walk, Nos. 5–11 (early-18th-c. group), 44, and 67 (early 18th c.).

2. *Rotherhithe area:*

St Mary, St Mary Church Street (1714–15; tower 1738–47).

St Marychurch Street. The Peter Hills School (early 18th c.).

Mayflower Street, Nos. 6 and 26–34 (remains of fine street dated 1721–6).

Rotherhithe Street, No. 141 (late-18th-c. warehouse); No. 265 (mansion of *c.*1750 with frontispiece and belvedere).

APPENDIX I

BETHNAL GREEN

St Matthew, St Matthew's Row (Dance the Elder, 1743–6; restored after bombing).

St John, Cambridge Heath Road (Soane, 1825–8; C.B.C.; interior wholly remodelled).

Victoria Park Square, Nos. 16–18 (very early 18th c.).

Old Ford Road, Nos. 2–4 (late-18th-c. terrace); Nos. 17–21 (mid-18th-c. terrace).

CAMBERWELL

1. *Camberwell area:*
St George, Wells Way (Bedford, 1822–4; C.B.C.).

Camberwell Road. Nos. 56–84 and 117–155 (terraces, c.1800); No. 86 (Coade stone reliefs from Dr Lettsom's house in Camberwell Grove).

Peckham Road, Nos. 30–34 (three linked houses, set back behind lawn), and No. 33, with other houses, opposite (terrace, pair, and another house); all c.1790.

Camberwell Grove. Grove Chapel (D. R. Roper, 1819); Grove Crescent (after 1815); and several late-18th- and early-19th-c. groups of houses. No. 220, the modernized remains of a 'cottage ornée'.

2. *Peckham area:*
Friends Meeting House, Highshore Road (1826).

Licensed Victuallers' Asylum, Asylum Road (1827–31).

Queen's Road, Nos. 4–10 (early 18th c., including a semi-detached pair).

3. *Denmark Hill area:*
[1]Denmark Hill. Nos. 150–4. Remains of formal group of houses, c.1780; centre house has colonnade-porch, an early example of this South London type. *Derelict in 1962.*

Champion Hill, No. 23. Durlstone Manor Hotel (late-18th-c. villa with Doric colonnade-porch).

4. *Dulwich Village area:*
Dulwich College Picture Gallery (Soane, 1811–14).

1. Actually in Lambeth.

Dulwich Village. Mixed Georgian development on the east side, including Nos. 57 (villa of c.1820), 59 (c.1740), and 97–105 (mostly early 18th c.)

Village Way. Pond House (Palladian lodge of c.1750, with Victorian additions).

College Road. Bell House (Palladian, 1767).

Pond Cottages (off College Road), No. 3 (mid-18th-c. front in red and blue bricks).

Dulwich Common. 'Northcroft' (double villa of c.1820) and other stucco villas.

CHELSEA

Royal Hospital. Ancillary buildings by Soane, including the Stable Block (1814) and the Secretary's Office (1818–19).

Duke of York's Headquarters (Sanders, 1801).

1. *Riverside area:*

   Cheyne Walk. No. 2 (refronted, but interiors are early 18th c.); Nos. 3–6 (group of important houses, 1717–18); No. 16 ('Queen's House', 1717); Nos. 19–26 (terrace of c.1760); Nos. 46–8 (c. 1711); Nos. 91–4 (group, dated 1771–7; No. 92 is an unusual composition with canted bay and Venetian windows).

   Cheyne Row, Nos. 24 and 26, and 30–4 and others on east side are part of street begun 1708.

   Upper Cheyne Row, Nos. 24–8 (c.1716 much altered).

   Lawrence Street. Nos. 23 and 24 (early-18th-c. pair with doors under single pediment).

2. *King's Road area:*

   St Luke, Sydney Street (Savage, 1820–4; Gothic).

   King's Road, No. 211 Argyll House; G. Leoni, 1723); Nos. 213–15 (1720) and 217 (c.1750).

   Royal Avenue (17th-c. lay-out on axis of Royal Hospital) leading to St Leonard's Terrace.

   St Leonard's Terrace (Nos. 14–31 c.1765 and later).

   Sydney Street. Early-19th-c. street with some contemporary shops (especially No. 119).

   Smith Street. Late 18th c. Nos. 6–16 have unusual fronts with sunk panels.

   Paulton's Square (uniform small houses, c.1830).

3. *Hans Town area:*
  Sloane Street, Cadogan Place, and Hans Place, laid out by Henry
  Holland from 1771. A few of the original houses (two windows wide and very plain) survive. Nos. 104–6 Sloane Street
  are a trio of one-window fronts with fan tympana; No. 139
  has the same motif differently treated; No. 123 has an unusual
  doorway (all *c*.1780).

DEPTFORD

St Paul, Deptford High Street (Archer, 1712–30).
General Baptist Church. Deptford Church Street (1674; remodelled in 18th c.).
¹Albury Street. Substantial remains of a street of small houses,
  c.1725, with finely carved doorways.

FINSBURY

1. *Clerkenwell area:*
  St James, Clerkenwell (James Carr, 1788–92).
  Clerkenwell Green. Former Middlesex Sessions House (T. Rogers
    after J. Carter, 1779–82; much altered).
  Corporation Row, Nos. 35–45 (mid 18th c., much altered).
  Sekforde Street. Early-19th-c. street. Ironworks adjoining No. 26.
  Charterhouse Square, Nos. 4–5 (early 18th c. with Regency
    doorways), 12–14 (late 18th c.), and 22 (*c*.1775, with Coade
    ornaments).

2. *Old Street–City Road area:*
  St Luke, Old Street (1727–32; architect unknown).
  St Barnabas, King Square (T. Hardwick, 1822–3; C.B.C.;
    classical with spire). Planned relationship to King Square.
  Wesley's Chapel. City Road (1777–8).
  Old Street. Former St Luke's Hospital (more recently Bank of
    England printing works; Dance the younger, 1782–4). Nos.
    72–4 (shop-front of *c*.1785).
  Helmet Row. St Luke's Vicarage (1774 with doorcase of *c*.1730).
  King Square. Early 19th c. Only west and part of south side
    survive in 1962.
  City Road. Honourable Artillery Company's Headquarters
    (1735; wings added 1828). No. 47 John Wesley's House
    (*c*.1770).

1. Actually in Greenwich.

APPENDIX I

Chiswell Street. Whitbread's Brewery (incorporating early-18th-c. house; Porter Tun Room, 1774); Nos. 44 etc. (late-18th-c. terrace adjoining brewery).

3. *New River area:*

St Mark, Myddelton Square (W. C. Mylne, 1825–7; C.B.C.; Gothic).

Northampton Square. Begun 1802. Uniform and nearly intact.

New River Company's estate includes Claremont Square (1821) and Myddelton Square, Amwell Street, Mylne Street, and Chadwell Street; all plain, impressively uniform compositions of the 1820s.

Percy Circus (*c.*1830). Gauchely planned on a sloping site. Now partly destroyed.

Wilmington Square (begun 1818). Uniform and complete.

Lloyd Baker estate comprises Lloyd Square and Lloyd Baker Street (semi-detached brick houses of interesting design; 1819 onwards).

FULHAM

St John, Walham Green (J. H. Taylor, 1827–8; C.B.C.; Gothic).

Fulham Palace. East block by S. P. Cockerell (1814, for Bishop Howley).

Hurlingham House (*c.*1760, with stuccoed river front of 1797).

Parsons Green. Belfield House (early 18th c.).

New King's Road. Nos. 128–60 ('Elysium Row'; dated 1738; Nos. 237–47 (1795; later window openings).

GREENWICH

1. *Greenwich area:*

St Alphege, Greenwich Church Street (Hawksmoor, 1712–14).

Royal Naval College. All the significant buildings are of the 17th c., completed, in some cases, in the early 18th. The most conspicuous exterior Georgian additions are the Greek Doric colonnades attached to the Queen's House and leading to wings, the work of Daniel Alexander (1807–10). The interior of the Chapel is by William Newton acting for James Stuart (1779–89).

National School (1814) next St Alphege Churchyard.

Queen Elizabeth's Almhouses, Greenwich High Road (1819).

Nelson Road and Church Street. Stucco façades (improvement scheme of 1826–9) and Market (1831), all by J. Kay.

Greenwich High Road, Nos. 98, 100, etc. (early 19th c.).

Stockwell Street, Nos. 10–11 (early 18th c.).

Croom's Hill, Nos. 2–4 (early 18th c.); Nos. 6–12 (two fine pairs, 1723); Nos. 14–36 (various dates); No. 52 (17th–18th c.); Nos. 54–60 (terrace of c.1760); Manor House (c.1700).

Gloucester Circus, Circus Street, Royal Hill, King George Street. Small houses, mostly early 19th c.

Chesterfield Walk. Macartney House (early 18th c., altered by Soane, 1802).

Ranger's House (fine early-18th-c. brick mansion with wings of c.1754).

West Grove, No. 17, and Point House.

Park Vista, Manor House (early 18th c.) and Vicarage (mostly 18th c.).

Greenwich Park Street. Park Terrace (1823).

Maze Hill, Nos. 47–9 (early 18th c.); Vanbrugh Castle, the architect's own house (1717–c.1726).

Mycenae Road. The Woodlands (stone-built country villa, 1772–4).

2. *Blackheath area:*
St Michael, Blackheath Park (G. Smith, 1830; Gothic).

Blackheath Road, Nos. 25–9 (stucco villas, c.1820).

[1]Blackheath Hill, Nos. 87–91 (mixed group, c.1790); Nos. 106 and 108 (c.1760).

[1]Dartmouth Row, Nos. 21 and 23 (Spencer House and Percival House; originally one house, c.1750); Nos. 20–2 (irregular group); Nos. 28–36 (group of various dates; No. 30 has an interesting Palladian front of c.1730).

[1]Eliot Place. No. 1 ('Heathfield House'; c.1820, with entry behind piers); No. 6 (central pedimented house); Nos. 7 and 8 ('Eliot Place 1792').

Blackheath Park. Estate development on wide avenue, with St Michael's Church and good classical villas by George Smith (c.1825–30).

[1]Montpelier Row, Nos. 1–16 (late-18th-c. terrace).

[1]South Row. Colonnade House (c.1790, with colonnade).

Paragon. Crescent of large semi-detached houses, linked by colonnades (designed by Michael Searles, c.1790).

1. Actually in Lewisham.

Paragon House (*c*.1790).

HACKNEY

1. *Mare Street area* (*north to south*):
St John the Baptist, Mare Street (J. Spiller, 1791–7, steeple, 1811).
Mare Street, No. 387 ('Manor House', late 18th or early 19th c.);
No. 195 (18th-c. mansion).
Spurstow's Almshouses (1819).
Paragon Road, Nos. 71–83 (terrace of houses connected by
porches, *c*.1810; unusual design).

2. *Clapton Road area* (*south to north*):
Clapton Square (*c*.1820). Semi-detached and terrace houses sur-
vive on north and west sides.
Lower Clapton Road, No. 162 (stucco villa of *c*.1800); Nos.
145–53 (semi-detached trio, *c*.1820).
Linscott Road. Former London Orphan Asylum (W. S. Inman,
c.1823; now Salvation Army Congress Hall).
Clapton Common, Nos. 43–7 (terrace of *c*.1800) and 49–67 (ter-
race of *c*.1740).
Springfield Park. Mansion (stucco villa of *c*.1820).

3. *Homerton area:*
Sutton Place (uniform terrace of *c*.1820).
Homerton High Street, Nos. 140–2 (pair, *c*.1750).
Homerton Row. Baptist Chapel (1822).
Hassett Road. Convent of the Sacred Heart (incorporating a
house of *c*.1790).
Berger's Paint Works, with early-19th-c. warehouse and clock
turret of 1805.

HAMMERSMITH

1. *River front:*
Upper Mall, Nos. 12 and 14 ('Sussex House', *c*.1726); No. 26
('Kelmscott House', *c*.1785); No. 36 ('Rivercourt House',
1808 with earlier features).
Lower Mall, No. 10 ('Kent House', *c*.1760 and later); No. 22
(*c*.1780).
Hammersmith Terrace (mostly *c*.1770, but perhaps begun
1755).

2. *West Hammersmith:*

St Peter's Church (Lapidge, 1827–9; C.B.C.).

Ravenscourt Park. The Mansion (*c.*1720 with earlier features).

St Peter's Square. Stuccoed houses in linked groups of four (*c.*1825–30).

HAMPSTEAD

1. *Hampstead Village area:*

St John, Church Row (J. Sanderson, 1745–7; lengthened and re-oriented 1878).

Church Row, Nos. 16–28 (houses of *c.*1720); Nos. 5–12 (*c.*1720 and later. No. 5 is weatherboarded; No. 12 has a Doric pilaster order executed in brick).

Hampstead High Street. Vane House (17th c., stuccoed, with entry by Soane); Stanfield House (*c.*1730); Nos. 68–75 (early and late 18th c.); Nos. 82 and 83 (early 18th c.).

Heath Street, Nos. 60–2 (*c.*1730 with late-18th-c. porch); Nos. 92–8 (various dates); Nos. 113–25 (irregular group of 18th-c. cottages).

The Mount (off Heath Street), No. 5 (early 18th c., with wrought-iron gate); Nos. 8–12 (18th or early 19th c.).

Holly Hill, Nos. 16–24 (late-18th-c. cottages).

Holly Bush Hill, Nos. 2, 3, and 4 (late-18th-c. houses with angular bays); No. 5 (1797 for George Romney; weatherboarded).

Holly Mount (early 18th c. and later; gardens over vaults in Holly Hill).

Windmill Hill. Terrace of four houses (*c.*1730).

Mount Vernon, Nos. 1–7 (*c.*1800–10, including terrace of four houses).

Holly Place. Lay-out of small houses, dated 1816, with R.C. Church (front *c.*1830) in centre.

Benham's Place (cottages, dated 1813).

Prospect Place. Two pairs of narrow timber-frame houses with stuccoed fronts and weatherboarded backs (*c.*1815).

Frognal, No. 94 (The Old Mansion, *c.*1700 and later); Nos. 104 and 106 (pair, *c.*1760); No. 108 (formerly three houses, mid. 18th c.); No. 110 (perhaps early 18th c.); Nos. 103, 105, and 107 (three contiguous premises, incorporating the house built by Flitcroft for himself, *c.*1745).

Upper Terrace, Nos. 1–4 (terrace of *c.*1740).

Lower Terrace, Nos. 1–4 (late-18th-c. group).

The Grove, Old Grove House (early 18th c., much altered); Admiral's House (early or mid. 18th c., with many excrescences).

New End, Nos. 10–14 (early 18th c.).

New End Square, Burgh House (mansion of 1703; fine iron gates).

Elm Row, Nos. 1–5, with No. 110 Heath Street (canopied balcony) and No. 1 Hampstead Square (all about 1720–30).

Hampstead Square, No. 1 (see Elm Row above). Nos. 3, 12, and Vine House are early-18th-c. mansions.

Cannon Place, Cannon Hall (early-18th-c. mansion).

Squire's Mount. Terrace of houses (c.1720–30).

Well Walk, Nos. 32–40 (mid 18th c.); No. 46 (with late-18th-c. Gothic front).

East Heath Road, No. 11 (Foley House; c.1750 and later).

Heath Side. Heath Lodge and Heath Side (pair, c.1810); No. 1 East Heath Road and South Heath (pair with pediment, c.1770).

2. *South End area:*

St John, Downshire Hill (1818, much altered).

Downshire Hill. Ranges of brick and stucco houses of mixed types, c.1815 onwards.

Keats Grove. Development similar to Downshire Hill above.

South End Road, Nos. 71–107 (range of mixed types of early-19th-c. cottages).

Rosslyn Hill, Nos. 22–4 (semi-detached pair, dated 1702).

Pond Street, Nos. 19–21 (late-18th-c. pair); Nos. 33–5 (early 18th c. with carved Doric doorcases).

3. *Belsize area:*

Belsize Grove, Nos. 26–38 (terrace, c.1825).

Belsize Lane, No. 5 (Hunter's Lodge; late-18th-c. ornamental cottage).

4. *Vale of Health:*

Vale Lodge and houses adjoining (late-18th- and early-19th-c. cottages).

HOLBORN

1. *St Giles area:*

St Giles-in-the-Fields (Flitcroft, 1731–4).

APPENDIX I

St George, Bloomsbury Way (Hawksmoor, 1716–23).

British Museum (Smirke, 1823–47).

Bloomsbury Square, Nos. 5 and 6 (c.1740, probably by Flitcroft);
Pharmaceutical Society's premises (Nash, c.1777–8, with pilastered stucco front).

Great Russell Street, Nos. 99–106 (17th c. remodelled in 18th c.).

Southampton Place. Rows of uniform houses (c.1740–50).

Bedford Square, Bedford Place, Bedford Way, Torrington
Square, Woburn Square. *See* ST PANCRAS.

2. *Holborn north area:*

St George, Queen Square (1703–23; much altered 1867–8).

Queen Square. Georgian houses of various dates on the west
side.

Old Gloucester Street, No. 44 (c.1710).

Great Ormond Street, Nos. 1–15 and 2–16 (early-18th-c. groups);
Nos. 40 (c.1740) and 41 (richly carved doorcases, c.1730–40).

Lambs Conduit Street, Nos. 29–37 with return in Dombey Street
(mid 18th c.).

Dombey Street. Nos. 8–15 (mid-18th-c. terrace). *See also* Lambs
Conduit Street.

Theobalds Road, Nos. 14–22 (c.1750).

Bedford Row. Nearly complete Georgian Street. Nos. 36 and 43
are probably late 17th c. (No. 36 has one of the earliest fanlights in London); the prevailing date of the remainder is
c.1720, except where rebuilt at various times; No. 11 has a
painted staircase.

Great James Street. Northward continuation of Bedford Row.
Mostly c.1720.

Millman Street. Extends northwards from Great James Street,
but of the old houses Nos. 2–12 only survive.

John Street. Mid-18th-c. street partly rebuilt. Continues northward as Doughty Street (*see* ST PANCRAS).

Red Lion Square. Only two original houses survive (Nos. 14 and
15; both refronted in early 19th c.).

Gray's Inn. Mostly 17th c. Georgian parts are Verulam Buildings
(1805–11) and Raymond Buildings (1825). In Field Court, iron
gates and piers (1723).

Warwick Court, No. 8 ('Warwick House'; stone front of c.
1810).

Hatton Garden, Nos. 16–18 (early 18th c.).

Ely Place. Close of 1773, built by E. Cole.

4. *Lincoln's Inn area:*

New Square, Lincoln's Inn (1691 onwards).

Carey Street, No. 60 (early 18th c. with painted staircase).

Stone Buildings, Lincoln's Inn (Taylor, 1774–80; completed 1843).

Lincoln's Inn Fields, Nos. 12, 13, and 14 (Soane, 1792, 1812, and 1824 respectively; No. 13 is Sir John Soane's Museum); Nos. 57 and 58 (Henry Joynes, *c.*1730 in imitation of Lindsey House, attributed to Inigo Jones, adjoining). No. 65 (T. Leverton, 1772).

Took's Court (off Cursitor Street). Nos. 14 and 15 (*c.*1720 with fine brickwork).

Staple Inn. Inner Court, dated 1734 and 1757–9.

ISLINGTON

1. *Islington area:*

St Mary, Upper Street (L. Dowbiggin, 1751–4, but all except the tower rebuilt after bombing).

Islington High Street, Nos. 80 (mid 18th c.) and 84–94 (mid-18th-c. terrace).

Colebrooke Row. Terrace houses in groups of various dates from *c.*1715 to *c.*1830. The earliest are Nos. 56 and 57 (pair, *c.*1715, with bracketted hoods to doors); Nos. 1–28 range between *c.*1810 and *c.*1830; Nos. 34–6 are *c.*1775 but much altered; Nos. 41–53 are *c.*1760, some retaining pedimented Doric doorcases; Nos. 60–65 are *c.*1770.

Duncan Terrace (opposite the above). Terrace houses in groups of various dates from 1791 to *c.*1830. The earliest are Nos. 50–8 ('New Terrace 1791') and 46–9 (similar style and date). Nos. 1–45 proceed in groups from *c.*1800 to *c.*1830.

Charlton Place. Late 18th c., with the west side curved ('Charlton Crescent 1795').

Camden Walk. Uniform mid-18th-c. *Derelict in 1962.*

Cross Street. Mid-18th-c. houses with pedimented Doric doorcases. Nos. 23, 33, and 35 have later doorcases imitating Adam work in the Adelphi.

Essex Road, Nos. 246–290 ('Annett's Crescent', early 19th c.); Nos. 294–300 (two early-19th-c. stucco villas and a house with veranda).

2. *Canonbury area:*

Canonbury Square. Formed by J. Leroux. *c.*1800; plain houses, mostly uniform.

Compton Terrace (east side of Upper Street). Built by Leroux from 1806.

Canonbury Place. Dated 1780 on rainwater heads. No. 1 has Adam-style pilastered front. All stuccoed (unusual at this date). Canonbury House (brick and stone), *c.*1780.

Alywne Villas. Plain terrace houses including 'Canonbury Terrace 1824'.

Canonbury Grove. Various early-19th-c. formations, including Nos. 13–22 (*c.*1810; unusual composition, apparently uncompleted).

3. *Highbury area:*

St Mary Magdalene, Holloway Road (W. Wickings, 1812).

St John, Holloway Road (Barry, 1826–8; C.B.C.; Gothic).

Highbury Place. Successive terraces comprising thirty-nine houses, built from *c.*1774, onwards and designed by J. Spiller (No. 39 was his own house).

Highbury Terrace. Series of linked terraces (centre block dated 1789).

4. *Barnsbury area:*

Holy Trinity, Cloudesley Square (Barry, 1826–8; C.B.C.; Gothic).

Cloudesley Square and adajacent streets (e.g. Cloudesley Road, Place, and Street, Stonefield Street, Barnsbury Street): good, plain work of *c.*1820–30.

Offord Road, Nos. 85–103 (terrace of *c.*1810).

Hemingford Road, Nos. 44–78 (unusual stuccoed terrace of quasi-semi-detached houses, *c.*1825–30).

Barnsbury Square, with Mountfort Crescent, *c.*1820 (but much rebuilt).

Barnsbury Park. Semi-detached type as in Barnsbury Square, No. 8 (detached stuccoed villa).

Liverpool Road. Almost continuously lined with late-18th- and early-19th-c. terraces, including Nos. 264–92 ('Park Place Islington 1790'), 295, etc. ('Park Terrace 1822'), 281–5 ('Morgans Place 1818'), 84–124 ('Trinidad Place 1834'), 71–197 ('Gloucester Terrace', *c.*1820).

KENSINGTON

1. *Kensington Palace:*

The Orangery (Hawksmoor, 1704–5), The Cupola Room and several other apartments built 1718–26 and decorated by William Kent.

2. *High Street area:*

St Barnabas, Addison Road (Vulliamy, 1827–9; C.B.C.; Gothic).
Kensington Square. Nos. 11 and 12 are the earliest (*c.*1700);
    No. 29 (good late-18th-c. doorway); No. 43–44 (mid 18th c.)
Holland Street. Nos. 18–26 (row of early-18th-c. houses).
Earl's Terrace and Edwardes Square. Early-19th-c. lay-out. The
    terrace is set back from the road. Behind it the square con-
    sists of small houses. In the square garden is a Doric garden-
    house.

3. *South Kensington:*

Holy Trinity, Brompton (Donaldson, 1826–9; C.B.C.; Gothic).
Pelham Crescent and Pelham Place (Basevi, *c.*1830, on the
    Smith Charity estate).
Alexander Square (1827–30, on the Thurloe Estate) and streets
    adjoining.
Brompton Square. Narrow horseshoe of ordinary houses, *c.*1820,
    open to Brompton Road.

LAMBETH

1. *South Bank area:*

St John, Waterloo Road (F. Bedford, 1823–4; C.B.C.).
York Road. General Lying-in Hospital (H. Harrison, 1828).

2. *Lambeth Palace area:*

Pratt Walk (off Lambeth Road), Nos. 4–8 (1775).
Stangate Street, Nos. 6–22 (cottages with ornamented doorways,
    *c.*1785); *derelict in 1962.*
Walnut Tree Walk, Nos. 57–63 (1755; coupled doorways of
    remarkable design).

3. *Kennington area:*

St Mark, Kennington (D. R. Roper, 1822–4; C.B.C.).
Kennington Park Road, Nos. 116–132 (symmetrical arrangement
    of semi-detached houses at entry to Cleaver Square). Various
    late-18th-c. terraces. *See also* SOUTHWARK).
Cleaver Square. Laid out *c.*1788, but the houses mostly early
    19th c.

Clapham Road, Nos. 17–24 (*c*.1800) and other terraces built between 1800 and 1825.

Harleyford Road, St Mark's School (J. Bailey, 1824–5).

Camberwell New Road. Various early-19th-c. terraces.

Foxley Road (off Camberwell New Road), Nos. 32–48 (linked semi-detached pairs, 1824).

Cowley Road (off Vassall Road), Nos. 9–21 (terrace of small houses with unusual panelled stucco fronts).

Kennington Lane, No. 363 (probably by J. M. Gandy, *c*.1825).

Kennington Road. Various late-18th-c. terraces, notably the range of thirty houses comprising Nos. 233–91 (*c*.1795, formerly Chester Place).

4. *South Lambeth area:*
South Lambeth Road, No. 87 (incorporating Beaufoy's Vinegar Works, late 18th c.); No. 274 (Beulah House, 1791–8); Nos. 281–300 (terrace of 1790–1); *derelict in 1962.*
Wandsworth Road, No. 30 (mansion of 1758; later porch).

5. *Brixton area:*
St Matthew. Brixton Hill (C. F. Porden, 1822–4; C.B.C.).
Brixton Road. Various terraces built between 1800 and 1825.

6. *Tulse Hill and Norwood area:*
St Luke, Upper Norwood (F. Bedford, 1823–5; C.B.C.).
Brockwell Park Mansion (D. R. Roper, 1816).

LEWISHAM

St Mary, Lewisham (J. Gibson, 1775–7, much altered internally. Fine south porch).

Lewisham High Street, No. 246. Late-18th-c. mansion.

Manor House, Old Road, Lee (very fine 18th-c. mansion, 1788, now Public Library, with colonnade-porch).

Merchant Taylors' Almshouse, Lee High Road (Jupp, 1826).

[1]Lewisham Way. 'Stone House' (late-18th-c. country villa of unusual character; architect unknown).

PADDINGTON

St Mary, Paddington Green (J. Plaw, 1788–91).

1. Actually in Deptford.

Connaught Square and adjacent streets (built *c*.1828–30; first stage of development on the Bishop of London's estate).

Sussex Gardens, Nos. 1–35 and 2–36 (formerly Oxford and Cambridge Terraces; tree-lined street of terraces). *In process of demolition, 1962.*

Orme Square. Laid out *c*.1818, but the original symmetry is obscured by Victorian alterations.

POPLAR

All Saints, East India Dock Road (J. Hollis, 1821–3). Rectory in Newby Place of same date.

St Matthias. Victorian (1867–70) but encloses Tuscan columns and ceilings of East India Company's Church of 1776.

East India Docks, 1805–6. Entrance gateway (reconstructed 1915) with domed cupola.

West India Docks. A few warehouses by W. Jessop, 1799–1802, remain.

Priscilla Road. Draper's Almshouses, dated 1706. *Derelict in 1962.*

ST MARYLEBONE

1. *Cavendish–Harley area:*
The Oxford Street fringe has been entirely rebuilt. North of Cavendish Square as far as Marylebone High Street, west as far as Baker Street, and east to Regent Street and Portland Place, the area is still predominantly Georgian in spite of much rebuilding. Mostly commonplace speculators' work ranging between 1760 and 1830.

St Peter, Vere Street (the Oxford Chapel; Gibbs 1721–4).

St Marylebone Church (Hardwick 1813–17). Planned relationship to York Gate.

All Souls, Langham Place (Nash, 1822–4; C.B.C.). Planned relationship to Regent Street.

Cavendish Square, No. 3 (*c*.1720), Nos. 11 and 12, 13 and 14 on north side with Corinthian columns and pediments (*c*.1770); No. 20, a modern building, encloses a painted architectural staircase of *c*.1720; No. 17 has a Palladian front of *c*.1730.

Harley Street. No. 2 is an exceptional house with front of *c*.1800. Nos. 26 and 28 (corner of Queen Anne Street) *c*.1760. The remainder 18th to early 19th c.

Wimpole Street, Upper Wimpole Street, and Devonshire Place.
Mostly 18th to early 19th c. No. 24 Upper Wimpole Street has
remarkable ceilings, c.1790.

Queen Anne Street, Nos. 9–13, 14, and 19 (c.1760).

Chandos Street, Chandos House (Adam, 1769–71).

Mansfield Street, Nos. 5–15 and 16–32 (Adam, 1770–5). Opposite the end of the street are Nos. 61–3 New Cavendish Street
(John Johnson, 1775).

Portland Place (1776–c.1780). Street composition with façades
by James Adam. Ruined by continual alteration and much
rebuilding.

Stratford Place (off Oxford Street). Street, partly rebuilt, and
small square leading to a great mansion (usually called Derby
House) at the north end. Designed by R. Edwin, 1773.

2. *Portman area:*

Still predominantly late 18th to early 19th c. but such regular
units as there were have been disrupted.

St Mary, Wyndham Place (Smirke, 1823). Planned relationship
to Bryanston Square.

Portman Square, Nos. 12, 13, and 14 (Wyatt, c.1775–80; much
altered); No. 20 (Home House, now Courtauld Institute;
Adam, 1775–7). The remainder of the square has been or
shortly will be rebuilt.

Baker Street, Nos. 89–115 (west side) and 94–124 (east side) are
the much altered remains of an unusually fine regular street,
with Coade ornaments.

Gloucester Place. A long street of late-18th- to early-19th-c.
houses extending from Portman Square on the south, across
Marylebone Road to Dorset Square. Ordinary quality but
remarkable for its completeness.

Montague Square. A long narrow 'square', fairly complete.

Bryanston Square. Long and narrow, though a little wider than
the last. On an axial line which runs from St Mary's Church
on the north, through Wyndham Place and Bryanston Square
to Great Cumberland Place. The Square has symmetrically
treated east and west sides, with Ionic centres and ends (J.
Parkinson, 1811) but has been partly rebuilt.

Manchester Square. Formerly a Square of uniform houses
1776–88 but now largely rebuilt.

Dorset Square and Blandford Square (early 19th c.) are part of
a continuation of this area north of Marylebone Road.

3. *St John's Wood area:*
St John's Wood Chapel (T. Hardwick, 1813).
Nearly the whole of the original villa building in this area has disappeared but there are some vestiges of the 1820–30 period.
Lodge Road, Nos. 32–40 (small detached houses, *c.*1820–30).
St John's Wood Road, Nos. 31–7 and 38–54 (detached and semi-detached villas, *c.*1825).
Grove End Road, Nos. 47 and 49 (semi-detached pair, *c.*1820; the most characteristic survivor of the early villas).
Melina Place and Elm Tree Road, off Grove End Road. Disorderly villa and cottage development, *c.*1820–30.
Loudoun Road, No. 12 (*c.*1820). *Derelict in 1962.* Nos. 18–26 (Gothic houses, *c.*1830).
Marlborough Place, Nos. 24–32. Gothic houses as in Loudoun Road.
Circus Road, No. 39. House with veranda in large garden, *c.*1825.
Abbey Road, Loudoun Road, and the streets between. Villa development, mostly after 1830, but with a few earlier houses at the street crossings (e.g. Clifton Hill, Carlton Hill).
Woronzow Road. Gothic houses at junction with Norfolk Road, *c.*1830.
Hamilton Terrace, Hall Road, Abercorn Place. Harrow School estate development, begun *c.*1809. The southern stretch of Hamilton Terrace is a mixed array of terraces, detached and semi-detached houses of the 1815–30 period. Nos. 11–18 Cunningham Place and 25–32 Aberdeen Place are vestiges of a more regular development, probably of earlier date, on the same estate.

4 *Regents Park area*[1]:
Starting at Gloucester Gate, on the west, and proceeding clockwise the main surviving architectural features are as follows (by Nash unless otherwise stated): Gloucester Terrace (1827); St Katherine's Hospital (Ambrose Poynter, 1827); Cumberland Terrace (1826); Cumberland Place (1826); Chester Terrace (1825); Cambridge Terrace (1825); St Andrew's Place (1826); St Andrew's Terrace (1823); Park Square (1823–5); Park Crescent (1812–22); Ulster Terrace (1824); York Terraces, East and West, and York Gate (1821–2); Cornwall Terrace (Decimus Burton, 1821); Clarence Terrace (Decimus Burton, 1823); Sussex

1. Partly in the Borough of St Pancras.

Place (1822); Hanover Terrace (1822–3); Kent Terrace (1827); Lodge at Hanover Gate.

The surviving villas in the Park include: Hanover Lodge (architect unknown; partly rebuilt); Grove House (now 'Nuffield Lodge'; D. Burton, 1822–4); The Holme (Dr Burton, for his father, James Burton, c.1818); St John's Lodge (J. Raffield, c.1818).

Park Villages, East and West. Begun by Nash c.1824 and completed by J. Pennethorne. Detached and semi-detached houses in various styles.

ST PANCRAS

1. *North Bloomsbury area:*

   St Pancras, Euston Road (Inwood, 1818–22).

   University College, Gower Street (Wilkins and Gandy-Deering, 1827 with later additions).

   Foundling Hospital. Colonnades of the Hospital (built 1742–52; demolished 1926) in Coram's Fields, Guilford Street.

   Bedford Square. Uniform square with pilastered centres (T. Leverton, from 1776). No. 1 is separately designed and has a fine interior.

   Russell Square. A few unaltered houses (Burton, 1800–14) remain on the west side.

   Tavistock Square. West side (Cubitt, c.1824) is a formal composition preserved as façade to new building. Related to this are the following (all Cubitt): the return front of Tavistock Square (No. 29, with causeway paved in one stone of prodigious size) to Endsleigh Place linked to the return of Gordon Square; Nos. 36–46 and 55–9 Gordon Square; Endsleigh Street; block in angle of Upper Woburn Place and Endsleigh Gardens (Cora Hotel, etc.).

   Woburn Square (Sim, 18829). Both sides substantially intact.

   Torrington Square (Sim, 1821–5). Nine houses only on the west side survive.

   Byng Place. Courtauld House (originally Coward College; Cubitt, 1832, altered).

   Woburn Walk (formerly Woburn Buildings; Cubitt 1822). Uniform shopping passage with return to Duke's Road.

   Mecklenburgh Square. East side (J. Kay, 1812) is a formal composition. Destroyed parts are being rebuilt to original design.

   Heathcote Street, No. 12 (detached stucco villa).

Guilford Street, Lansdowne Terrace, Bernard Street, Coram Street, and Marchmont Street still consist largely of the original houses (Burton and others, around 1810). Nos. 70–3 Guilford Street (Burton) have a Doric façade intended as a decorative termination to Queen Square.

Grenville Street, No. 16. Shop-front (spoilt by modern bars).

Regent Square. Rebuilt except the south side.

Cartwright Gardens, originally Burton Crescent (Skinners' Company Estate; Burton, from c.1807).

Doughty Street. Uniform street of c.1790. Both sides intact south of Guilford Street.

2. *Gray's Inn Road area:*

Gray's Inn Road, Nos. 258, etc. Cubitt's premises (Messrs Holland, Hannen, and Cubitt) since 1815 but much altered.

Frederick Street, Nos. 48–52 (Cubitt, c.1815–20). Stucco fronts with verandas.

3. *Fitzroy area:*

Fitzroy Square. Stone-fronted east and south sides by R. Adam, 1790. North and west sides later.

Charlotte Street. Mostly rebuilt. No. 76 is a survivor of many houses of this type in the south part of the street. Colville Place, on the east, is a pedestrian street, c.1820.

Goodge Place. Four-storey houses with some doorcases of c.1740–50 but later fronts.

Whitfield Street. Nos. 131, 135, 147, and 149. Group of late-18th-c. shop-fronts.

Percy Street. Vestiges of a regular street of c.1760.

4. *North St Pancras area:*

St Mary, Eversholt Street (Inwood, 1822–4; C.B.C.).

All Saints, Campden Street (Inwood, 1822–4; C.B.C.; now leased to the Greek Orthodox Church).

St Aloysius R.C. Church (c.1808; façade 1830).

Euston Square, north side, with Euston Grove. Remains of stucco terraces.

Fortess Road. Nos. 36–94 ('Fortess Terrace', early 19th c.).

St Pancras Gardens, Pancras Road. Tomb of the Soane family, 1816.

5. *Highgate area:*

Ken Wood House (Iveagh Bequest). Mansion reconstructed by

R. Adam, 1768, with additions by G. Saunders, *c*.1795.

Whittington College, Archway Road (G. Smith, 1822, Gothic).

Grove Terrace, Highgate Road (late 18th c.).

[1]Highgate Hill, Nos. 106–108 (early 18th c. pair); No. 110 (early 18th c.); Nos. 128–30 (late 17th or early 18th c. pair with modilion eaves cornice).

[2]Highgate High Street, Nos. 17–21 (terrace of 1733); No. 23 (*c*.1730).

Holly Terrace (off West Hill); terrace of late-18th-c. houses.

Pond Square, Nos. 1–6 (18th-c. cottages).

South Grove, Nos. 14 and 17 ('Old Hall', 1671 and later). ('Moreton House', 1715).

The Grove, Nos. 1–6 (late-17th-c. semi-detached pairs, much altered in the 18th c.).

[2]North Hill. Nos. 47–9 (early Georgian).

[2]Southwood Lane. Woolaston Paunceford Almhouses (1722). Nos. 2–12 (row of mid-18th-c. houses).

SHOREDITCH

St Leonard, High Street (G. Dance I, 1736–40).

St John the Baptist, New North Road (F. Edwards, 1824–6; C.B.C.).

Shoreditch Training College, Pitfield Street. Formerly Haber-dashers' Almshouses (D. R. Roper, 1825).

Geffrye Museum, Kingsland Road, formerly Ironmongers' Alms-houses (1715).

High Street, Shoreditch. Nos. 2 and 196 are early-18th-c. sur-vivors in a long street.

Charles Square, Rebuilt except for No. 16 (fine house of *c*.1725).

Hoxton Street, Nos. 124 and 126 (early-18th-c. pair behind modern shops).

Hoxton Square (laid out soon after 1683). Nos. 32, 49, and 50 are perhaps late 17th c.

SOUTHWARK

1. *Bankside and Borough area:*
St George the Martyr, Borough High Street (J. Price, 1734–6).

1. Actually in Islington.
2. Actually in Hornsey.

Holy Trinity, Trinity Church Square (F. Bedford, 1823–4; C.B.C.).

Guy's Hospital. Begun 1722. East wing 1738–9; west wing (R. Jupp) 1774–80.

Bankside, Nos. 49–52 (17th and early 18th c.); Nos. 51–2 dated 1712 but much modernized.

Hopton Street. Hopton's Almhouses (1752). No. 61 (c.1702).

St Thomas Street. Chapter House of Southwark Cathedral (former chapel of St Thomas's Hospital, 1702–3). Nos. 2–14 1819).

Stamford Street. Former Unitarian Chapel (Greek Doric portico). Nos. 42–8 (c.1803; terrace).

Glasshill Street. Drapers' Almhouses (1820).

Blackfriars Road, Nos. 179–189 (late-18th-c. terrace).

Union Street, Nos. 59–61 (late-18th-c. shop-front; 18th-c. malting house behind).

St George's Circus. Laid out by Mylne, with obelisk now moved to Mary Harmsworth Park, near by.

2. *Newington and Walworth area:*

St Peter, Walworth Grove (Soane 1823–4; C.B.C.).

Imperial War Museum (former Bethlehem Hospital). Built 1812–15 (J. Lewis); wings demolished at conversion into Museum. Dome added 1838–40.

West Square (off St George's Road) north, east, and west sides (1791–4).

Old Kent Road, No. 155 (Rolls Estate Office; Michael Searles, c.1795).

Surrey Square (off Old Kent Road). Nos. 20–54 (terrace by Searles, 1795, with ornamented pediment).

New Kent Road. The Paragon (remains of a crescent of linked pairs of houses by Searles). Nos. 154–70 (late-18th-c. terrace).

Kennington Park Road, Nos. 86–8 and 114–32 (1789) and other terraces.

Walworth Road, Nos. 140–52 (remains of late-18th-c. terrace with ornamented pediment).

STEPNEY

1. *Spitalfields area:*

Christ Church, Spitalfields (Hawksmoor, 1714–27).

Fournier Street. Mostly built 1722–8. Nos. 2 (Christ Church Rectory; Hawksmoor 1726–9) and 14 are the best houses.

Wilkes Street, Nos. 17–25 (1723).

Folgate Street and Elder Street. Mostly built between 1717 and 1727.

Spital Square. No. 20 (1732; doorway and fine entrance hall, c.1789).

Artillery Lane, No. 56 (exceptionally fine shop-front, c.1757).

Brick Lane. Truman, Hanbury, Buxton and Co.'s Brewery Directors' House, c.1740; Vat House, c.1805).

2. *Whitechapel area:*

Whitechapel Road, Nos. 30 and 32 (house and shop; Mears and Stainbank, Bellfounders) with No. 2 Fieldgate Street and adjoining warehouse (mostly mid and late 18th c.; the most remarkable group of its kind in London).

Leman Street, No. 66 (large town house, c.1760). *Derelict in 1962.*

Alie Street, Nos. 30–44 (c.1720, row behind modern shops, except No. 34 which has finely carved doorcase.

Braham Street (off Leman Street), Nos. 5–11 (early 18th c.).

3. *Tower Hill area:*

Royal Mint (J. Johnson; completed, with lodges, by Smirke, 1807–9).

¹Trinity House (S. Wyatt, 1793–5; interior reconstructed after damage).

St Katherine's Dock. Warehouses by Telford (1827–8). Offices by Hardwick demolished.

4. *Ratcliff Highway area:*

St George-in-the-East (Hawksmoor, 1714–22).

Wellclose Square. North side: Nos. 1–6 (early 18th c. much altered). East side: No. 45 (early-19th-c. warehouse); Nos. 41 and 43 (late 18th c.). South side: No. 36 (c.1700), and adjoining houses, similar but much altered; No. 33 retains original staircase (c.1700).

Swedenborg Square. All early-18th-c. houses except the north side (early 19th c.). *Derelict in 1962.*

Cable Street. Nos. 104–224 (late-18th-c. row; No. 220 is a large house; No. 214 has contemporary shop-front).

Butcher Row. Royal Foundation of St Katherine (late-18th-c. mansion).

1. Actually in the City of London.

5. *Wapping and Shadwell area:*

St John, Wapping (John Johnson, 1756; tower only survives).

St Paul, Shadwell (John Walters, 1817–21).

St John's School, Scandrett Street (*c.*1760 with later additions). *Derelict in 1962.*

Raine's House, Raine Street (school, founded 1719).

London Docks. Warehouses by D. A. Alexander, 1796–1831. Wapping Pierhead (terraces, 1811, flanking entry to Docks, now filled up).

6. *Stepney area:*

Stepney Green. Nos. 29–35, early-18th-c. row. No. 37 (*c.*1700, mansion with hooded doorway, fine ironwork, staircase, and panelling). Nos. 61 and 63 (remains of a terrace of *c.*1740).

Mile End Road, No. 113 (survivor from a terrace of *c.*1730).

Albert Gardens (off Commercial Road). Regular three-sided square of small early-19th-c. houses.

Arbour Square (off Commercial Road). Formerely a regular square of small early-19th-c. houses, but north and east sides have been rebuilt.

7. *Limehouse area:*

St Anne, Limehouse (Hawksmoor, 1714–25).

Narrow Street, Nos. 78–86, 92, 102, and 104 (*c.*1730).

STOKE NEWINGTON

Stoke Newington High Street, Nos. 187, 189, and 191 (three large early-18th-c. houses). No. 187 is an exceptionally fine example with carved doorway and good staircase. *Derelict in 1962.*

Stoke Newington Church Street. Iron gates of Old Abney House. Nos. 81–7 (terrace of *c.*1740) and 89–91 (terrace of *c.*1770).

Clissold Park. Clissold House (villa by J. Woods, *c.*1820).

[1]Balls Pond Road. Nos. 131–5 ('Brunswick Terrace 1812'); No. 100 (Metropolitan Benefit Socities Asylum, 1829; Gothic).

WANDSWORTH

1. *Wandsworth area:*

All Saints, Wandsworth High Street (mostly rebuilt 1779–80).

1. Actually in Islington.

St Anne, St Anne's Crescent (Smirke, 1820–2; C.B.C.).
Friends' Meeting House, Wandsworth High Street (1778).
Wandsworth Plain, Nos. 1–6 (Church Row; fine terrace of
  c.1723).
Garratt Lane, No. 14 (front of c.1760 on older structure).

2. *Clapham area:*
  St Paul, Clapham (C. Edmonds, 1815).
  Holy Trinity, North Side, Clapham Common (K. Couse, 1776).
  North Side, Clapham Common. Nos. 11–23 (terrace of c.1720–
    30).
  Old Town, Clapham. Nos. 39, 41, and 43 (early 18th c.).
  Rectory Grove, Clapham. Nos. 8 and 10 (late 18th c.); No. 52
    ('Thurston House', c.1780).

3. *Tooting area:*
  Church Lane, Tooting. Hill House (late-18th-c. villa).

4. *Roehampton area:*
  Roehampton Lane. Roehampton House (Archer, 1710–12; now
    part of Queen Mary's Hospital). Manresa House (villa by
    Chambers, c.1760; now a Jesuit College).
  Mount Clare (large villa, built 1772; portico added 1780).

WOOLWICH

St Mary Magdalene (1732–8).
Royal Arsenal. Gun Foundry, Model Room, and entrance to
  Gun Boring Factory (all probably by Vanbrugh, 1717 on-
  wards). Entrance from Beresford Square (1829).
Royal Military Academy (J. Wyatt, 1805–8).
Royal Artillery Barracks (1775–1802).
Connaught (R.A.S.C.) Barracks. (Originally Royal Ordnance
  Hospital, c.1780 and 1806, and Grand Depot Barracks, c.1803
  and 1814).
Thomas Street. St Mary's Rectory (Papworth, 1809).
Rotunda, Woolwich Common (designed by Nash, for St James's
  Park, 1814 and re-erected here 1819).
Severndroog Castle (triangular belvedere by W. Jupp, 1784, to
  celebrate capture of Malabar).

Books

THE bibliography of London architecture is practically co-terminous with the bibliography of London, for architecture touches the life of London at every point. The following list is an essential nucleus of titles which may be useful to those who wish to consult the sources of information which I have chiefly used in writing this book. Less essential and more out-of-the-way sources I have given in the foot-notes to the text. I have divided the list to conform with the three main aspects of the subject as treated in this volume – Architecture, Biography, and Topography.

ARCHITECTURE

Britton, J., and Pugin, A. C., *Illustrations of the Public Buildings of London*, 1825. A magnificent record, with steel-engraved plans, elevations, and perspectives.

Elmes, James, *Metropolitan Improvements*, 1827. Described at the beginning of Chapter 15.

London Interiors, 1841-4. A useful companion to *Metropolitan Improvements*, which deals only with exteriors.

Malton, T., *A Picturesque Tour through the Cities of London and Westminster*. Some of the aquatints are reproduced in this book.

Rasmussen, S. E., *London: the Unique City*, English edition, 1937. Published in Penguin Books 1960. A perceptive and illuminating analysis by a Danish architect.

Richardson, A. E., and Gill, C. L., *London Houses from 1660 to 1820*. A useful anthology of photographs and plans.

Rowlandson, T., and Pugin, A. C. *The Microcosm of London*, 1808, etc. An incomparable mirror of Georgian life and architecture. A facsimile reprint was published in 1904.

ARCHITECTS

Colvin, H. M., *A Biographical Dictionary of English Architects, 1660-1840*, 1954.

Bolton, Arthur T., *Robert and James Adam*, 1922.

Davis, T., *The Architecture of John Nash*, 1960.
Downes, K., *Hawksmoor*, 1959.
Little, B., *The Life and Work of James Gibbs*, 1955.
Stroud, D., *The Architecture of Sir John Soane*, 1961.
Summerson, John, *John Nash, Architect to King George IV*, 1935
(2nd ed. 1949). Deals exhaustively with Regent Street, Regent's
Park, etc.

TOPOGRAPHY

The Survey of London. This great work now comprises 16 mono-
graphs and 30 Parish volumes. It is the definite description of
the fabric of London but has only covered a small part of the
County.
Wheatley, A. B., and Cunningham, P., *London Past and Present*,
1891. The standard topographical dictionary of London.
London Topographical Society, *The London Topographical Record*
(vols. 1–18, in progress) and other publications, including a facsimile of Rocque's map of 1746.

The following books are standard works on the areas of London
with which they deal:
Allen, T., *History and Antiquities ... of Lambeth*, 1827.
Allport, D., *Collections illustrative of ... Camberwell*, 1841.
Barratt, T. J., *The Annals of Hampstead*, 1912.
Blanch, W. H., *Ye Parish of Camerwell*, 1875.
Brayley, E. W., *Topographical History of Surrey*, 1841–8. Vol. 3
deals with London south of the Thames.
Ellis, Sir H., *History and Antiquities of the Parish of ... Shoreditch*,
1798.
Faulkner, T., *Historical and Topographical Account of Fulham*,
1813. *Historical and Topographical Description of Chelsea*, 1829.
History and Antiquities of Hammersmith, 1839. *History and Anti-
quities of Kensington*, 1820.
Lewis, S., *History and Topography of the Parish of St Mary's, Isling-
ton*, 1842.
Lysons, D., *Environs of London*, 1792–1811.
Park, J. J., *Topography and Natural History of Hampstead*, 1818.
Pinks, W. J., *History of Clerkenwell*, 1881.
Prickett, F., *History and Antiquities of Highgate*, 1842.
Robinson, W., *History and Antiquities of Stoke Newington*, 1820.
Smith, T., *A Topographical and Historical Account of ... St Mary-
le-Bone*, 1833.
Walcott, M. E. C., *Westminster: memorials of the City*, 1849.

APPENDIX 2

Walford, F., *Greater London*, 1894.

MAPS

The principal maps for the study of Georgian London are:
   John Rocque's maps, first published 1746.
   R. Horwood's map, published 1794.
   Cruchley's maps, 1826 onwards.

PRINTS, DRAWINGS, AND PHOTOGRAPHS

The Crace Collection in the British Museum (printed catalogue, 1878) and the collections in the London Museum and at County Hall are the most important sources for prints and drawings. The Gardner Collections was unfortunately dispersed, but valuable parts of it are to be found in the town halls and libraries of many boroughs. Both the London County Council and the National Monuments Record have important collections of London photographs.

Index

INDEX

Plates

a. COVENT GARDEN: Inigo Jones, 1631-5. 'Piazzas' now demolished; church rebuilt 1795

b. LINCOLN'S INN FIELDS: Lindsey House, 1640, and, on the left, house in the same style, c. 1740

a. MANSION HOUSE: George Dance, the elder, 1739-53. Front attic removed 1842

b. FENCHURCH STREET, about 1750, showing a typical City street as rebuilt after the Great Fire

NEVILLE'S COURT. House of about 1670 with porch and sashes probably
of the early eighteenth century. Destroyed 1940–1

3

a. Plate from *The Builder's Jewel* by Batty Langley,

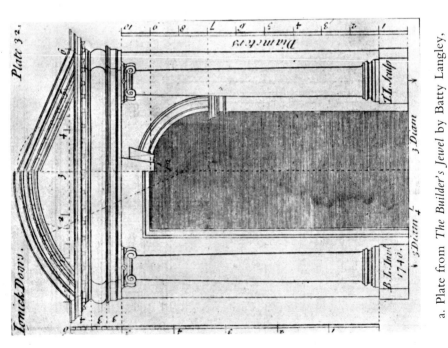

b. GREAT ORMOND STREET, doorcase of No. 42.

4

BERKELEY SQUARE, No. 44: William Kent, for Lady Isabella Finch, 1744-5

St Mary-le-Strand: James Gibbs, 1714-17

a. St Martin-in-the-Fields: James Gibbs, 1721-6. Model preserved in the church

b. St Martin-in-the-Fields: James Gibbs, 1721-6

CHRIST CHURCH, SPITALFIELDS: Nicholas Hawksmoor, 1714-29

a. St Paul's, Deptford: Thomas Archer, 1712-30

b. St John's, Smith Square: Thomas Archer, 1714-28. Gutted 1941

St George's, Hanover Square: John James, 1720–4. On the right, No. 30 St George Street

CAVENDISH SQUARE, north side. The houses at either end (destroyed) are by Edward Shepherd (c. 1720) for the Duke of Chandos. Those in the centre were built shortly before 1771 as a speculation

a. HORSE GUARDS: John Vardy after William Kent, 1750–8. In the distance, the Treasury, also by Kent, 1734–42

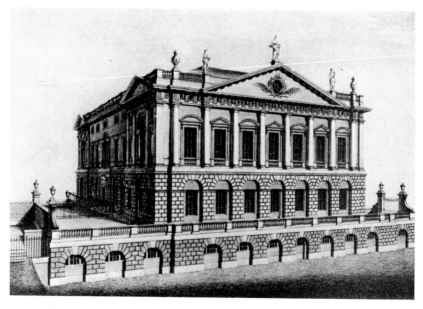

b. SPENCER HOUSE: John Vardy, from designs by General Gray, 1756–65

BURLINGTON HOUSE: Lord Burlington, with Colen Campbell, 1718-19.
Gateway, colonnades, and wings destroyed 1866; main block altered 1872

WESTMINSTER BRIDGE, centre arch: C. Labelye, 1738–50. Demolished
1861

a. MIDDLESEX HOSPITAL: James Paine, 1755–75. Remodelled during nineteenth century and demolished 1928

b. FOUNDLING HOSPITAL: T. Jacobsen, 1742–52. Demolished, except gateways, 1928

No. 37 PORTLAND PLACE: James Adam, about 1775. The porch, balcony, and attic are later. Bombed 1940; demolished after partial collapse 1943

a. Plate from the Coade 'catalogue' in the British Museum. Executed examples of this doorway exist in Bedford Square and many other parts of London. Compare also the Baker Street example, figure 16

b. Plate from the Coade 'catalogue' in the British Museum. This relief panel was used by James Wyatt at his own house (destroyed) in Foley Place.

JOHN ADAM STREET (formerly John Street), Adelphi, with the Royal
Society of Arts (1772–4) on the left and No. 7 Adam Street in the distance

a. THE ADELPHI: the brothers Adam, 1768 onwards. Demolished 1937

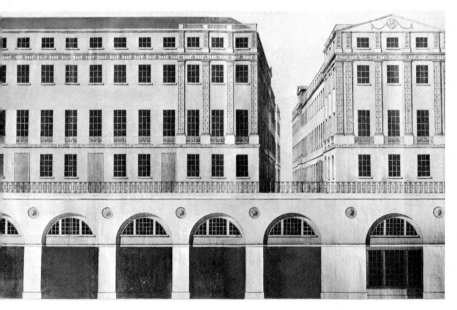

b. THE ADELPHI TERRACE. Detail from original drawing, *c.* 1768

a. SOMERSET HOUSE: Sir William Chambers, from 1775. East wing completed by Sir Robert Smirke, 1835, west wing by Sir James Pennethorne, 1856

b. SOMERSET HOUSE, south front of the Strand block: Sir William Chambers, 1775-80

SOMERSET HOUSE, detail of Strand loggia: Sir William Chambers, 1775–80

CARRINGTON HOUSE, Whitehall: Sir William Chambers, *c.* 1769.
Demolished 1886

Montagu House, Portman Square: James Stuart, 1777–82. Destroyed
1941

a. NEWGATE GAOL: George Dance, the younger, 1770-8. Demolished 1902

b. HAY HILL, showing (*left and right*) houses by Sir Robert Taylor, about 1760, and beyond (*right*) the house built for himself by John Nash, about 1812

ALL HALLOWS, LONDON WALL: George Dance, the younger, 1765-7. Photographed before partial destruction in 1940-1 and subsequent rebuilding

BANK OF ENGLAND, seen through the arcade of the Royal Exchange. *Left:* Façade by G. Sampson, 1732-6. *Right:* Façade by Sir Robert Taylor, 1766-70

a. CARLTON HOUSE: Henry Holland, 1783-5. Demolished 1826

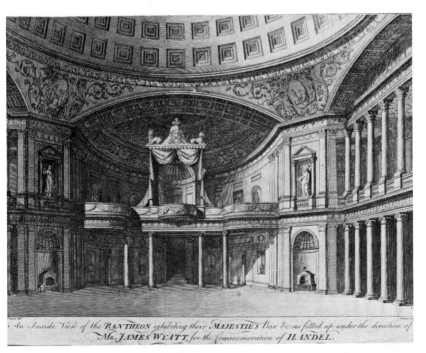

An Inside View of the PANTHEON exhibiting their MAJESTIE'S Box &c as fitted up under the direction of Mr. JAMES WYATT, for the Commemoration of HANDEL.

b. THE PANTHEON: James Wyatt, 1770-2. Destroyed by fire 1792

a. BANK OF ENGLAND, Five Per Cent Office: Sir John Soane, 1818–23. Demolished 1925–30

b. COURT OF CHANCERY, Westminster: Sir John Soane, 1820–4. Demolished 1882

DULWICH ART GALLERY, the Mausoleum: Sir John Soane, 1811-14.
Photographed before destruction in 1944 and subsequent rebuilding

Patterns for Window Guards and Balcony Railing executed in London

Plate from L. N. Cottingham, *The Ornamental Metal-worker's Director*, 1823, illustrating types of window-guard and balcony railing common in London after Waterloo

a. FITZROY SQUARE, east side: Robert Adam, 1790-5

b. MECKLENBURGH SQUARE, east side: Joseph Kay, 1812

a. YORK GATE, Regent's Park: John Nash, about 1822

b. PARK CRESCENT, Regent's Park: John Nash, 1812–22

COUNTY FIRE OFFICE, Regent Street: Robert Abraham, under John Nash, 1819

HYDE PARK CORNER, 'PIMLICO' Arch and Screen: Decimus Burton, 1825. Arch re-sited 1888

a. BRITISH MUSEUM: Sir Robert Smirke, 1823-47

b. BRITISH MUSEUM, detail of colonnade, completed 1847

a. LONDON UNIVERSITY (now University College): William Wilkins with J. P. Gandy-Deering, 1827-8

b. NATIONAL GALLERY: William Wilkins, 1832-8

36

a. LONDON INSTITUTION: William Brooks, 1815–19. The domed observatory was not executed. Demolished 1936

b. LONDON INSTITUTION, interior of library. Demolished 1936

a. St Luke's, Chelsea: James Savage, 1820-4

b. St Pancras: W. and H. W. Inwood, 1819-22

c. Hanover Chapel, Regent Street: C. R. Cockerell, 1823-5. Demolished 1897

ST PETER'S, Regent Square: W. and H. W. Inwood, 1824-6. Derelict in 1962

a. ALL SAINTS, Camden Town:
W. and H. W. Inwood, 1822-4

b. HOLY TRINITY, Marylebone
Road: Sir J. Soane, 1824-8

c. ST MARY'S, Wyndham Place:
Sir R. Smirke, 1823-4

d. ST JOHN'S, Waterloo Road:
F. Bedford, 1823-4

a. CATHOLIC CHAPEL, Moorfields: John Newman, 1817–20.
Demolished 1899

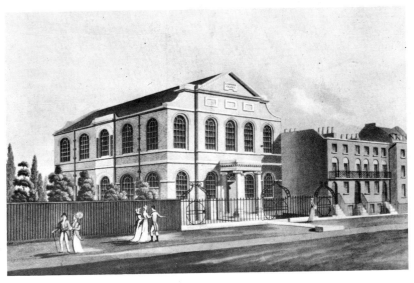

b. LAMBETH CHAPEL, Lambeth Road, built about 1817. Demolished

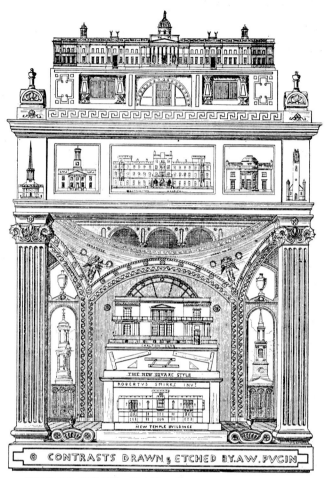

SELECTIONS FROM THE WORKS OF VARIOVS CELEBRATED BRITISH
ARCHITECTS

Plate from A. W. Pugin, *Contrasts in Architecture*, 1836. This composition is a satire on the mannerisms and idiosyncrasies manifested in some of the buildings dealt with in Chapters 15, 16, and 17. At the top of the composition is the National Gallery, resting on an 'attic' made up of details from two blocks (by Soane and Abraham) in Regent Street. The remainder of the plate is enclosed within a frame caricaturing Dance's 'Ammonite' order, as employed in the Shakespeare Gallery, Pall Mall. In the frieze are (*left to right*): All Souls, Langham Place; St Philip's, Regent Street; Westminster Hospital; 'The Holme', Regent's Park; and St Mary's, Haggerston. In the space between the columns, Soanic arches, pendentives, and acroters provide a setting for the Carlton Club and the Inner Temple Library, while to left and right are the Steeples of St Peter's, Regent Square, and St John's, Waterloo Road

a. LANCASTER HOUSE: Benjamin Wyatt, 1825–41, succeeding R. Smirke (c. 1821)

b. LANCASTER HOUSE, Grand Staircase: Benjamin Wyatt, 1827; completed by Barry, 1838–41

a. WATERLOO BRIDGE: John Rennie, 1811–17. Demolished 1937–8

b. SOUTHWARK BRIDGE: John Rennie, 1815–19. Demolished 1914

a. United Service Club: Sir R. Smirke, 1816-17. Demolished 1855

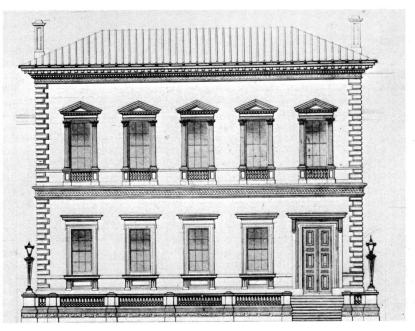

b. Travellers' Club: Sir Charles Barry, 1829-32

45

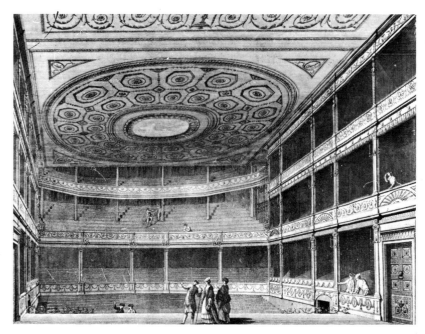

a. DRURY LANE THEATRE: Robert Adam, 1775–6. Demolished 1791

b. DRURY LANE THEATRE: Henry Holland, 1791–4. Destroyed by fire 1809

a. COVENT GARDEN OPERA HOUSE: Sir R. Smirke, 1808-9. Destroyed by fire 1856

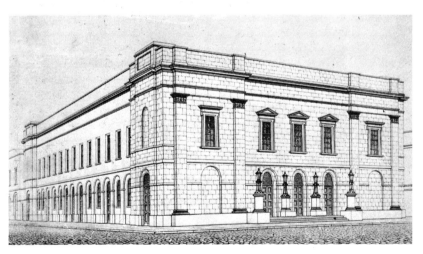

b. DRURY LANE THEATRE: Benjamin Wyatt, 1811-12. The exterior before the addition of portico and colonnade by other architects

a. COVENT GARDEN MARKET: Charles Fowler, 1831-3

b. LONDON DOCKS: warehouses by D. A. Alexander, various dates
between 1802 and 1831